African-American
HUMANISM
an anthology

African-American
HUMANISM
an anthology

edited by
Norm R. Allen Jr.

Prometheus Books ◆ Buffalo, New York

Published 1991 by Prometheus Books

With editorial offices located at 700 East Amherst Street, Buffalo, New York 14215, and distribution facilities located at 59 John Glenn Drive, Amherst, New York 14228.

Library of Congress Cataloging-in-Publication Data

African-American humanism : an anthology / edited by Norm R. Allen, Jr.
     p.   cm.
Includes bibliographical references.
ISBN 0-87975-658-6
    1. Humanism. 2. Humanists. 3. Afro-Americans. I. Allen, Norm R.
B821.A36   1991
144'.08996073—dc20   91-3642
                                            CIP

Printed on acid-free paper in the United States of America

Contents

Introduction

Norm R. Allen, Jr.

Historically, African Americans have been regarded as a deeply religious people. And many people have maintained that every noble effort and action that has ever been undertaken to uplift the African-American community has come from an individual or organization directly affiliated with the black church.

Today there is a movement among people of color to develop curricula that emphasize multicultural approaches to learning. For too long, America's educators have been trained to teach students from a one-sided, Eurocentric point of view. This push for multicultural education is highly laudable, but it should also be noted that whites are not the only people capable of distorting or neglecting history. For while it is true that the black church has been very influential in shaping the lives of African Americans, humanism has had its role to play as well.

This latter point, however, has often been overlooked. Why has so little been said or written about black deists, humanists, agnostics, freethinkers, rationalists, atheists, etc., and how their intellectual freedom enhanced their effectiveness as leaders and thinkers? If it is important to include blacks in the nation's history textbooks, is it not also important to acknowledge the humanistic or nontheistic beliefs of blacks who have made history? If it is important to examine the ways in which religion has influenced individuals and nations, is it not equally important to examine the ways in which humanism has shaped our thought? Why, for example, is so much importance given to the religious beliefs of Malcolm X and Martin Luther King, while so little is known about the atheism of A. Philip

Randolph? And why is so little attention given to the fact that humanistic ideals influenced King, Malcolm X, W. E. B. Du Bois, Frederick Douglass, and many other great black leaders? If multicultural education is to be taken seriously, it must be all-inclusive. If people sincerely wish to educate students properly, standards of fairness and objectivity must be applied consistently.

This collection has been compiled to highlight a grossly neglected side of black thought and history. Before the history of black people can be understood, the *entire* history must first be made known —including the history of *black freethinkers.*

Many rationalists are fiercely independent, and some tend to reject all labels and categories: they would not wish to be considered humanists, freethinkers, etc. For this reason, humanism must be briefly defined for the benefit of the reader.

Humanism entails a belief in reason, science, democracy, openness to new ideas, the cultivation of moral excellence, a commitment to justice and fairness, and a belief in the inherent worth of humanity. But whether they be religious or secular, humanity—not divinity—is the *primary* concern of humanists. They think freely and do not feel morally obligated to adhere dogmatically to every tenet of any religion or religious text. Humanists have varied backgrounds and often embrace a variety of political, economic, and social points of view: capitalism, socialism, communism, libertarianism, African communalism, nationalism, accommodationism, Pan-Africanism, democratic principles, republican principles, liberalism, radicalism, moderate principles, conservatism, Afrocentrism, Eurocentrism, and a host of others. Contrary to popular opinion, all secular humanists do not hate—or even criticize—religion. Many work very closely with religious individuals and organizations. Some simply have no use for religion and focus mainly on improving and enjoying life in the here and now.

Indigenous Africans have often been deemed very religious, but humanism has a long history on the African continent. For this reason, the reader will find the essays on Africa and Africans to be both surprising and refreshing. Black humanists—more so than their white counterparts—often feel alone in their opinions: some have been shunned by family and friends for holding "heretical" views. In this volume, a number of African-American humanists have been given the opportunity to express their views openly and honestly. A straightforward approach to the study of the ideals of African-American humanists will add considerable depth to our understanding of the black experience and their ongoing quest for freedom, justice, and equality.

Part One

Biographical Essays
On African-American Humanists

1

Frederick Douglass:
Abolitionist and Political Leader

David Howard-Pitney

Frederick Douglass (1817–1895), the great black abolitionist and political leader, made enormous contributions to the liberation of African-Americans and to the cause of human freedom generally in the nineteenth century. From 1841 to 1895 he was unquestionably Afro-America's leading spokesperson and an eloquent champion of equality in America. He served black Americans foremost as a peerless orator and propagandist in the crusade against slavery and for constitutional rights, and his rhetoric and leadership were instrumental in the great gains blacks made in these areas during the Civil War era.

Although seeking abolition and furthering African-Americans' welfare comprised the heart of his mission, Douglass also vigorously supported the overall cause of social reform, and his abiding commitment to human welfare, freedom, and dignity was eminently catholic, never provincial. He declared his broad concern for humanity and immediate priority of serving blacks in the maiden issue of his abolitionist newspaper, *The North Star,* writing that "while our paper shall be mainly Anti-Slavery, its columns shall be freely opened to . . . discussion of all measures and topics of a moral and humane character, which may serve to enlighten, improve, and elevate mankind."[1]

15

Like many mid-century American reformers, Douglass supported several of the diverse but interrelated "sisterhoods of reform" which prominently included abolitionism, women's rights, and the temperance (anti-alcohol) crusade. He was notably a committed feminist and an advocate of equality for women. Douglass considered every struggle for human freedom connected and complementary and justified by the same universal egalitarian principles. Underlying all his reformist thought and activities was an egalitarian humanism that cherished human freedom, abhorred anything restricting the realization of people's full potential, and posited a rational, orderly universe progressing toward freedom and morality.

Douglass's famous hatred of slavery began early in his life as a Maryland slave; already by age seven, he keenly felt the injustice of his bondage. This was true despite his being a relatively privileged slave. He performed light household tasks during childhood, and his master's wife taught him to read. He learned the skilled caulking trade and was hired out by his master to work in the Baltimore ship works. Although this position gave him relatively great freedom and mobility for a slave, Douglass intensely resented that his master kept his earnings. In general, the more that Douglass learned of the world, the more he detested slavery and racial prohibitions, the more he grew restless and dissatisfied with his lot.

A turning point in his life came when his master tried to cure Douglass's rebelliousness by sending him to work as a field hand in the country under an infamous "Negro breaker," William Covey, who habitually brutalized slaves in his charge. After an especially hard flogging, Douglass vowed never again to submit to physical mistreatment. The next time Covey attacked him, Douglass courageously defended himself and defeated the tyrant. After that brave defiance, Covey never again beat him and Douglass was recalled to Baltimore. This episode taught Douglass the value and efficacy of resisting oppression.

Douglass escaped from slavery in 1838 at age eighteen, fleeing by boat and train to Philadelphia before halting in Bedford, Massachusetts. Douglass sought work as a caulker in Bedford but found himself barred by race from any such well-paid, skilled employment. Sobered by exposure to Northern white prejudice, Douglass nevertheless eagerly commenced his new life as a free Northern black and searched for new modes of resisting racial slavery and injustice.

Douglass was deeply influenced by the African-American slave culture from which he sprang. His oratorical style showed the imprint of the preachers and storytellers from his childhood and youth. He had often witnessed black preachers swaying revival crowds, and he personally shared the slave culture's religiosity. After his conversion at thirteen, black Christianity became a source of strength and comfort for Douglass and the Bible a revolutionary text for social liberation. He continued his entwined religious and antislavery commitments in the North.

Evangelical Protestantism served as Douglass's springboard to black abolitionism and later to general Northern abolitionism and social reform. Both movements were considerably based in churches. The interconnected development of strong attachments by African-Americans and Anglo-Americans to evangelical Protestantism in the two generations before the Civil War made possible an interracial moral vocabulary for condemning slavery.

William Lloyd Garrison, the famous white social reformer, was a pivotal figure, who helped initiate Douglass's entry into interracial antebellum reform. In 1841 Douglass attended an American Anti-Slavery Society convention to hear Garrison deliver a flaming message. Douglass was thrilled by this experience. "The Bible was his textbook," Douglass said of Garrison, and the lesson drawn from it was simply that prejudice against color is rebellion against God. "You are the man—the Moses raised up by God, to deliver His modern Israel from bondage," he thought, entranced, while listening to Garrison.[2]

Upon joining the American Anti-Slavery Society, Douglass quickly sank deep roots into Northern abolitionism and middle-class culture, particularly of the New England social-reformist variety. Amalgamating with that culture, his ideas and rhetoric incorporated the three chief strands of mid-nineteenth-century American thought: Protestantism, the Enlightenment, and Romanticism. The moral fervor spawned in the revivalism of the Second Great Awakening was a vital force in contemporary social reform. American evangelicals contributed a new stress on human volition and moral agency and an intense social millennialism. Enlightenment and Romantic thought advanced complementary ideas about the efficacy of human action, the potential for human malleability and perfectibility, and the coming of a rational and moral universe. Religious and secular ideologies alike encouraged attitudes and actions supporting social reform.

Douglass soon became a leading orator of the Northern and transatlantic abolitionist movement, speaking against slavery before hundreds of public gatherings throughout the Northern states and in Great Britain. Publication in 1845 of his first autobiography, *Narrative of the Life of Frederick Douglass, an American Slave,* further spread his fame.

In 1847, Douglass separated his activities from the American Anti-Slavery Association and became an independent advocate for abolition. In Rochester, New York, he founded the first of several newspapers he edited, *The North Star.* Douglass took this step for several reasons. The first was his growing suspicion that white abolitionists were unwilling to let a black exert major public and intellectual leadership within the movement. Also, by the 1850s, he had started to abandon reliance on moral persuasion as the sole acceptable means of pursuing abolition. Douglass began advocating political means for achieving an end to slavery, a position rejected as morally impure by the followers of Garrison. He was encouraged in this direction by his involvement during the 1840s and 1850s with the Negro Convention Movement. Black leaders such as Henry H. Garnet were political abolitionists who advocated cooperating with the "Free Soil" political antislavery forces spreading through the Northern states. A smaller group also joined Garnet in justifying and supporting slave rebellions in pursuit of liberation. Douglass gradually came to accept both positions.[3]

Despite such tactical shifts, the basic arguments that Douglass made against slavery and racism were quite consistent. Slavery and racism, the two worst evils of American society, violated every tenet of morality and civilization, he held, and must never be accepted or tolerated but ceaselessly attacked and resisted. Douglass considered racism irrational, unnatural, and perverse; he called it "a moral disorder" and the product of a "diseased imagination." Racism was mentally disabling, as it clouded one's clear apprehension of reality and lessened one's capacity for sound reasoning and moral judgment. "Few evils are less accessible to the forces of reason," he repined, "than a long-standing prejudice." Racial contempt was not a natural phenomenon based on real, inherent racial differences, but was based on social conditioning, especially learned association between color and social condition. There was no natural revulsion among whites toward blackness. "Color is innocent enough," Douglass insisted, "but things with which it is coupled make it hated"—the undesirable traits associated with blackness being "slavery, ignorance, stupidity, servility, poverty, [and] dependence." When these circumstances would "cease to be coupled with color," he predicted, "there will be no color line."4

While Douglass denounced white racism in hundreds of speeches and statements, his most systematic analysis and rebuttal of white racist thinking was an 1854 address he gave to a college literary society, "The Claims of the Negro Ethnologically Considered."5 He made this speech to refute the then prestigious views of the "American school of ethnology," which lent scientific backing to common racist beliefs in the biological limitations of Africans and their sharp distinctiveness from allegedly superior Anglo-Saxons and Teutons. The cardinal proposition of Douglass's speech was "that the Negro is a man" identical in natural ability and potential with every other branch of humanity. He challenged the American school's polygenesis theory, which held that Africans had originated independently from Caucasians and descended from a separate evolutionary line. Polygenesis defied Christian teachings about the brotherhood of man, he contended, as well as the findings of science and common sense, all of which supported the time-honored view that Africans were "a part of the human family . . . descended from a common ancestry, with the rest of mankind."

The underlying cause of racism was slavery which, by causing black debasement, also caused color prejudice. Slavery's inhumane exploitation of African people had to be rationalized by denying the humanity of blacks, which white ethnologists were doing. Because of slavery, Douglass claimed, the temptation "to read the Negro out of the human family" was very strong among American whites who tried to cover their guilt by "making the enslaved a character fit only for slavery."

Racism clearly perverted the "science" and distorted the findings of the American school of ethnology. Douglass found its writings full of "pride of race" and "conspicuous contempt for Negroes." Refusing to consider blacks capable of civilized achievement, these white scholars resorted to specious arguments to identify the builders of the pyramids, not as Africans but Caucasians, an obvious twisting of fact and logic to support racist presuppositions. Douglass proudly reclaimed for African-Americans the heritage of ancient Egypt and

Africa as founts of racial pride and proof of blacks' past and potential greatness.

Douglass always urged blacks to achieve socially, thus demonstrating their capability and worth, and to dispel racist notions about their supposed innate limitations. In his own impressive bearing and oratorical brilliance, Douglass was a potent symbol of the black ability to achieve once freed of slavery's stultifying effects. He vigorously advocated black social and economic self-help and entreated African-Americans to make the most of every opportunity to rise through enterprise to middle-class status. Blacks needed to do more than make moral appeals and assert their natural, or "theoretical" equality, he taught. They needed also to prove their equality in deeds, since white prejudice would "gradually yield to the pressure of wealth, education, and high character" among blacks.[6]

Douglass endorsed black nationalist themes and social strategies mainly because he deemed appeals to race pride and unity to be most effective for inspiring those efforts for black accomplishment which he thought necessary to help end racism. While holding that "in a natural state of society, there would be no necessity of separate action," he insisted that, until this ideal state was attained, blacks had a duty and "right to associate with each other to promote our interests."[7] At the same time, though, Douglass's final social goals were broader and more inclusive than aiding any single group or race, even his own. What he hoped for in America was the eventual birth of a universal democracy in which racial identity would be irrelevant; his highest social goal and priority was to help bring about this future egalitarian society.

Although he championed the fight for black liberation and self-development and considered these goals complementary, even prerequisites, to achieving general social justice, Douglass's support for nationalistic racial endeavors occasionally conflicted with his final assimilationist-integrationist goal for his people. Sometimes he criticized racial separatism. He warned that overemphasis on black pride and identity could lead to clannishness among blacks which could reinforce America's racial hyperawareness. Blacks would never ultimately succeed by limiting their activities and interests to narrowly racial concerns. "Our policy," he advised African-Americans, "should be to unite with the great mass of the American people in all their activities, and resolve to fall or flourish with our common country."[8] Black nationalism to Douglass was a positive but temporary force that he would willingly sacrifice to advance his higher raceless social ideal. When racial loyalty conflicted with his broader social goals and vision, Douglass usually subordinated racial nationalism to transracial Americanism and both of these, when necessary, to humanism.

Douglass relied on protest and moral appeal along with black achievement in the long run to end the anomaly of racism. Racism was for Douglass a perplexing aberration in the order of things, which fundamentally had no place in the progressive universe in which he believed and acted. It was irrational, immoral, and reactionary and so would inevitably be overcome by history's providential tide. To emphasize racism's impermanence, Douglass made much of his belief that some whites had surmounted it already and that more would surely follow. Impressed by the egalitarianism of white abolitionists with whom he had worked in Great Britain, Douglass claimed to have found "no prejudice against color in England," save what was carried there from America "as a moral disease from an infected country." Douglass could therefore say of racism: "It is American, not European; local, not general; limited, not universal, and must be ascribed to artificial conditions, and not to any fixed and universal law of nature."[9]

Douglass masterfully wove together the eclectic strands of mid-nineteenth-century American Protestantism, Englightenment-Romanticism, and social reformism in his powerful assaults on slavery and caste. Abolitionism epitomized true religion for him; it truly *was* his religion. Douglass viewed abolitionism as the synthesizing of religion and ethics with natural law and reason, while racism violated every moral, humane, and progressive principle. He felt no conflict among these value systems, since he believed all genuine religious and humanistic impulses supported freedom and, therefore, abolitionism.

Douglass reached maturity in an age before the Darwinian controversy of the latter nineteenth century opened a great fissure between naturalistic and theistic explanations of the world. The authority and claims of religion and science in the first half of the century were regarded by most Americans as fully consonant and mutually supportive.[10] Religion was clearly a positive force to Douglass who breathed in easily the evangelical air of both the African-American and Anglo-American cultures in which he lived, and he naturally expected the church to be in the forefront of abolitionism and every humanitarian movement.

Although Douglass embraced "true" religion, which was necessarily active in alleviating human suffering and promoting dignity, he often excoriated institutionalized religion. Most particularly, he blasted away at the white churches that either supported or temporized slavery and so served oppressors' interests. The shameful betrayal of Christian ethics by churches that acting as "the bulwark of American slavery, and the shield of American slavehunters" outraged him. "I would say, welcome infidelity! welcome atheism! welcome anything," Douglas exclaimed, in "preference to the gospel, as preached . . . [by persons who] convert the very name of religion into an engine of tyranny and barbarous cruelty."[11]

Douglass also criticized many black churches. He complained that most black churches were poorly led and the clergy ignorant, uneducated, and ill-trained. He lamented the characteristic anti-intellectualism, antirationalism, and mindless emotionalism of much that passed for black Christianity. The African-American church was often otherworldly, apolitical, and socially conservative, Douglass complained; it often encouraged people to be so passively dependent on divine action that they failed to achieve good.

Douglass's own persuasion moved from a God-centered, humanly passive religion toward a human-centered creed stressing the efficacy of human will, good works, faith in human progress, and the perfectibility of humankind. By the 1850s, Douglass was a thoroughgoing religious liberal, or humanist. His liberal Protestantism coexisted comfortably with Enlightenment ideals of natural law and reason. Douglass's humanistic worldview was anchored in both Christian theology and natural rights philosophy, and his experience with religion helped form and support his humanistic faith.

Frederick Douglass's thought and rhetoric harnessed the most potent and socially progressive forces of African-American and Anglo-American culture. For the half century between 1841 and 1895, he led African-Americans in both courageously resisting slavery and protesting racism. As a moral leader, skillful propagandist, and major political figure,[12] he played a key role in bringing about emancipation and recognition of blacks' citizenship rights during the Civil War and Reconstruction eras. In his bold and eloquent calls to end racism and extend equal rights, moreover, Douglass mightily served not only the just cause of blacks but that of American democracy and of human freedom everywhere.

NOTES

1. Frederick Douglass, "To Our Oppressed Countrymen," *The North Star* (3 December, 1847), in *The Life and Writings of Frederick Douglass,* ed. Philip S. Foner, 5 vols. (New York: International Publishers, 1950, 1971) 1:283.

2. Frederick Douglass, *Life and Times of Frederick Douglass: Written by Himself* (New York: n.p., 1892; reprint, n.p., 1962), 78–79.

3. For a brief summary of Douglass's conversion to political abolitionism, see Waldo E. Martin, Jr., *The Mind of Frederick Douglass* (Chapel Hill: University of North Carolina Press, 1984), 57–58.

4. Frederick Douglass, "The Color Line," 1881, in Foner, ed., *Life and Writings* 4:342–43, 350.

5. Frederick Douglass, "The Claims of the Negro Ethnologically Considered," in Foner, ed., *Life and Writings* 2:308, 291, 295–96.

6. Frederick Douglass, "The Future of the Colored Race," in Foner, ed., *Life and Writings* 4:195.

7. Frederick Douglass, "Prejudice and Opportunity," *Frederick Douglass's Paper* (12 August 1853), in *The Frederick Douglass Papers,* ed. John W. Blassingame (New Haven: Yale Unviverity Press, 1982) 2:449.

8. Frederick Douglass, "The Nation's Problem," (16 April 1889), in *Negro Social and Political Thought, 1850–1920,* ed. Howard Brotz (New York: Basic Books, 1966), 318–19. Because of his dream of a future transracial America, Douglass adamantly opposed all African-American emigration or colonization schemes.

9. Frederick Douglass, "The Color Line," 1881, in Foner, ed., *Life and Writings* 4:351–52.

10. The widely assumed compatibility between religion and science in this era is described in George M. Marsden, "Everyone One's Own Interpreter? The Bible, Science, and Authority in Mid-Nineteenth-Century America," in *The Bible in America: Essays in Cultural History,* eds. Nathan O. Hatch and Mark A. Noll (New York: Oxford University Press, 1982), 79–100, especially 81–87.

11. Frederick Douglass, "The Meaning of the Fourth of July for the Negro," in Foner, ed., *Life and Writings* 2:197.

12. From the Civil War to his death, Douglass was a loyal and active Republican party member. He held several major federal political ap-

pointments, including Marshall of the District of Columbia and U.S. Ambassador to Haiti.

SELECT BIBLIOGRAPHY

Blight, David W. *Frederick Douglass's Civil War: Keeping Faith in Jubilee.* Baton Rouge: Louisiana State University Press, 1989.

Douglass, Frederick. *The Frederick Douglass Papers.* Edited by John W. Blassingame. Serial I, vols. I-3. New Haven: Yale University Press, 1979, 1982, 1986.

———. *Life and Times of Frederick Douglass: Written by Himself.* New York: n.p., 1892; reprint ed., n.p., 1962.

———. *The Life and Writings of Frederick Douglass.* Edited by Philip S. Foner. 5 vols. New York: International Publishers, 1950, 1971.

———. *Narrative of the Life of Frederick Douglass, an American Slave: Written by Himself.* Boston: Anti-Slavery Office, 1845.

Douglass's Monthly (Rochester) 1859–1863.

Frederick Douglass's Paper (Rochester) 1851–1859.

Huggins, Nathan I. *Slave and Citizen: The Life of Frederick Douglass.* Boston: Little, Brown, 1980.

Martin, Waldo E. *The Mind of Frederick Douglass.* Chapel Hill: University of North Carolina Press, 1984.

New National Era (Washington, D. C.) 1870–1873.

The North Star (Rochester) 1847–1851.

Preston, Dickson J. *Young Frederick Douglass: The Maryland Years.* Baltimore: Johns Hopkins University Press, 1980.

Quarles, Benjamin. *Frederick Douglass.* Washington, D. C.: Associated Publishers, 1948.

2

W. E. B. Du Bois:
Black Scholar and Social Activist

David Howard-Pitney

William Edward Burghardt (W. E. B.) Du Bois (1868–1963) was a towering figure in African-American thought and letters; his combined achievements as a scholar, writer, social critic, and leader are unmatched. As the leading African-American intellectual for decades, he greatly influenced two generations of black thinkers and artists. The poet Langston Hughes testified to this impact when he stated that "my earliest memories of written words are those of Du Bois and the Bible."[1] Although he preferred the scholarly role, duty called DuBois to the political arena to fight racism and injustice and to assist attempts by blacks to improve their lot. He was a pioneer of the modern civil rights movement. Indeed, Du Bois ranks with Frederick Douglass and Martin Luther King, Jr., among the greatest champions of black rights and liberty in United States history. Besides being a key leader of the domestic black freedom struggle, Dr. Du Bois inspired many internationally as they struggled against racism and colonialism and for socialism, peace, and democracy. His long career was totally committed to freedom, justice, and a profound sense of social duty and service.

A Renaissance man in his activities and universalist in sympathies, W. E. B. Du Bois was a great humanist. His diverse accomplishments spanned seven decades and his work, because of its tremendous scope and complexity, transcends simple categorization. He was, among other things, an outstanding scholar, penetrating social critic and theorist, superb propagandist, and gifted writer. He was, to varying degress and at different times, a racial integrationist, a black nationalist favoring voluntary self-segregation, and a cultural pluralist; he was a scientific empiricist and a moral idealist; he was also a liberal reformist and an evolutionary socialist; and finally a Communist. Some scholars have described the nature of his thought, because of its change and complexity, as essentially "paradoxical." Others have correctly noted, however, that underlying the complex, shifting, even contradictory nature of his ideas and contemporary positions was constant courageous opposition to oppression and an unswerving dedication to democracy and freedom.[2]

W. E. B. Du Bois was born in the small town of Great Barrington, Massachusetts, where he led a happy childhood. Aware of being black, he nonetheless felt himself a fully accepted member of the community and took part in town activities with no thought of discrimination. Not until high school did he begin to perceive social snubs from whites. His reaction then, as whenever he encountered racial rejection and exclusion, was to adopt an attitude of pride and disdain. "They were the losers who did not ardently court me and not I," he told himself. He also responded by seeking to beat whites wherever possible—especially in the academic realm where his brilliance shone immediately.[3]

Abolitionism was a major inspiration to Du Bois. He gave his high school valedictory address, for example, on the white abolitionist, Wendall Phillips, whose life and work in promoting black welfare and changing white attitudes fascinated Du Bois. In studying Phillips, Du Bois recalled, "I took a long step toward a wider conception of what I was going to do." He also took a pilgrimage as a young man to hear the aging black abolitionist hero Frederick Douglass speak. Throughout his life, Du Bois drew on the inspirational example of abolitionism, which ever epitomized for him social morality and duty in action.[4]

Alexander Crummel, the black abolitionist and clergyman, was a significant influence on Du Bois and other young black intellectuals during the 1890s. Crummel preached black pride, solidarity, and self-help. Crummel, who had lived in Liberia for a decade, helped awaken

Du Bois's interest in Africa and Pan-Africanism. For Du Bois, in his early professional years, Crummel was a shining example of an African-American intellectual devoted to work, service, and sacrifice for his race.[5]

Attending all-black Fisk College in Nashville, Tennessee, solidified Du Bois's budding racial nationalism and his desire to help and serve black people. Even before leaving Great Barrington, he had begun to imagine a heroic role for himself as a race leader with a great duty to perform. "I very early got the idea that what I was going to do was prove to the world that Negroes were just like other people."[6]

Du Bois decided to serve blacks as a man of culture and scholarship. He planned to study the racial problem to assist blacks and educate whites out of racial ignorance and prejudice. Believing that his "mighty task" required "the best in organized learning,"[7] Du Bois graduated from Fisk and Harvard colleges and attended the University of Berlin where he studied philosophy, history, and sociology. He received his doctorate in history from Harvard in 1894.

Du Bois believed in the power of science and education to foment social reform and progress, and he conducted trailblazing historical and sociological research on African-Americans. Some of his leading scholarly works include: *The Suppression of the African Slave Trade in the United States* (1896), *The Philadelphia Negro* (1899), the Atlanta University Publications on black social conditions (an annual series that Du Bois edited between 1898 and 1913), and *Black Reconstruction in America* (1935). *The Philadelphia Negro* was the first thorough empirical study of an African-American community, and his editorship of the Atlanta University Publications continued his pioneering sociological work. *Black Reconstruction*, written in the 1930s, stressed blacks' positive achievements during national Reconstruction and made an original class analysis of the era's politics. Although not initially well received by the white-dominated history profession, *Black Reconstruction* was ahead of its time and boldly set forth the main points of the revisionist interpretation of Reconstruction that became standard during the 1950s and 1960s.

Du Bois first achieved great fame in the twentieth century for his key role in reviving militant African-American protest and demands for equality. His book, *The Souls of Black Folk* (1903), electrified the black intellectual community partly because it departed from the accommodationist position associated with the dominant black figure of the time, Booker T. Washington. Washington advised blacks to accommodate rather than protest forms of public inequality such as segregation. Du Bois, on the other hand, advised that blacks seek singlemindedly to achieve education and economic success through private self-help efforts. This clarion of protest became the chief symbol of the growing number of African Americans in the early twentieth century who dared to challenge Washington and demand their rights as citizens.

Driven by duty down from academia's lofty towers into the thick of public combat, Du Bois edited journals devoted to controversial social and political issues and helped launch a new black protest organization, the Niagara Movement. Resigning from Atlanta University in 1910, Du Bois, along with other Niagara members, joined white reformers to establish the National Association for the Advancement of Colored People (NAACP).

The peak of Du Bois's impact on both black and white American public opinion was from 1910 to 1934 during his tenure as editor of the NAACP's official journal, *Crisis.* Du Bois immediately established editorial independence in *Crisis* and made it the organ of his own thought and opinion. Largely because of his ideas and masterful expression, *Crisis* was a great and immediate success.

Du Bois's contributions to the journal were the single most important segment of his literary corpus.[8] Du Bois penned a torrent of slashing editorials protesting the rise of race prejudice, discrimination, and violence in the United States. Often combatively, sometimes acidly, always brilliantly, he exposed in each issue the glaring racial evils in American society. He was openly controversial and believed that it was his mission in *Crisis* "to tell the nation the crying evil of race prejudice" so that, alerted, it might reform. "It is a hard duty," he contended, "but a necessary one—a divine one."[9]

Crisis, based in New York City, soon became a center of African-American culture and art. It was the chief black literary journal of its day. Through literary contests, reviews, and publicity, Du Bois introduced many promising black artists to the American public. *Crisis* was the main outlet for black literature and art before the Harlem "New Negro" Renaissance of the 1920s; even here *Crisis* played a significant role in this movement.

Du Bois himself wrote many novels, poems, short stories, plays, and pageants. While he wrote creative works of unquestionable power (some of his poems such as "A Litany for Atlanta" [1906] and "The Burden of Black Women" [1908] powerfully convey their author's outrage over gross injustice), Arnold Rampersad is right to say that Du Bois "never attained complete competence as a great poet or novelist." But Rampersad also observes that "his efforts in those roles combine with his other works to extend our understanding of the history and character of his people, and indeed, of humanism itself."[10]

Du Bois's creative literary endeavors serve in different format the same social goals as do his other works and activities. All his novels treat social topics. For examples: *The Quest of the Silver Fleece* (1911) is a sociological fiction that traces the role of cotton in shaping the lives of blacks and whites in the United States; the massive *Black Flame* trilogy (1957, 1959, 1961) relates the experiences of an African-American man between 1876 and 1956 and includes many historical events and persons; and *Dark Princess* (1928) involves a worldwide conspiracy of dark peoples to overthrow white rule. Even his less successful imaginative writings are revealing of his deepest social commitments and dreams for blacks and the world.

Du Bois's greatest literary legacies are his writings in *Crisis* (1910–1934) and immortal *The Souls of Black Folk* (1903). The latter book, his masterpiece, is filled with majestic, unforgettable prose. *Souls* is an evocative montage of nonfiction and fiction on various aspects of African-American culture and history. Included among its many moving essays is a piece on black spirituals, a glowing tribute to Alexander Crummel, and an emotionally wrenching reflection on the death of his firstborn. Shifting among the voices of the learned scholar, the passionate polemicist, the lyrical poet, and the mystic seer, the total effect of *Souls* is to inspire awe and appreciation for the richness and beauty to be found in African-American life as well as the pain and oppression blacks endured. Like all great works, *Souls* is timeless. It has gone through many reprintings and editions and is hailed as an international classic.

Du Bois encouraged black artists to draw the subjects of their work, as well as their inspiration, from black life; he urged them to direct their art mainly to the sensibilities and needs of black people. Du Bois felt that artists, like all privileged blacks, should dedicate their work to advance the people and their well-being. Black artists had a crucial role to play in society: nourishing black pride and distinct aesthetic values. To fulfill their mission, black artists should not conform to white Western standards but must be "inspired with new ideals." By following the distinctive vision, the black artist "dreams a splendid future" and "mighty prophecy" which is necessary for "that sort of world we want to create for ourselves and for all America" and the world.[11]

An ardent black nationalist, Du Bois felt special pride in, love for, and identity with, his people. He believed that they had a great mission and destiny to fulfill. Because of their suffering and oppression, blacks were uniquely motivated to bring about social changes that would be beneficial not only to themselves but to the whole of humanity.

Du Bois championed united black social action and economic self-help. In the decades between the First and Second World Wars, he advocated constructing a self-sufficient separate group economy for American blacks, an economy in which blacks would collectively focus on gaining economic advance and independence. Developing proposals for establishing a system of all-black producer and consumer cooperatives was one of Du Bois's highest priorities, especially in the Depression era of the 1930s. By 1934, Du Bois's vocal support for black "voluntary self-segregation" as the most effective means of promoting racial advance prompted a confrontation with the NAACP board of directors, which led to his resignation as editor of the *Crisis*.

Another feature of Du Bois's black nationalism was his lifelong interest in Africa. He wrote extensively on it. In 1961, at the age of ninety-three, for example, he went to Ghana to direct production of a multivolume *Encyclopedia Africana;* he eventually adopted Ghanaian citizenzhip and worked on the project until his death in 1963.[12]

Du Bois also exerted leadership in organizing the international Pan-African movement. He was the secretary of the first Pan-African Congress held in 1900 and helped organize Pan-African congresses of black representatives from around the world in 1919, 1921, 1923, 1927, and 1945, earning him recognition as the "father" of Pan-Africanism. Africa's collective fight to overthrow European colonialism and to establish independent nations that would secure human rights made it "the Spiritual Frontier of humankind," paving the way to universal freedom and democracy.[13] Du Bois believed that Pan-Africanism was destined to expand and have a unifying effect on black people everywhere, emboldening them to break the bonds of white domination.

Socialism was another of Du Bois's intense convictions, one that grew stronger over time. He considered socialism to be the right course and the surest sign of hope for the future. He was attracted to its goal of economic justice and spirit of social and racial egalitarianism. Du Bois accepted socialism's critique of capitalist exploitation of workers and rule by private wealth and greed. In 1907, he declared himself a "Socialist-of-the-Path," someone who supported socialism's broad goals and principles, but stopped short of joining any particular socialist organization. For most of his life, Du Bois was a reformist, a Fabian-type socialist, whose preferred model of socialism was the British Labour party. Long a moderate middle-class socialist, he believed that socialism should be evolutionary, not revolutionary, and accomplished by peaceful, democratic means.

Du Bois typically combined his racial and socialist goals. In developing their own internal economy, African-Americans, he stressed, must not "try the old paths of individual exploitation, but develop a class of rich and grasping brigands of industry," and "reproduce in our own group all the industrial hell of Old Europe and America." After World War I, Du Bois was increasingly certain that economic cooperation represented "the new spirit" that was eventually "going to work itself out in the white world." Furthermore, he predicted that blacks "can evolve a new and efficient industrial cooperation quicker than any other group," because in America "the colored group is not yet divided into capitalists and laborers"; instead it shared an "interclass sympathy" that would allow it to build the just economy that the whole world needed. "We who have had least class differentiation in wealth can follow in the new trend," he claimed, "and indeed lead it."[15] Though Du Bois's commitments to African-Americans and to socialism were usually consonant, if one of these concerns conflicted with the other, as sometimes happened during the war years of the 1940s, his greatest commitment was to race.

Largely for this reason, for decades Du Bois dissented from orthodox Marxism and the Communist party. He argued that Marxists fundamentally erred by assuming the interracial solidarity of the working class. The irrational prejudice of white workers prevented them from uniting with blacks to fulfill the universal promise of economic democracy. Du Bois denounced the alliance between jingoistic white capitalists and laborers who shared psychological and economic interests in exploiting workers of color overseas.[16]

After the Second World War, however, Du Bois's priorities shifted; interracial socialism eclipsed his once preeminent concern for race. "Not from the inner problems of a single social group . . . can the world be guided," he concluded. Instead, he "began to enter into a World conception of human uplift . . . centering about the work and income of the working class irrespective of color or nationality."[17]

Beginning in the late 1940s and continuing to his death over two decades later, Du Bois grew most concerned with colonial imperialism.[18] Racism and colonialism were the offspring of capitalism as well as the main obstacles to peace and social progress, he insisted. He pictured the United States leading an imperialistic and militaristic campaign to stem worldwide progress toward socialism and to keep control of colonial workers of color. Frightened by the Korean War and possible nuclear annihilation, Du Bois clamored for peaceful coexistence with the Soviet Union.

Fearlessly voicing and organizing on behalf of these unpopular views, Du Bois was shunned by all but the American Left during the Cold War-McCarthy years. He was harassed by the federal government for his peace activities and, in the hysterical antiradical climate, became a pariah to middle-class leaders and organizations. Even the NAACP banned him from speaking before its chapters. Du Bois felt betrayed, having been rejected by middle-class African-Americans: ruefully recalling his later years in America, he wrote, "The colored children ceased to hear my name."[19]

In 1961, at the invitation of President Kwame Nkrumah, Du Bois traveled to the West African nation of Ghana to undertake the *Encyclopedia Africana* project. Just before he left, he publicly joined the Communist party. Du Bois did so for two important reasons. First, he had finally concluded that capitalism was congenitally undemocratic and incapable of reforming itself, and that communism's attitude toward capitalism was closest to his own. Second, he wished to make a political statement against McCarthyism and set an example of non-intimidation for other dissenters by publicly announcing his decision to become a Communist.[20] He died in Ghana two years later.

A constant theme in Du Bois's evolving thought was his determination to resist racism. Early in his career he confidently expected science to end racism swiftly and to establish democracy. Even after Du Bois had concluded that science alone was insufficient for this task and that "agitation," "boycott," and "organization"—the tools of protest—were also needed, he still expected quick and dramatic results from his efforts. When he "founded . . . the *Crisis,*" he recalled, "my basic theory had been that race prejudice was primarily a matter of ignorance . . . [and] that when the truth was properly presented . . . race hatred must melt and melt quickly before it."[21]

Unanticipated disappointing events in the twentieth century undermined Du Bois's once sanguine view about democracy's rapid triumph over racism. He reflected, "Upon this state of mind after a few years of conspicuous progress fell the horror of World War," the first major blow to his liberal reformist faith in human reasonableness. Then there followed the economic holocaust of the Great Depression. By 1940, the "scope of change and unreason in human action" seemed far more vast to him than it once had. From contemporary events and reading Marx and Freud, Du Bois grew to appreciate the existence of "more powerful motives less open to appeal and reason" than mere ignorance. These deeply rooted, more intractible forces were "economic motives" based on exploitation sanctioned by racism, and psychological forces ("unconscious acts and irrational reactions") based on inherited, centuries-old beliefs and habits. In view of capitalism's powerful resurgence after the Second World War, Du Bois saw little reason to expect dramatic, imminent victories. Of course, Du Bois never lost hope or ceased working for progress: such a defeatist attitude would have meant spiritual death. Nevertheless, his life ended with his belief that "not sudden assault but long siege" was required in the battle against racism and for social justice and democracy, and that for this, much "time was needed."[22]

Du Bois's basic philosophical and ethical position was internally consistent, even though he combined a scientific iointellect with an idealistic, poetic soul. On the one hand, he was an empiricist/materialist who turned reflexively to naturalistic understandings and explanations of human behavior. He was thus attracted to "scientific socialism" and the Marxist idea that history is determined by economic forces. Du Bois was not religious in any traditional sense; indeed he was something of an anticleric.[23] At the same time, he believed in a creative force directing the universe and in the immortality of the soul, and there was an undeniably spiritual dimension to Du Bois's imagination and expression.

Despite his distaste for religious orthodoxy, Du Bois relied heavily on biblical language and imagery in his many writings, especially his creative ones. This predilection appears quite pronounced, for example, in the short story titled "Jesus Christ in Georgia," and in the remarkable set of poem-sermonettes he called "Prayers for Dark People." Of course, it is conceivable that Du Bois simply used religious motifs as an effective rhetorical device to reach and effect his audience, but the passionate intensity that usually characterizes such passages strongly suggests that he found religious symbols and nomenclature deeply expressive of his own highest hopes and longings.[24]

Social morality and duty formed the bedrock of Du Bois's values. He felt duty-bound to serve humanity, and he believed in the nobility of work, service, and sacrifice. "Love is God and Work is His prophet," he declared. "We make the world better by the gift of our service and our selves. So in some mystic way does God bring realization [of a better world] through sacrifice."[25]

Although Du Bois detached his ethics from religion, his basic moral ideals were formed early in life during his exposure to denominational religion. As a child Du Bois had attended a Congregational church in New England with his mother, and Puritanism was an important part of his social inheritance. He retained throughout his life the impact of that Puritan social ethic. Du Bois almost perfectly embodied such key Puritan behavioral ideals as diligence, discipline, and sacrifice for divine social ends; he internalized Puritanism's insistence on the individual's responsibility to the community and the people's duty to accomplish God's will on earth.[26]

Du Bois devoted both his life and his great genius to making the world a better place for blacks and for all people. His was a trek that led to many struggles and social debates. He was a persistent advocate of black liberation, women's rights, the labor movement, and peace. He produced groundbreaking scholarship, helped found the black civil rights movement, increased national understanding of racial issues, fought courageously for peace, and launched modern Pan-Africanism. In these and other ways, Du Bois worked tirelessly and selflessly for human progress. Faith continually sustained him, faith that "always human beings will live and progress to greater, broader, and fuller life."[27]

At a public gathering on his ninetieth birthday, Du Bois advised his great-grandson about what to do in life. Find worthwhile work, he urged the youngster; work that brings not just money but satisfaction from "the supreme sense of a world of men . . . inevitably going forward, and you, yourself, with your hand on the wheels. Make this choice, then, my son, . . . [and] never falter." At the same time, he cautioned the boy to expect that "the forward pace of the world which you are pushing will be painfully slow. But what of that; the difference between a hundred and a thousand years is less than you now think. But doing what must be done, that is eternal."[28] All his life, W. E. B. Du Bois did whatever he thought must be done or said to advance humanity; that is why the inspiration of his words and deeds endures.

NOTES

1. Langston Hughes, "Tribute," in *Black Titan: W. E. B. Du Bois,* eds. John Henrik Clarke, et al. (Boston: Beacon Press, 1970), p. 8.

2. The best-known proponent of the "paradox" interpretation of Du Bois is August Meier, *Negro Thought in America, 1880–1915* (Ann Arbor: University of Michigan Press, 1963), ch. 11, "The Paradox of W. E. B. Du Bois." More recently Manning Marable and others have stressed an underlying moral and intellectual unity; see Marable, *W. E. B. Du Bois: Black Radical Democrat* (Boston: Twayne Publishers, 1986). Manning's book is the best biography of Du Bois.

3. W. E. B. Du Bois, *Dusk of Dawn: An Essay Toward an Autobiography of a Race Concept* (New York: Brace, 1940; reprint ed., 1968, 3rd printing, 1969), p. 14.

4. Du Bois, *Dusk of Dawn,* p. 20. Examples abound of Du Bois's attachment to abolitionism. His biography, *John Brown* (Philadelphia: George W. Jacobs, 1909), reveals his deep identification with the abolitionist martyr and his tendency to compare all progressive social causes to abolitionism. In the 1950s, Du Bois often compared the communist and abolitionist movements.

5. On Crummel's influence on Du Bois, see Marable, *W. E. B. Du Bois,* pp. 38–40. Also see Du Bois's own reverential tribute to Crummel in *The Souls of Black Folk: Essays and Sketches* (Chicago: A. C. McClurg, 1903), ch. 12.

6. W. E. B. Du Bois, "Reminiscences of William Edward Burghardt Du Bois." Interview by William T. Ingersoll, 1963, Columbia Oral History Collection, Columbia University, p. 8; *Dusk of Dawn,* p. 20.

7. W. E. B. Du Bois, "My Evolving Program for Negro Freedom," in *What the Negro Wants,* ed. Rayford W. Logan (Chapel Hill: University of North Carolina Press, 1944), pp. 37–38.

8. This is the opinion of, besides this writer, Herbert Aptheker, the most knowledgeable student of Du Bois; see *Selections from "The Crisis,"* ed. Herbert Aptheker, vol. 1, 1911–1925 (Millwood, N.Y.: Kraus-Thomson, 1983), p. xvii.

9. W. E. B. Du Bois, "The Crisis," *Crisis* (10 November 1910).

10. Arnold Rampersad, "W. E. B. Du Bois as a Man of Literature," *American Literature* (March 1979): 68. Excellent commentaries on Du Bois's creative literature appear in Rampersad, *The Art and Imagination of W. E. B. Du Bois* (Cambridge: Harvard University Press, 1976); Herbert Aptheker, *The Literary Legacy of W. E. B. Du Bois* (White Plains, N.Y.: Kraus-Thomson, 1989); and *Creative Writings of W. E. B. Du Bois,* ed. Herbert Aptheker (White Plains, N.Y.: Kraus-Thomson, 1985), pp. ix-xii. The latter book is part of the excellent series, *The Complete Published Works of W. E. B. Du Bois,* comp. and ed. Herbert Aptheker, 37 vols. (White Plains, N.Y.: Kraus-Thomson, 1973–1986), to which all students of Du Bois are enthusiastically referred.

11. W. E. B. Du Bois, "Criteria for Negro Art," *Crisis* (October 1926).

12. Herbert Aptheker, "W. E. B. Du Bois and Africa," in *Racism, Imperialism, and Peace,* eds. Marvin Berlowitz and Carol Martin (Minneapolis: MEP Publications, 1987) gives an incisive analysis of Du Bois's writings and views on Africa.

13. W. E. B. Du Bois, "Africa," *Crisis* (April 1924). See Marable, *W. E. B. Du Bois,* pp. 99–107, for a description of Du Bois's contributions to Pan-Africanism.

14. W. E. B. Du Bois, "Socialist of the Path," *The Horizon* (February 1907). In this period, he often wrote complimentary things about the Socialist Party of America and even joined it for a while in 1911. On the other hand, Du Bois was politically pragmatic and usually did not advise that blacks waste votes on unelectable parties. He also often criticized socialists for inconsistency and failure to practice their racial egalitarian principles. See Marable, *W. E. B. Du Bois,* pp. 108–13, on Du Bois's early relation to socialism.

15. W. E. B. Du Bois, "Thrift Calls," *Crisis* (January 1921); "Cooperation," *Crisis* (November 1918); "The Class Struggle," *Crisis* (August 1921); *Dusk of Dawn,* p. 217.

16. W. E. B. Du Bois, "Black and White Workers," *Crisis* (March 1928). See Marable, *W. E. B. Du Bois,* pp. 111–12 and 142–43, on Du Bois's long-held reservations regarding Communists.

17. W. E. B. Du Bois, *In Battle for Peace: The Story of My 83rd Birthday* (New York: Masses and Mainstream, 1952), p. 180.

18. Du Bois's book, *Color and Democracy: Colonies and Peace* (New York: Harcourt, Brace, 1945), well exemplified his major interest of the period.

19. W. E. B. Du Bois, *The Autobiography of W. E. B. Du Bois: A*

Soliloquy on Viewing My Life from the Last Decade of Its First Century, ed. Herbert Aptheker (New York: International Publishers, 1968), p. 395.

20. For discussion of the factors in Du Bois's public decision to join the Communist party, see Marable, *W. E. B. Du Bois,* pp. 210–12.

21. Du Bois, *Dusk of Dawn,* pp. 6, 282.

22. Du Bois, *Dusk of Dawn,* pp. 6–7.

23. Du Bois generally regarded institutional religion as a bastion of unreason and reaction that buttressed the *status quo.* He was a humanist and a rationalist, not a theist or a supernaturalist. Antirational dogma repelled him, and he ceased participating in organized worship as a young adult. Yet he sincerely appreciated (though always as an outsider) the fervent religiosity of black folk, as is clear in *The Souls of Black Folk* and elsewhere. He also recognized the black church's role as a vital social institution and source of comfort and strength for African-Americans.

24. W. E. B. Du Bois, "Jesus Christ in Georgia," *Crisis* (December 1911), reprinted in *Creative Writings of W. E. B. Du Bois,* pp. 79–84; *Prayers for Dark People,* ed. Herbert Aptheker (Amherst, Mass.: University of Massachusetts Press, 1980).

There is considerable agreement among better and more recent students of Du Bois's work regarding its deeply spiritual aspects. See, e.g., Marable, *W. E. B. Du Bois,* p. ix, and Aptheker, "W. E. B. Du Bois and Religion: A Brief Reassessment," *Journal of Religious Thought* (Spring-Summer 1982): 5–11.

25. Du Bois, *Dusk of Dawn,* p. 326; *Prayers for Dark People,* p. 13.

26. Arnold Rampersad offers valuable insights into Du Bois's reflection of Puritan social ethics as well as the influence of denominational religion generally on his moral philosophy in *Art and Imagination of W. E. B. Du Bois,* pp. 5–8, 21–27, and 41.

27. W. E. B. Du Bois, "Last Message to the World" (26 June 1957), *Encyclopedia Africana* Secretariat Information Report No. 6, September 1962; reprinted in *W. E. B. Du Bois Speaks: Speeches and Addresses,* ed. Philip S. Foner, 2 vols. (New York: Pathfinder Press, 1970) 2: 326.

28. W. E. B. Du Bois, "Advice to a Great-Grandson," *National Guardian* (5 March 1958); reprinted in *W. E. B. Du Bois Speaks,* 2: 291–93.

SELECT BIBLIOGRAPHY

Primary Sources

Du Bois, William Edward Burghardt. *Africa: Its Geography, People and Products.* Girard, Kansas: Haldeman-Julius, 1930.

Du Bois, William Edward Burghardt, ed. *Atlanta University Publications on the Study of Negro Problems*. Atlanta University, 1898–1913.

——. *The Autobiography of W. E. B. Du Bois: A Soliloquy on Viewing My Life from the Last Decade of Its First Century*. Ed. Herbert Aptheker. New York: International Publishers, 1968.

——. *Black Reconstruction: An Essay toward a History of the Part Which Black Folk Played in the Attempt to Reconstruct Democracy in America, 1860–1880*. New York: Harcourt, Brace, 1935.

——. *Color and Democracy: Colonies and Peace*. New York: Harcourt, Brace, 1945.

——. *Crisis* (New York City) 1910–1934.

——. *Dark Princess: A Romance*. New York: Harcourt, Brace, 1928.

——. *Darkwater: Voices From Within the Veil*. New York: Harcourt, Brace, & Howe, 1920.

——. *Dusk of Dawn: An Essay toward an Autobiography of a Race Concept*. New York: Harcourt, Brace, 1940.

——. *The Horizon* (Washington, D.C.) 1907–1909.

——. *In Battle for Peace: The Story of My 83rd Birthday, With Comments by Shirley Graham*. New York: Masses & Mainstream, 1959.

——. *John Brown*. Philadelphia: George W. Jacobs, 1909.

——. *Mansart Builds a School*. New York: Mainstream, 1959.

——. *The Ordeal of Mansart*. New York: Mainstream, 1957.

——. *The Philadelphia Negro: A Social Study*. Boston: Ginn and Co., 1899.

——. *The Quest of the Silver Fleece: A Novel*. Chicago: A. C. McClurg, 1911.

——. *The Souls of Black Folk: Essays and Sketches*. Chicago: A. C. McClurg, 1903.

——. *The Suppression of the African Slave-Trade to the United States of America, 1638–1870*. New York: Longmans, Green, 1896.

——. *The World and Africa: An Inquiry into the Part Which Africa Has Played in World History*. New York: Viking, 1947.

Secondary Sources and Edited Volumes

Aptheker, Herbert, ed. *Against Racism: Unpublished Essays, Papers, Addresses by W. E. B. Du Bois, 1887–1961*. Amherst: University of Massachusetts Press, 1985.

——, ed. *Annotated Bibliography of the Published Writings of W. E. B. Du Bois*. Millwood, N.Y.: Kraus-Thomson, 1973.

Aptheker, Herbert, ed. *The Complete Published Works of W. E. B. Du Bois.* 37 vols. White Plains, N.Y.: Kraus-Thomson, 1973–1986. The best source for reprints of Du Bois's original writings and book editions. Aptheker's introductions and annotations are very helpful. *Selections from "The Crisis,"* for example, is a wonderful collection.

———, ed. *The Correspondence of W. E. B. Du Bois.* 3 vols. Amherst: University of Massachusetts Press, 1973.

———. *The Literary Legacy of W. E. B. Du Bois.* White Plains, N.Y.: Kraus-Thomson, 1989.

———. "W. E. B. Du Bois and Africa." In Marvin Berlowitz and Carol Martin, eds., *Racism, Imperialism, and Peace.* Minneapolis: MEP Publications, 1987.

———. "W. E. B. Du Bois and Religion: A Brief Reassessment." *Journal of Religious Thought* 59 (Spring-Summer 1982): 5–11.

Clarke, John Henrick, et al., eds. *Black Titan: W. E. B. Du Bois.* Boston: Beacon Press, 1970.

De Marco, Joseph P. *The Social Thought of W. E. B. Du Bois.* Lanham, Md.: University Press of America, 1983.

Du Bois, Shirley Graham. *His Day is Marching On: A Memoir of W. E. B. Du Bois.* Philadelphia: J. B. Lippincott, 1971.

Foner, Philip S., ed. *W. E. B. Du Bois Speaks: Speeches and Addresses.* 2 vols. New York: Pathfinder Press, 1970.

Harding, Vincent. "W. E. B. Du Bois and the Black Messianic Vision." *Freedomways* 9 (1969): 44–58.

Horne, Gerald. *Black and Red: W. E. B. Du Bois and the Afro-American Response to the Cold War, 1944–1963.* Albany: State University of New York Press, 1986.

Lester, Julius, ed. *The Seventh Son: The Thought and Writings of W. E. B. Du Bois.* 2 vols. New York: Random House, 1971.

Logan, Rayford W., ed. *W. E. B. Du Bois: A Profile.* New York: Hill & Wang, 1971.

Marable, Manning. *W. E. B. Du Bois: Black Radical Democrat.* Boston: Twayne Publishers, 1986.

Moore, Jack B. *W. E. B. Du Bois.* Boston: Twayne Publishers, 1981.

Moses, Wilson J. "The Poetics of Ethiopianism: W. E. B. Du Bois and Literary Black Nationalism." *American Literature* (November 1975): 411–27.

Rampersad, Arnold. *The Art and Imagination of W. E. B. Du Bois.* Cambridge: Harvard University Press, 1976.

3

Hubert H. Harrison:
Intellectual Giant and Freelance Educator

J. A. Rogers

That individuals of genuine worth and immense potentialities who dedicate their lives to the advancement of their fellow men are permitted to pass unrecognized and unrewarded from the scene, while others, inferior to them in ability and altruism, receive acclaim, wealth, and distinction, is common—yet it never ceases to shock all but the confirmed cynic. Those with a sense of right and wrong, of fitness and incongruity—whether they be wise men or fools—will forever feel that this ought not to be.

Shakespeare was so little regarded during his lifetime that no one bothered to record the details of his life, and today most of what is said about him is pure conjecture. Gregor Mendel, whose experiments were to revolutionize biology and agriculture, was practically unknown until sixty years after his death. Of course, there are some of genuine worth who do not die obscure and who do win gradual recognition while alive. But why are so many who we feel really ought to be up, down; and why are so many who certainly ought to be down, up?

Reprinted with permission of Macmillan Publishing Company from *World's Great Men of Color,* vol. II, by J. A. Rogers. Copyright © 1947 by Helga M. Rogers, copright renewed © 1975.

Hubert Henry Harrison is the case in point. Harrison was not only perhaps the foremost Afro-American intellect of his time, but one of America's greatest minds. No one worked more seriously and indefatigably to enlighten his fellow men; none of the Afro-American leaders of his time had a saner and more effective program—but others, unquestionably his inferiors, received the recognition that was his due. Even today only a very small proportion of the Negro intelligentsia has ever heard of him.

Harrison was born [in 1883] in St. Croix, Virgin Islands, of apparently unmixed African descent. His birthday, April 27, was also that of Herbert Spencer, by whose philosophy he was profoundly influenced. At sixteen he made a tour of the world as a cabin boy, and at seventeen came to New York, where he worked as a hall boy in a hotel, as an elevator operator, and in similar positions. With an avid desire for learning, he spent his spare time reading and went to a public night school. He was the brightest scholar in a class composed almost wholly of white people. Professor Hendrick Karr, his instructor, said of him:

> Harrison is the most remarkable Negro I have ever met. In the examination for the diploma—and it was rigid—he passed perfect at one hundred percent—the only student in his class having that rating. He will be heard from in the future if learning has anything to do with success.

Shortly afterwards he took the competitive examination for the Post Office Service, and passed with ease. Unable financially to enter college, he spent his leisure hours absorbing all he could of sociology, science, psychology, literature, and the drama.

Harrison remained at the Post Office for four years. The routine of sorting letters was not for a man of his caliber. But in a land so color-conscious and alive with race prejudice, what opportunities, if any, were there for a youth whose skin had been dyed so deeply black by nature? The only outlet for his talent, ambition, sympathy, and deep sense of justice seemed to lie in concentration on the problems affecting himself and his people.

He saw that Negro leaders were treating their injustices as a purely racial question, and that their program was nebulous, consisting largely of complaint or advice to submit. The Negroes, these leaders would whine, had been brought to America against their will;

they had supported the nation in all its crises—and just look how badly they were being treated for their pains! The remedy they suggested was work and submission, which they argued, would bring wealth.

Harrison, on the other hand, searched much more deeply. He realized that the Negro's ill-treatment transcended color differences; he knew that the black man in his time of ascendancy had exploited the white, and would do so again if the opportunity came. Color, he argued, was only the surface expression, and underneath it lay the world-old exploitation of man by his fellow man, which manifested itself now under the guise of tribal and national relationship, now under religion, political belief, sex, color, or anything else available.

His study of modern science and sociology enabled him to see that the Socialists had a clearer vision of this truth than either of the two great American political parties. Consistently, also, the Socialists were advocating the improvement of the economic lot of humanity, regardless of race or color. He thereupon joined the Socialists, who were few in number, but very militant. This latter feature pleased him most.

He showed such zeal that he rose rapidly to be one of the recognized leaders. His all-around knowledge; his grasp of economics; the logic of his thought; his fearlessness; his ability as a speaker, all brought increasing recognition to the party. He took an active part in promoting strikes, one of them at the Paterson, New Jersey, silk mills. It is true that the exploited white workers in those mills objected to working with Negroes, but Harrison, with his wider vision, saw that the cause of the black worker was also that of the white worker, and he hoped to make the white workers see that some day. With Elizabeth Gurley Flynn, Bill Haywood, Morris Hilquitt, and other party leaders, he labored for the emancipation of the workingman.

His activities were not confined to Socialist gatherings. He spoke wherever an audience could be had on subjects embracing general literature, sociology, Negro history, and the leading events of the day. He wrote also for such radical and antireligious periodicals as *The Call, The Truth-Seeker,* and *The Modern Quarterly,* being perhaps the first Negro of ability to enter this field.

While the older Negro leaders were taking generally a backward or a conservative point of view or agitating along purely racial lines, Harrison continued to speak of the Negro "problem" in its universal aspect, making it one with the protest of oppressed humanity everywhere.

He applied the latest scientific theories to the position of the Negro, and found much in Marx, Buckle, Spencer, Nietzsche, Schopenhauer, Lenin, Bertrand Russell, Dewey, and others to support his own ideas. At the Modern School (later located at Stelton, New Jersey) he was appointed adjunct professor of comparative religion, lecturing on the natural history of religion and expounding modern socialistic ideals and tendencies.

His views on religion and birth control were often opposed by Catholics and Protestants alike, and at his open-air meetings he and his friends were obliged to defend themselves physically from mobs at times. But he fought back courageously, never hesitating to speak no matter how great the hostility of his opponents.

He continued to work with the Socialists until he found that they, too, were becoming infected by color prejudice. Most of the original leaders were still sincere, but certain of them, tired of the struggle, were surrendering to the newer ones, who were either for barring Negroes from their ranks altogether, or for dealing with their wrongs pianissimo in the hope of attracting more adherents. The Socialists, too, he felt, were becoming capitalistic-minded, at least in their attitude toward the Negro, and therefore, he was convinced, they could not be relied on to treat Negroes fairly should they ever come into power. He left them in 1917.

Retiring to Harlem among his own people, he founded the Liberty League together with its organ, a newspaper called *The Voice*. He continued his open-air addresses, stressing the economic side of the color question, which brought him much opposition from Negro press, pulpit, and politics. The Negro preachers, and sometimes their white colleagues, objected to his theories on evolution—which were Darwinian—and would summon the police to break up his meetings.

Nevertheless, crowds flocked to hear him. His auditors would stand hours at a time shifting from foot to foot, entranced. He had a way of presenting the most abstract matter in a clear and lively fashion, so that the least of his hearers were not only spellbound by his powerful delivery but also understood what the man was talking about. His vast knowledge and keen logic were a delight to the sophisticated.

For a livelihood he sold literature. So able was he in this respect that on one occasion he disposed of 100 copies of a book on sociology at $1 each within an hour on Lenox Avenue in Harlem. The feat was all the more remarkable in view of the fact that the purchasers were Negroes, who, as a group, were very little inclined to buy books.

Harrison also gave open-air addresses in parts of the city inhabited by white people. At Ninety-sixth Street and Broadway a large crowd of whites usually assembled to hear him, and at Wall Street, the world's money center, he had an even larger audience. Some of America's wealthiest men, attracted by his eloquence, would stop to hear his dissertations on philosophy, history, economics, and religion.

One of the men who was very much influenced by Harrison was Marcus Garvey, later the most prominent of Negro agitators. Garvey's emphasis on racialism was due in no small measure to Harrison's lecturers on Negro history and his utterances on racial pride, which animated and fortified Garvey's views. Harrison's slogan became "Race First"—in opposition to his earlier socialistic one of "Class First." He explained this change by saying that since the Socialists were mostly Americans who had been reared in an atmosphere of color prejudice, they habitually thought "White First," hence, whenever their economic interests were involved they were usually ready to sacrifice the Negro. Thus, he reasoned, if Negroes thought in terms of "America First," or "Class First," they would be neglecting their own interests—at least until the time that the whites—socialist-minded and otherwise—underwent a real change of heart. Hence, he said, in self-defense, Negroes must think "Negro First."

Harrison's views profoundly influenced the Messenger Group, headed by A. Philip Randolph and Chandler Owen, two leaders who did more than anyone else to focus the attention of the government and of thinking whites on the injustices suffered by Negroes during the [First World War]. While the old leaders capitulated and urged the members of the race to submit while the war was on, these two brilliant young men spoke out fearlessly. Largely because of opposition from the War Department, The Messenger Group received nationwide publicity; by showing that progress toward obtaining justice lay not in barren agitation about race, or in dying and going to a white man's heaven, but in awareness and intelligent application of economic laws, it opened new vistas to the minds of thinking Negroes and not a few whites.

The Garvey movement and the Messenger Group, the first racial, the second economic in doctrine, had only radicalism in common and later became enemies. Both, however, represent eras in the progress of the Afro-American, and both were fructified by the spirit and teaching of Harrison.

In 1926 Harrison became a staff lecturer of the Board of Education of the City of New York. He gave a series of lectures at New York City College, making several addresses at New York University as well. Several times he was the principal speaker at the Sunrise Club, a fortnightly gathering of some of the most brilliant minds of the city. Fluent on almost any subject, he was best in topics dealing with world problems in relation to the darker races.

Under average height, Harrison was sturdily built. His head attracted instant attention, the more so as his forehead, which was a shade lighter in color than the rest of his face, seemed illuminated. It was unusually large and so fully rounded out in its upper portion that it seemed to bulge from pressure within.

His health was excellent, though at times he suffered from vertigo while speaking and had to steady himself. Small wonder, for he spent the night in reading, even after his strenuous three-hour lectures. He would retire at daybreak, sleep for two or three hours, and start the day all over again.

He made many enemies among the more conservative Negro leaders, especially those who derived support from wealthy whites. When he died, the two leading Negro magazines, the *Crisis* and *Opportunity*, ignored him, though at the same time, the *Crisis* gave space to the death of Tiger Flowers, Negro pugilist.

Harrison was not without his faults. The life of any leader, scrutinized detail for detail, does not look like the handsome image presented by ecstatic admirers after flaws have been removed and bits retouched. As the saying goes: "No man is a hero to his valet." The process of debunking history that has been going on since World War I has spared neither Jesus nor Washington—yet who would deny their essential greatness?

One of the many charges made against Harrison was that he called himself a "Doctor of Science," although he had not received that degree from a university. This charge seemed to be well founded —yet the fuss stirred up about it was out of all proportion to its significance, and handicapped him seriously. It is not for this writer to dwell upon the ethical implications of the case, yet in justice to Harrison it should be pointed out that in America especially, it is common for many who can barely read or write to adopt titles such as "Doctor" or "Professor," and this is particularly true among the Negro clergy, where "D.D.'s"* are really superabundant. Often an individual who displays a certain amount of learning is addressed by a title, and in the Southern states that of "Colonel," for instance, is a form of courtesy. Harrison first entered a university as a lecturer, which, considering the fact that he had no formal education or prestige therefrom, would be regarded as quite an achievement by anything but a warped mind. There is no proof that he received a degree from the University of Copenhagen, as he said, yet it is obvious that he felt this ruse necessary in order to win favor in the eyes of those who worship degrees, holding them to be symbols of genuine scholarship. The sad commentary here is not so much on Harrison as on the academic system and the picayune minds it produces. Few graduates of any university excelled Harrison in erudition, and after a thorough investigation of the matter, it seems as if Harrison was not so much a delinquent as a victim of professional jealousy on the part of those who, by all rules of common decency, should have given a handicapped colleague a boost instead of a kick.

Inconsistencies in politics might be another point against Harrison. An ardent Socialist, he turned Democrat—a considerable change, to be sure. Yet when a principle for which one has labored hard and long fails economically, and when one has a wife and five young children to support, who can deny the reasonableness of practical considerations? If Harrison expected an appreciable material increase from his switch to the Democrats, it was not forthcoming. His enthralling oratory should have paid him well, yet, like so may scholars, he was so thoroughly wrapped up in his work that this aspect of the situation quite escaped him. Whatever money he received usually drifted to him as food to a polyp attached to the piles of a pier. Harrison's lifelong enemy, like that of most scholars, was poverty. Destiny sent him into this world very poor. And as if this were not enough, she gave him a critical mind, a candid tongue, a family to support; a passion for knowledge, and on top of all that, a black skin, and sent him to America. Surely, a more formidable string of handicaps would be hard to conceive.

---

*Doctor of Divinity—Ed.

Most of the enmity against Harrison was incurred by his devastating candor. In this respect he was an *enfant terrible*. He spoke out freely what he thought, and more often than not it was with such annihilating sarcasm and wit that those whom he attacked never forgave him. Before he began his attacks, he usually collected "the evidence," as he called it, consisting of verbatim utterances, verbal or printed, of the prospective victim. This type of ammunition was deadly. There was, however, no personal malice in Harrison's shafts. Like a true sportsman, he was willing to shake hands with an opponent as soon as he descended from the platform, and was surprised and hurt that the other was not.

In his personal contacts Harrison was kindly and good-natured, and both among the common people and the broad-minded intellectual whites he had many friends. He was happiest and at his best on a "soapbox" surrounded by admiring listeners and a heckler or two to match in a combat of wits. He would usually squelch these amid outbursts of laughter from his audience.

He momentarily forgot names, but his memory was astounding. In the course of his addresses he would reel off quotations from poets great and obscure, cite passages from Spencer, Darwin, Huxley, and other scientists and scholars without an error; in jokes and anecdotes he was to the point.

Unlike most persuasive speakers, he was also an able writer. At the age of twenty-four he was writing book reviews for the *New York Times*—a remarkable achievement for a beginner. He also contributed articles and reviews to the *New York Sun, Tribune, World,* and other metropolitan dailies, as well as for periodicals, including *The Nation, The New Republic,* and *Masses*. He was assistant editor of the last magazine for four years, and editor of Garvey's *Negro World* for another four years. Through this medium he did much to stimulate learning in various parts of the world. Every week he compiled a list of books on literature, science, drama, and learning in general as recommended reading. His best editorials and articles were published in two booklets: *The Negro and the Nation* and *When Africa Wakes*.

In his last years he suffered acutely from poverty. His clothes became shabby and his shoes heavily patched, quite in contrast to the appearance of many other Negro leaders, less sincere and less capable than he. All that he owned at the time of his death were his favorite books.

If the day ever dawns when mankind values truth and learning more than money and the superficial amenities of life, then men like Harrison will be at least assured of what nature freely gives to the animals in their haunts, namely, food and shelter. Then what is so glibly called civilization will really deserve its name. In the pursuit of an ideal surely no more can be demanded of one than to sacrifice literally everything, as Harrison did.

Harrison had many admirers. The following are some of the tributes paid to him while still alive:

New York University Daily News: "Dr. Harrison's address on 'India's Challenge to the Powers,' was enlightening, authentic, and imposing."

Miss Ernestine Rose, librarian of the Harlem branch library, at which Harrison often spoke: "I appreciate very deeply Dr. Harrison's keen and intensely living mind; his wide and varied culture and his intellectual contribution to the expressed thought of his day."

The New York Times (September 11, 1922): "Hubert Harrison, an eloquent and forceful speaker, broke all records at the Stock Exchange yesterday."

Burton Roscoe, literary editor of the *New York Tribune* (June 4, 1923): "Mencken asked me to introduce him to Dr. Hubert Harrison, who sat next to me at the dinner, and very soon Dr. Harrison was the center of the most serious discussion of the evening; for Theodore Dreiser, Heywood Broun, Ludwig Lewisohn, Charles Hansen Towne came over for the pleasure of talking with the distinguished Negro."

William Pickens, winner of the Ten Eyck prize for oratory at Yale University: "Here is a plain black man who can speak more easily, effectively, and interestingly on a greater variety of subjects than any other man I have ever met even in the great universities. . . . I know nothing better to say than that he is a walking encyclopedia of current human facts. . . . If you have brains you will give him the palm as an educational lecturer. . . . If he were white, and I say it boldly, he might be one of the most prominent professors of Columbia University, under the shadow of which he is passing his days."

Hodge Kirnon: "He was the first Negro whose radicalism was comprehensive enough to include racialism, politics, theological criticism, sociology, and education in a thoroughgoing and scientific manner."

The obituary notices were striking. The *New York News* (December 31, 1927) said:

> Thousands of New Yorkers will miss the philosophy of the most brilliant street orator that this metropolis has produced in the last generation. The soul of Hubert Harrison knew neither black nor white, race nor religion. If a more universal man has been created in our day we have not met him. His fund of philosophy, ready wit, his measured and melodious utterances disarmed all those who came to scoff, and turned them into his admiring followers. He was a potent and living example of the potential equality of the black man.

Rev. Ethelred Brown: "In Hubert Harrison we had a man so human, so natural, that because of this we forgot for a while that we stood in the presence of an intellectual giant."

The *Pittsburgh Courier*:

> It was a revelation to see Hubert Harrison mounted on the street corner ladder and surrounded by a crowd of several hundred Negroes discussing philosophy, psychology, economics, literature, astronomy, or the drama, and holding his audience spellbound. His achievement should prove an inspiration to many young Negroes, for despite the handicap of poverty, he became one of the most learned men of his day, and was able to teach the wide masses of his race how to appreciate and enjoy all the finer things of life, to glance back over the whole history of mankind, and to look forward "as far as thought can reach."

REFERENCES

Harrison, Hubert Henry. *The Negro and the Nation.* New York: Cosmo-Advocate Publishing Company, 1917.

———, ed. *The Voice of the Negro,* Vol. I, no.1 (April 1927). New York: International Colored Unity League.

———. *When Africa Awakes.* New York: The Purro Press, 1920.

4

Joel Augustus Rogers: A Leading Scholar, Thinker, and Motivator

Mike McBryde

ROGERS ON THE CONCEPT OF RACE

Realizing that prejudice usually stems from ignorance, the African-American historian Joel A. Rogers (1883–1966) dedicated his life to building a greater understanding among diverse peoples. He realized that doctrines of selfishness and racial hatred were in conflict with open mindedness.

What made Rogers so remarkable was his incredible perception. Adept not only in English but in foreign languages as well, he managed to expose the subtle racism that existed in the mainstream scholarship of his time. In a straightforward and fearless manner, Rogers attacked pseudoscientific propaganda and racial ideologies that are still, despite changes, being used today. His books and articles have influenced W. E. B. Du Bois, Haile Salassie, Elijah Muhammad, and Malcolm X. This intellectual giant was also largely responsible for the sense of pride that exists in the African-American community today. Seen from a racist's point of view, Rogers's work would be considered somewhat dangerous, because his books tended to lead toward the eradication of the black self-doubt that was especially prevalent earlier in this century. He examined the racist double standards that are still keeping the many black people ignorant about their past.

Rogers noted that while the rising dictator Adolph Hitler originally claimed that the concept of racial superiority was a hoax, two great and ostensibly democratic nations—America and Britain—had been using it to oppress people of color for centuries. Later, when the fascists and Nazis themselves advanced this destructive doctrine, America and Britain were quick to denounce them, hypocritically proclaiming "liberty and justice for all." At the same time, Rogers observed that America, Britain, and other white nations, fearful of miscegenation, used "race" as a fetish to keep their citizens and subjects divided. Rogers, therefore, began his study of "race" mixing. He noted that mankind, beginning as a single family, eventually separated into several branches. Social thinkers as diverse as Aristotle, Arthur Sansen, and William Shockley maintained that, after distinct nations and laws had evolved, these branches were no longer parts of the same family. But Rogers denounced this belief by affirming that racial understanding, racial sympathy, is the key to permanent world peace.[1]

Rogers cited evidence of fear of miscegenation in the plays of Shakespeare (some example of which will be presented in the next section) and the writings of the ancient Greeks. He noted that Joseph-Arthur de Gobineau, Thomas Jefferson, Abraham Lincoln, and many other famous political thinkers had used the concept of race to divide humanity; and it is this kind of thinking that deeply influenced Hitler, a devoted student of American racial thought. Rogers wrote: "People are governed . . . by myths, and of all the myths . . . racial superiority is the sweetest. Any number of otherwise intelligent people, some of them of the highest scientific pretensions, can be found who believe that their own race is elevated far above the rest of humanity . . . ."[2] Rogers's arguments thus worked to dispel the myth that whites were "pure" until their contact with the "colored races" following the discovery of the New World. His works (especially volume 3 of *Sex and Race* and *Nature Knows No Color Line*) proved that whites and blacks had intermixed since prehistoric times, and that claims of racial purity were unsubstantiated. Indeed, Rogers argued that many historical figures who were believed to have been whites, had African roots. They included the Egyptian queen Hatshepsut, the pharaoh Thutmosis, and the Carthaginian general Hannibal.

Rogers devoted at least five decades to uncovering many unknown facts about the history of people of African descent. He realized early that not only were his people in the dark regarding their identity, but that they did not know where they were headed or how to free themselves from their collective slave mentality. He wondered how a people could have respect for themselves if they adhered solely to another people's standards of beauty. He wondered, too, how a people could successfully compete with others if their world had been shattered by others' greed, religion, selfishness, and brutality. Rogers was one of those rare and talented yet troubled individuals who was determined to find the answers to his questions. He kept calling attention to the fact that Africa was not respected by mainstream historians. He asserted that white history, with its Eurocentric bias was used to deny blacks, Indians, and other people of color their right to self-determination while at the same time forcing them to renounce their culture and their roots. Rogers noticed that people of color tended to identify with the white world rather than their own.

Rogers had grown up in a society that was indifferent to the grievances of black people. The world in which he lived seemed like one that was growing increasingly decadent and full of contradictions. But while acknowledging that blacks had been brutally victimized, Rogers believed that if they succumbed fully to a philosophy of victimization, they would eventually destroy themselves.

ROGERS'S VIEWS ON THE BLACK SLAVE MENTALITY, THE COLOR BLACK, AND THE CAUSES AND EFFECTS OF SLAVERY

Rogers argued that the emancipation of a people didn't necessarily happen with a mass exodus or the signing of a document. It had to occur first in the minds of a people. He came to this realization after some interesting experiences both in the church and in the classroom, where he found rampant hypocrisy. In the classroom, the only facts presented regarding the achievements of blacks were chosen by whites. If they were lucky, children were taught about Crispus Attucks, Frederick Douglass, and Booker T. Washington; but great African contributions to world civilization were ignored. The children didn't learn that people of African descent conquered mighty nations and taught science and mathematics. Subsequently, most people were led to believe that blacks had never created a worthwhile civilization.

After discovering the ancient source material, Rogers often wondered why scholars would continue to deny historical truths that, if properly taught, could motivate an entire people. He knew that wise men studied history not simply as an academic discipline but as a way of affirming national pride. History formed the basis upon which all nations realized themselves as nations; upon which all people built their cultural foundations; and upon which all legacies were continued. Rogers could therefore not understand why white economists, ethnologists, and sociologists, as well as historians, would always adduce the law of "cause and effect" to help explain white societal ills that derived from, say, the Civil War; but whenever the mental effects of slavery were discussed to explain the plight of blacks, some of these same scholars would hypocritically snarl: "Don't mention something that happened 150 years ago; it has no bearing on what is happening today. Slavery is over." Yet how was it possible for four centuries of fear, rape, torture, self-abnegation, family separation, and dehumanization to have no effect on the way African Americans viewed themselves?

The respected historian Arnold J. Toynbee criticized other whites for trivializing the devastating psychological impact that slavery had on the minds of African Americans, as compared with the various forms of slavery that had been practiced in other cultures. Toynbee wrote:

> From first to last, the Negro's suffering at the hands of English-speaking peoples of the Western world has probably been greater in the aggregate than those of the Greeks and Orientals and barbarians who were enslaved by the Romans. The horrors of the Delian slave market in the 2nd century B.C. are hardly to be compared with those of "the middle passage" on transatlantic slave ships in the eighteenth century of the Christian Era; and even if we allow that the next stage of the slaves' career, the conditions of servile life and labor on the plantation of modern America, may not have been as bad as those of ancient Italy, we must add that the Roman slave at least saw his horizon (i.e., freedom) faintly yet distinctly illuminated by a gleam of light which has never been offered to the Negro survivor of the transatlantic voyage nor to any of his descendants even in the third or fourth generation.[3]

But even Toynbee, Rogers revealed, was not free from racial prejudice. In Rogers's promotional literature he noted that Toynbee had written that of the "21 primary" races, the black race was the only one without a contribution to any civilization.

Rogers revealed that the stigma attached to being black and the subsequent self-abnegation were European inventions, and that the contempt that many American blacks had for their hair texture and other physical features was not to be found in African societies. He realized that as a group, African Americans were a sick people, and that those who had graduated from college or become "successful" were perhaps the sicker members of that group. During slavery, whites created a value system for the slaves that brought about the loss of their collective sense of pride. Original source material allowed Rogers to discover that if "Uncle Toms" were nonexistent before their enslavement by Europeans, the Europeans had to have created them. He desired to prove the Western intellectuals wrong about their assumptions regarding the so-called "Negro." His mission was essentially to remove the veil of ignorance that had been draped over the eyes of the Africans since the European had conditioned them to work against themselves.

Rogers wrote about the manner in which blacks were "programmed" by their slave masters: ". . . very, very little had been left psychologically of the original African. Uprooted from their native land and [culture], then scattered among the white population, there was nothing left for Negroes to do but adopt the language, customs, religion, and general teachings of the whites. They adopted these so much that it is a matter of record that the descendants of Africans born among the whites generally looked down on the newly arrived African. In short, though black without, they became white within."[4] As a result, Rogers noted, even in his day many African Americans preferred to boast of their European or Indian blood while ignoring their African ancestry. This problem still continues.

Rogers was heavily influenced by Carter G. Woodson, the "father" of Negro History Month. Woodson wrote: "When one controls a man's thinking you do not have to worry about his actions. You do not have to tell him to stand here or to go yonder. He will find his 'proper place' and will stay in it. You do not need to send him to the back door. He will go without being told. In fact, if there is no back door, he will cut one for his special benefit. . . . History shows that it does not matter who is in power . . . those who have not learned to do for themselves and have to depend solely on others, never obtain any more rights or privileges in the end than they do in the beginning."[5] Rogers was further influenced by what Woodson said about America's hypocritical double standards pertaining to freedom, independence, and equal opportunity: "A Negro with sufficient thought to construct a program of his own is undesirable, and the educational systems of this country generally refuse to work through such Negroes in promoting their [i.e., the African Americans'] cause."[6]

Rogers's greatest motivation for researching history and leaving a literary legacy for black intellectual advancement was his desire to dispel the myths associated with the color black. The negative attitudes toward black skin, he discovered, were originally manifestations of Eurocentric mythology and superstitions. Later, many whites would alter these superstitions and apply them stereotypically to blacks, thus affecting the collective mentality of the blacks for centuries. Such mental slavery was achieved by whites as a result of their repeated attempts to destroy several key elements of African self-awareness and traditional life. By the annihilation of a sense of group identity, unity would become impossible, and slavery could be more easily practiced. With African cultural traditions thus destroyed, the slaves' resistance to bondage was severely limited. Rogers further realized that the socialization process (i.e., media, religion, and education) was used to control slaves, and later, free blacks. Such a process resulted in an unnatural state of dependency and a near-amnesic loss of the slaves' African cultural memory. The slaves were trained to respond to the instructions of their masters. Such observations led Rogers to conclude that the power to define and determine a people's existence is ultimately the power to destroy them.

Rogers was such a dynamic historian because he was not primarily concerned with being accepted by the leading historians of his day. "The slave masters have done their jobs well," wrote Rogers.

This new African mind, the "creation," which took the European several centuries to "train" and to "mold," desires to have nearness to those that have little desire to see him succeed. He refuses, even today, in the broadest sense, to intelligently define his own reality, then act on that reality for future advancement. He is so well trained, in fact, that he is now convinced that he is less intelligent. He feels defeated.

Such has been the education of Negroes. They have been taught about history, but have never learned to think. Their conception is that you go to school to find out what other people have done, and then you go out in life to imitate them. What they have done can be done by others, they contend; and they are right. They are wrong, however, in failing to realize that what others have done, we may not need to do. If we are to do identically the same thing from generation to generation, we would not make any progress. If we were to duplicate from century to century the same feats, the world would grow tired of such a monotonous performance.[7]

By reading the works of Rogers, one will easily learn how the black man arrived at his present condition. "Because the newly enslaved Negro represented an ever present danger as a potentially violent rebel within the heart of white society, the system of slavery required a style of dominance over the black man [which was] more effective than the simple threat of physical punishment and torture. What was required was a form of brutality that rendered the mind of the black man useless except for those functions that were desired by whites—from devoted laborer to object of white sexuality. In a systematic process, whites attempted to dismantle the psychic integrity of their black slaves."[8]

The growing respectability of theories of white supremacy occurred simultaneously with attempts to impose on blacks feelings of inferiority. When blacks began to think of themselves as ignorant, childish laborers, they became docile and passive in the face of their oppression —docility and obedience were necessary for the slaves' survival. "Boy" became the epithet for black men. American literature and art portrayed blacks with these qualities and implied that, because they were ignorant and immature, they deserved their plight. "Sambo was created by whites, imposed on blacks, and then rejected by whites as a model unfit for dignified human behavior."[9] In *Nature Knows No Color Line,* Rogers gave evidence of the origin of color prejudice which began when Nordic or fair-skinned whites imposed their standards of beauty on the darker Spaniards, Portuguese, Greeks, and Italians.[10] The color white had become equated with purity, cleanliness, and Godliness. Conversely, blacks were forced to believe that everything associated with the color black was trivial or inferior.

By the time the colonialists had arrived in the New World they had already inherited many negative images associated with the word "black," as noted by Rogers. In the late fifteenth century, "soiled" and "filthy" became synonymous with "black." By 1536, "black" was synonymous with "deadly" and "malignant"; by 1581 "baneful," "sinful," "sinister," and "disastrous," also connoted blackness. In the late sixteenth century, Englishmen taught that "smut" meant "to make dirty." The devil was established as the "Black Prince" in 1563; in 1590 pagan practices fell under the title "black arts." This term was derived from the Latin word "nigromantia," which was a corruption of the Latinized Grecism "necromantia" (divination by corpses). Words such as "necromancy," "death," "secret," and "devilish" were also tied to the word "black." African blood was said to contain "poison" that could "taint" the supposed purity of European blood.

Even Shakespeare was not entirely free from this belief, as Rogers noted. In his first tragedy, *Titus Andronicus,* the murderous Machiavellian is portrayed as a black "Moor"—a member of a people about whom Rogers often wrote. Aaron, the black Moor, fathered an illegitimate child with his mistress Tamora, the beautiful white empress. The rest of Shakespeare's play seems to speak to the white male's fear of miscegenation—the underlying theme of most of Rogers's works. Tamora's nurse was appalled by the faithfulness of the Moor. In response to Aaron's question, "What is it she dost wrap and fumble in her arms?", Tamora replied: "O that which I would hide from heaven's eye." When Aaron inquired about the child's sex, the nurse screamed that it was "a devil . . . a joyless, dismal, black and sorrowful issue . . . as loathsome as a toad amongst the fairest breeders of our climate." Aaron the Moor screamed back: "Zounds, ye whore! Is black so base a hue?" In *Love's Labours Lost,* the king cried: "Black is the badge of Hell, the hue of dungeons and the soot of night." And the enraged Macbeth screamed at his servant, "The devil damn thee black."

Slavery engendered in black children born in the New World a self-abnegation that would last for many generations. Many black adults would pray that their children might be born with light skin and "good" (or straight) hair. This attitude is still pervasive in the African-American community today. In many cases, if a black woman gives birth to a baby who has straight hair, the mother's friends advise her on how to maintain the texture. Rogers spoke against this form of self-hatred by advocating self-knowledge and pride in his people's natural appearance. He believed that blacks had to reassert themselves by throwing off the shackles that had been imposed on them, i.e., European standards of beauty. He was aware, however, that such "psychological warfare" could not be easily overcome—especially when these negative beliefs were reinforced by the mass media.

ROGERS'S THOUGHTS ON RACIST HISTORICAL VIEWPOINTS

In *Sex and Race,* Rogers declared: "there is but one race . . . the human race." He pointed out that European laws were racist when they declared any child of mixed parentage—a mulatto—was a "Negro." He later revealed that many whites were so obsessed with the supposed purity of their own genes that they tended to ignore the anthropological facts that contradicted their claims. As already stated, Rogers denounced the racist scholarship of Toynbee, as well as the "Teutonic Germ Theory" (to be discussed below). Rogers countered claims that "white" implied higher intelligence and a greater degree of civilization by saying that, in reality, the farther away from northern Europe a culture was, the more likely that civilization was to have been highly civilized at an earlier stage in world history. He pointed out, for instance, that the ancient Egyptians (who belonged to an Africoid civilization), the Kushites, the Mesopotamians, and the East Indians (who were also largely Africoid), had highly developed civilizations when Europeans were still living in caves. By the time of the rise of Greek Civilization, Africa was already in decline. Indeed, it was the Greeks who were the inheritors of the older African, Asian, and Indian civilizations.

Rogers was a thorough advocate of humanism and believed in the inherent equality of mankind. This could be historically demonstrated by the fact that all races, including the European, had intermixed. He relied on accurate historical and physiological research to show, for instance, that what would come to be known as the "Aryan philosophy of race purity" had in fact no moral or scientific merit. By the same token, the bogus claim that any accomplishments made by blacks was due only to the substantial amount of "white blood" in their veins could be countered by the observance that therefore there must be black blood in white veins.

Rogers's many books exploded the myths supporting racist

ideologies, and exposed the humorous contradictions of the Western ethnologists and their apparent lack of self-esteem. Logically, a people who are truly secure with themselves should never feel compelled continually to besmirch the character of another, oppressed people. Perhaps it is that those who advance the pseudoscientific discipline of ethnology have traces of supposed "inferior blood" flowing through their own veins. A description of *Nature Knows No Color Line* states: "Starting with ancient Egypt . . . Greece and Rome, this book shows what the Negro had contributed, especially to Western European civilization . . . . For instance, there were the Moors, who invaded Europe in 711 A.D. and were the dominant power there for the next 500 years. Writings and paintings of those times show them as jet-black and wooly-haired. The Moors gave Europe one of its finest civilizations and rescued it from the Dark Ages. Not only have the Negroes contributed science and art to Europe, *but since they were once dominant, their blood entered into that of the whites,* and some were ancestors of Europe's leading families—including royal ones from Italy to Scandinavia . . ." [author's emphasis].[11]

Nonetheless, white supremacists continued to fear that their race would be bred out of existence by miscegenation. Universities in the American South received substantial support from racist historians whom Rogers briefly discusses in his first chapter of *Sex and Race*, vol. 1. Though these eminent white scholars were not involved with raping, lynching, and mutilating blacks, they managed nevertheless to pervert their disciplines in ways that would reaffirm racial myths that condoned the unjust treatment of blacks. Some of the pseudoscientific support for racism—before, during, and after Rogers's time—came from the American schools of anthropology, including many prominent scholars. Louis Agassiz wrote: "The indomitable, courageous, proud Indian . . . in how very different a light he stands by the side of the submissive, imitative Negro."[12] Rogers, however, noted that the Greeks and the Romans were influenced by African fashion, science, medicine, philosophy, and architecture. Likewise, many European religions share features of those of nonwhite peoples. Thus, Rogers was able to demonstrate that Europeans had a long history of imitating the very people whom many of them deemed inferior and "imitative." In his own words: "Had the Negro been an incompetent, unwilling worker . . . he would never have gotten the very name he did. It was his very assimilability, his capacity for progress, that caused the slaveholders to invent the doctrine of inferiority in order to keep him down."[13] Rogers further noted that there is no civilization—with the exception of tiny, isolated cultures —that hasn't borrowed from, imitated, or been influenced by other cultures at some time.

Ethnology, too, served to promote white hegemony. The "Teutonic Germ Theory" is one of the most notorious examples of the pseudoscientific nonsense to have emerged. Its leading proponent was Henry Baxter Adams; but Professor John Burgess explained it in greater detail. Burgess was an educator who taught political science and history at Columbia University for 36 years. Theodore Roosevelt had been one of his students. While doing research in Germany in the 1880s, Burgess learned of the the concept of German racial superiority. Later, he came to believe that Germans and Americans had marked similarities in their respective cultural and governmental achievements due to what he regarded as the similar racial make-up of Germany and the United States. He also believed that the two countries were blessed by God with the power to dominate the world. Americans, he thought, were originally a mixture of Teutonic and French strains, but the Latin (darker) racial component had been somehow lost due to contact with the wilderness. "The German people," he wrote, "stand closer ethnically, than any other people, to the American people."[14]

The depth of Burgess's devotion to a racist interpretation of history led him to discount even the grand influence of Greco-Roman political thought. He wrote: "Education can only be developed in what already exists in the seed and germ . . . . The Teutonic peoples possessed the proper germ with which to build politically stable governments; ideally they alone have political power . . . . The proof of this was found in the political stability which characterized any Teutonic people in the U.S., as opposed to the [darker] peoples in Southern Europe who are inclined to anarchy and crime . . . . They are the exact opposite of genuine [white] Americans."[15] Rogers provided striking evidence that European civilization was far more impressive in the South and in Mesopotamia (largely African, Semitic, and mulatto), as well as in Northeast Africa. "The ancestors of the Carthaginians," wrote Rogers, "were the Phoenicians, who were Negroid, their founder being Queen Dido. Dido is said to have refused to marry Iarbus, the Black King of Morocco . . . ."[16]

Rogers continues: "Concerning Queen Dido, this is said to have given Jerome Dowd, Professor of Sociology at Oklahoma University, an opportunity to read Southern color prejudice into classical history. Says Dowd, 'the attitude of the Caucasian toward intermixture with the Negro had not changed within the historic period. As far back as 700 B.C., the fair widowed Queen Dido of Carthage committed suicide rather than comply with her subjects to marry Iarbus, the swarthy monarch of Mauretania.' "[17] Rogers responds: "The first objection is that there is no proof as to Dido's color. She might have been anything from white to black. But supposing she was white, were it so unnatural and selfish as to wish her to marry a Negro? That meant the subjects had no such underlying color prejudice as Dowd endows them with. If Dido and her subjects were black, then would it be 'unnatural' for them to wish their queen to marry a black man? Besides, there are several versions of why Dido killed herself. According to Virgil, she committed suicide because her lover, Aeneas, deserted her."[18]

Following is one of the many contradictions in ethnological racial classification systems cited by Rogers:

The Ethiopians, who both in color, hair, and oft-times features, show more of the Negro trait than the African American, are classed by the ethnologists as white—a fact that most Ethiopians resent. . . . But instructions to the 1940 census-takers in America were that anyone with Negro strain, however slight, be set down as a Negro. Someone has rightly described a Negro in America as one light enough in color to ride in a white coach in America. . . . But if he speaks a foreign language, no matter how dark he is, he is classed as white. . . . In short, when one enters the field of ethnology one steps into a field of crooked thinking, where the main idea is to prove inferior and superior races. If the kind of science that is in ethnology went into engineering, no car would ever run, no airship would leave the ground, and no clock would run.[19]

Rogers was aware that categorizing people by race often led to genocide. In the 1880s, Burgess would have been dismissed as a fraud had he not influenced a future president and taught in a leading university. But at the end of the nineteenth century, his insistence that the "Teutons" were a superior race and that whites should separate themselves from the "lesser races" when necessary (and even exterminate them if they stood in the way of progress), found support in a society that was embarking on imperialistic ventures abroad while discriminating against blacks at home. Carter G. Woodson warned: "If a race has no history, if it has no worthwhile tradition, it becomes a negligible factor in the thought of the world, and it stands in danger of being exterminated."[20] The teachings of Burgess as well as other racist ideologies were later used to justify American imperialism in Cuba, Hawaii, and the Philippines.

Psychologists and many other white professionals, as Rogers clearly pointed out, were not above blending their otherwise objective research with racist thinking. But Rogers successfully challenged the notion of white intellectual superiority. One example of the misleading scholarship with which Rogers had to contend follows:

> [In an] intelligence test given in the Army in 1917 and 1918, Brigham proceeded to prove in his book *A Study of American Intelligence,* that "Nordic-white" racial types were more intelligent than both Negroes and Jews. Yet the data revealed not only that Northern blacks frequently did better on the tests than Southern blacks, but also better than literate Southern whites with Nordic blood. Instead of examining the environmental factors which may have caused the "discrepancy," psychologists explained it in terms of the percentage of Nordic blood that flowed through the Negroes' veins—concluding that intelligence varied in relation to "Nordic Inheritance."[21]

In 1952, Rogers wrote in his book *100 Amazing Facts About the Negro:* "The peoples of Southern Europe, including Italy and most of those of Eastern Europe and Russia, are more illiterate than Negroes in the U.S.A. In seventy years Negro illiteracy has fallen off about 80 percent. In 1870 it was 82 percent; in 1930, 16.3 In the U.S. Army intelligence tests during WW-1, Negroes of Pennsylvania, N.Y., Illinois, and Ohio led the whites of Mississippi, Kentucky, Arkansas, and Georgia by one to seven percent. . . . Afro-American illiteracy is three times higher than white [but] when certain states are matched against certain others, there are surprising comparisons. For example, Negroes of California, Minnesota, Nevada, South Dakota, Oregon, and Washington are less illiterate than the whites of Virginia, North Carolina, New Mexico, etc. . . . The Negroes of these several states are less illiterate by 100 to 400 percent than foreign-born whites of all states, save one."[22]

Rogers also adduced the evidence of white scholars who denounced the theory of white Nordic superiority; one such scholar was Joseph McCabe, who affirmed: "Primitive man . . . was a colored person . . . dusky. . . . Four thousand years ago, when civilization was already two thousand years old, white men were just a bunch of semisavages on the outskirts of the civilized world. If there had been anthropologists in Egypt, Crete, and Babylon, they would have pronounced the white race obviously inferior, and might have discoursed learnedly on the superior germ plasm of . . . colored folk."[23]

Another defender was Professor Dorsey, who said: "How low the savage European must have looked to the Nile Valley African looking north from his pyramid of Cheops. . . . Were the white an inherently superior race we should not have found it, at the beginning of authentic history, almost lost under a sea of underlife, but its superior qualities would have told at a far remote epoch; the Negro and the Mongolian expansion would have been checked long before, and history would have opened up with the Caucasian as the dominant element."[24] According to J. P. Widley: "They, the Negroes, once occupied a much wider territory then they do now and [had] a vastly greater influence. . . . The first Babylon seems to have been [populated by] a Negroid race. The earliest Egyptians seemed to have been Negroid . . . in the days before the Semite (mulatto) was known in either land. The blacks built up a great empire by the Ganges, before Mongol or Aryan. So, way down in the mud of beginnings . . . is the Negroid contribution to the fair superstructure of modern civilization."[25] Finally, Professor Toynbee, although he made statements about blacks that were clearly racist, admitted: "Our modern Western racialists have rationalized their Calvinism by substituting black and white for damnation and grace and expurgated it by omitting the divine cause—the result is not science but fetishism."[26]

Rogers, while pointing out the shortcomings of racist Western scholarship, never wrote with an air of black superiority. Realizing that many of his findings regarding racist teachings could produce hostility in black people, he was always quick to let it be known that not all white scholars were white supremacists. He once commented: "A few anthropologists such as Finot, Boas, Hershovits, Dorsey, and Hotten taught the opposite, but their voices were al-

most drowned out by the paranoiac screamings of the false prophets.
. . . It is my opinion, based on fairly wide experience, that the white
race, when not agitated by the cunning propagandists of capitalism,
is almost totally free from color prejudice, in any case it is less disturbed
by it than the blacks. In the many years I lived in Europe, I did
not once see a native European discriminate against a Negro, except
in the case of certain hotel proprietors who did it to please
Americans."[27]

ROGERS'S VIEWS ON RELIGION

Rogers became an atheist for a number of reasons. He believed that
a person had a right to believe in God, but he objected to the ways
in which many religious beliefs were practiced. In Rogers's estimation,
Christianity, as practiced by Westerners, did more to oppress, brainwash, and harm the black psyche than it did to motivate, unite, and
uplift black people. Many contradictions and double standards within
the Bible, for instance, caused him to wonder whether it truly was
the Word of God. He became especially curious when he discovered
that religious folklore from various cultures not only preceded many
of the stories in the Bible, but were so identical that it became very
clear to him that much of the Bible was not original. Rogers learned
that the Hebrews, in writing their version of the origin of man, copied
it from the legend of "Hadama and Hava" (Adam and Eve) that
came from eastern India. Rogers asked himself, "If God is rational,
why does there exist so much irrationality in his alleged word? The
American slaveholders, finding themselves forced to explain how the
teachings of Christ could be reconciled with the cruelties of slavery,
set their lackeys, the theologians, who were the 'scientists' of that
time, to find an explanation. . . . Turning to the Bible, the leading
'scientific' authority of that period, the servile divines discovered that
Cain had taken a wife from the land of Nod. Now, according to
the story of the Creation, which is Jewish folklore and nothing more,
there were only three people alive on the planet, Adam, Eve and
Cain. . . ."[28]

Rogers discovered blatant contradictions in both the text and
the practice of Christianity. He was disturbed by the notion that
blacks were the descendants of Ham, whose son Canaan had been

cursed by Noah. According to Genesis 9:25, Noah said: ". . . Cursed be Canaan; a servant of servants shall he be unto his brethren." In biblical times, prejudice was based on tribal, national, and religious differences, rather than color. But according to this myth, Noah had become drunk with wine and had fallen asleep in the nude. Ham supposedly laughed at him, while Shem and Japhith, Noah's other sons, covered Noah's body. For Ham's indiscretion, his eldest son Canaan was doomed to be a servant, as were all his offspring for generations to come. As Rogers put it: "Were not Negroes black, different in color from the whites? Blackness and servitude should go together like ham and eggs, or Siamese twins. Moreover, slavery was so philanthropic. It made 'good Christians' out of heathens and useful servants from savages. . . ."[29] Millions of Americans were exposed to "the myth of Ham." Rogers said: "I myself was taught in Sunday school, and by a Negro teacher, who valiantly defended the falsehood, quoting the Bible as the infallible authority. Of course, the Bible says no such thing. . . . The Canaanites, on whom this alleged curse of 'blackness' is supposed to have descended, were Asiatics, while the ancestors of the New World Negroes came from West Africa."[30]

Rogers's questions about Christianity were not answered to his satisfaction. The stories of Adam and Eve, Moses, Samson, and others were so identical to earlier stories from other cultures that they had to have been copied. Moreover, Rogers was deeply disturbed by the religious fanaticism he witnessed during his life. He wrote of an African-American graduate, twenty-six years old, from Tuskegee Institute, who in 1938 insisted that the "curse of Ham" myth was true. Rogers asked why the young man felt this way, and the graduate responded, "Because the Bible said so." Rogers also spoke of a white friend from Minnesota who had asked two Mormon missionaries from his home state if blacks could be admitted into their religion. They replied, "Yes, but we do not encourage them because their race is cursed by God himself." But as Rogers later discovered, the peoples of West Africa had a fitting reply to the curse of Ham. "You're wrong," said the natives to the missionaries and slave traders. "All men were originally black, but Cain killed Abel and God shouted at him, frightening Cain so much that he turned white and his features shrunk up, making him the first white man."[31]

Rogers did not become an atheist overnight, however. In his own words:

> As I look back on it now, I think it really began in my early childhood when it was firmly impressed on me by the ruling classes that black people were inherently inferior and that their sole reason for being was to be servants to white people and the lighter colored mulattoes [in his native Jamaica]. The blacks, I was told, had never accomplished anything in history, which of course, began with Adam and Eve, and that such signs of civilization they . . . showed were due to the benevolence of Christians . . . . The Christian blacks themselves said amen to this and joined in spreading the doctrine. My Sunday School teacher, an almost unmixed Negro, told us that black people were cursed to eternal servitude to white people because Ham had laughed at his drunken father, Noah. To clinch his argument he read to us from the Bible, which we were taught was infallible. Doubt but a single word, try to change but a title, and you were doomed to burn in hell forever. The slave masters and kidnappers had indeed done their work well. They had so incorporated their iniquities with the Christian religion that when you doubted their racism you were contradicting the Bible and flying in the face of God Almighty . . . ."[32]

Rogers's unmixed school teacher further claimed that the farther away one was from being white, the lower was his status in the eyes of God. But despite Rogers's initial fear of eternal torment, he could not refrain from asking questions—he was much too logical. He was taught that God was good, yet he was similarly taught that God had cursed millions of people simply because one human "ancestor" had laughed at his father because his father had made a fool of himself. This prompted Rogers to ask himself, "Was God so much in favor of the drunken father?"

To refute the myth of black inferiority further, Rogers noted that at school his black schoolmates were often brighter than their white counterparts. And while growing up, he saw black lawyers, physicians, and professionals who had attended the best Scottish universities. He asked himself, if the African strain was inferior to that of the whites, why were these blacks successful—even more so than some of the barefoot White adults? But in Sunday school Rogers was forced to keep quiet. Had he uttered one word of doubt, he could have been branded a traitor or infidel, which was considered worse than being a criminal, for a criminal could at least be saved from eternal torture. Rogers noticed that if someone did not believe the story of Jonah and the whale or the story of Moses and the parting of the sea, that person was not considered to be a good citizen.

Rogers, who was light-skinned, had been taught to look down on one dark individual with whom his father debated about the miracles of the Bible, which his father called "rubbish." Thus, Rogers's revolt against Christianity was based largely on his observation that racism and Christianity seemed to go hand in hand. A case in point is the segregation of black and white churches. He found the Mormon religion to be especially racist. There are Mormons who still harbor the notion that blacks cannot go to heaven because of their race. Rogers wrote:

> I ran across some Mormon missionaries in Germany in 1927 and a Minnesota white woman recently wrote me about their teachings in her state. In 1903 when burial services were being held in a Baptist church in Salt Lake City for Eugene Burns, a Negro, the grandson of Abel Burns, faithful servant of Joseph Smith, founder of Mormonism, Patriarch Miner, president of one of the quorums . . . walked up to the pulpit and to the consternation of mourners began a highly sensational discourse to prove that Burns, as a Negro, could not reach the state of exaltation necessary for entrance into heaven and that his soul was doomed from birth. The only Negro, Miner declared, that entered heaven was Burns's grandfather because of his fidelity [to] the prophet.[33]

BLACK GODS AND MESSIAHS

Rogers's studies in comparative religion indicated a direct connection between African and Indian gods and the accounts of Christ's nature and miracles. In the Appendix to his *Sex and Race,* vol. 1, Rogers wrote extensively on the subject of the black gods and messiahs. "The messiahs," he wrote, "some of whom lived centuries before Christ, had lives so close to that of Christ that it seems most likely that the story of the latter was adapted from them." Rogers first learned of the Africoid strain of the original Buddhas in the 1899 edition of the *Cambridge Encyclopaedia.* Referring to the first Buddha of the Hindu Pantheon, one excerpt reads: "The messiah was foretold by the prophets; he was the son of the Holy Spirit and the Virgin Maia; he was born in the village of Rajagritha; was recognized and worshipped by the Magi and the Kings; the messianic star stood over the place of his nativity; a brilliantly lit nimbus of light surrounded the holy infant's head; his complexion was black; his hair woolly; he was prematurely wise . . . his doctrines . . . were promulgated by ten disciples" (pp. 106–107).

This Buddha, like Jesus, some 1366 years later, came to reform mankind and save the world, where he remained until he was persecuted by the reigning king. And like Christ, he died at the age of thirty-three, descended into the netherworld where he remained for three days and three nights, and judged the dead. He then rose to a heavenly abode. The *Cambridge Encyclopaedia* also described Egyptian god Osiris as black-complected and woolly-haired. He was supposed to have been included in a slaughter of the innocents ordered by Typhon but he escaped. He performed a number of miracles; had ten disciples and was crucified on the vernal equinox; he descended to hell where he remained three days and three nights to judge the dead, then rose and ascended to heaven.[34]

The basic physical characteristics of people having African ancestry are woolly hair, thick lips, a broad nose, and jet black to very light skin. These traits were found in not a few idols and statues from the ancient world. Rogers was very familiar with the works of Sir Godfrey Higgins, who authored a two-volume work titled *Anacalypsis*. In Higgins Rogers found cited several ancient authors who had written about the ebony color of many of the Greek gods. "Bacchus, according to the ancient writers Ovid, Pausanias, and Anacreon, said his complexion was black, his hair woolly."[35] Black-skinned, woolly-haired Buddhas with flat noses and thick lips can still be found in museums throughout the world. As a rebuttal to many white scholars who still deny a black origin for the Buddhas, Rogers observed: "There is a tendency to deny that the ancient Buddhas were Negroes despite the fact that they are portrayed with Negroid hair and features. We are told that the curls on the heads of the Buddhas were originally snails that settled on the scalp to protect it from the burning sun. But is not the ethnological explanation less miraculous . . . ? Negroes still live in India. . . ."[36]

We may end with a quote from F. Wolford's *Asiatic Researches*, Vol. 3 (London 1799), which was cited by Rogers:

It is certain that very ancient statues of Gods in India have crisp hair and the features of the Negro. . . . I have seen many idols on which the woolly appearance of the hair was so well presented as to preclude all doubt. . . . The Brahmans ascribe these idols to the Buddhas, and nothing hurts them more than to say that any of their own gods had the figure of "Habashis" or Negroes; and even the hair of the Buddha himself for whom they have no small degree of respect, they consider to be twisted in braids, like the Midern Sannasis. But this will not account for the thick lips and flat noses of these ancient images; nor can it be reasonably doubted that a race of Negroes formerly had power and preeminence in India. In several parts of India the mountaineers still have [hair that is] curled and has a tendency to wool.[37]

CONCLUSION

Joel Augustus Rogers is a figure who has aroused curiosity and pride in both blacks and whites. His research did much to combat the feelings of white superiority. A world traveler, Rogers served as a newspaper correspondent during the Italian-Ethiopian War in the 1930s. For his help in improving race relations throughout the world and political involvement, Rogers received wide acclaim. In 1930, the Paris Society of Anthropology elected him as a member—one of its few black members since its inception in 1859. In the same year, he spoke at the International Congress of Anthropology which was opened by President Doumer of France. At his coronation Haile Selassie, the emperor of Ethiopia, awarded Rogers for his work. Greatly admired by many noted educators and officials, Rogers successfully redirected the thinking of many of those who read his works.

NOTES

1. J. A. Rogers, *Sex and Race,* vol. 1 (New York: Helga M. Rogers, 1952), foreword.

2. Ibid., p. 2.

3. Barry N. Schwartz and Robert Disch, *White Racism: Its History, Pathology and Practice* (New York: Dell Publishing, Co., 1970), p. 17.

4. J. A. Rogers, *Africa's Gift to America* (New York: Helga M. Rogers, 1961), p. 5.

5. Carter G. Woodson, *The Miseducation of the Negro* (Philadelphia: Hakim's Publications, 1939), back cover copy.

6. Ibid., pp. 133–34.

7. Ibid., p. 138.

8. Schwartz and Disch, *White Racism: Its History, Pathology, and Practice,* p. 18.

9. Ibid.

10. Rogers, *Nature Knows No Color Line* (New York: Helga M. Rogers, 1952).

11. Rogers, *Sex and Race,* vol. 1 (New York: Helga M. Rogers, 9th edition, 1967), on the book's jacket sleeve.

12. In Schwartz and Disch, *White Racism: Its History, Pathology, and Practice* p. 31. On the same page, Louis Agassiz speaks of Mongolians as being a "sneaky, cunning and cowardly race."

13. Rogers, *Sex and Race,* vol. 1, p. 25.

14. In Schwartz and Disch, *White Racism: Its History, Pathology, and Practice,* p. 31.

15. Ibid., p. 32.

16. Rogers, *Sex and Race,* vol. 1, p. 90.

17. Ibid. Rogers quotes from Professor Jerome Dowd's work, *The Negro in American Life* (New York: D. Appleton-Century Co., Inc., 1926).

18. Ibid.

19. Ibid., p. 37.

20. *Journal of Negro History* 11 no. 2 (April 1926). See *Negro History Bulletin* 47, no. 1 (January–March 1984): 6.

21. Schwartz and Disch, *White Racism: Its History, Pathology and Practice,* p. 33.

22. J. A. Rogers, *100 Amazing Facts About the Negro* (New York: Helga M. Rogers, 1957), pp. 5, 22–23.

23. Joseph McCabe, *Keys to Culture,* book 3 (Girard, Kans.: Haldeman Julius, Publishing, Co. 1927), p. 50.

24. Rogers, *Sex and Race,* vol. 1, p. 50. Rogers quotes from Wiley, *Race Life of the Aryans,* vol. 2 (1807), pp. 239–41.

25. Ibid., p. 264.

26. Ibid., p. 17.

27. Ibid.

28. Ibid., pp. 22–23.

29. Ibid., p. 23.

30. Ibid, p. 23. The information is repeated in *Sex and Race,* vol. 3.

31. J. A. Rogers, *World's Great Men of Color,* vol. 1 (New York: Helga M. Rogers, 1946; reprint Macmillan, 1972).

32. Rogers, *Sex and Race,* vol. 1, p. 4.

33. Ibid., p. 268, Appendix.

34. Ibid., p. 265, Appendix.
35. Ibid., p. 117.
36. Ibid.
37. Ibid., p. 268.

5

Cheikh Anta Diop:
Death Shall Not Find Us
Thinking that We Die

Ivan Van Sertima

I felt a strange sense of awe in his presence. It was the aura of nobility and graciousness, perhaps, the quiet air of intellectual authority; the legend of his life and his work that had preceded him. His eyes never left me as he spoke but though his gaze and his grip were firm, his voice was surprisingly soft. The sibilances of his French rose and fell upon my brain like waves of whispers.

"Monsieur Diop," was all I could say, "we meet at last."

It was a cool, blue London day, the light of a premature springtime loitering like a stranger on the streets of a winter morn. January 13, 1985 . . . about a year and a month before his death! We had exchanged long letters, we had spoken on occasion on the telephone, I had read his work in English, he my work in French.[1] He had followed avidly the issues of the Journal of African Civilizations. *Yet nearly a decade was to pass before we met face to face. That week in London we talked to packed houses. We dined, we discoursed,*

From *Great African Thinkers, Vol. I: Cheikh Anta Diop,* edited by Ivan Van Sertima and Larry Williams. Reprinted by permission of Transaction Publishers and the author.

we debated. Diop's great friend of many years, Carlos Moore, made us feel at times as though we were conversing in the same language. But in spite of the growing familiarity, my sense of awe and reverence in his presence persisted. I saw him more as a father than as a comrade-in-arms. I felt the long road that I would still have to walk. I could not shake off the impression of being in the shadows of an elder spirit.

It is not for us to say that the death of a man comes too early or too late. Fate is far too complex. But let us venture to say that we in America needed a guide and a teacher like Diop. Africa, above all, needed a leader like Diop. Had he lived to become President of Senegal, he might have piloted some of the nations of West Africa into the first stages of a federated state. His passing, therefore, is a very great blow to us all. Yet history teaches us that men like these do not die at the time of their deaths. Often it is that the fall of a great teacher or prophet is the beginning of the rise of his ideas. So be it with Diop . . .

He was born on December 23, 1923, in Diourbel, a little town in western Senegal. He was of a Muslim peasant family and attended Koranic schools. His hometown, Spady informs us, was the seat of a strong Muslim sect and brotherhood where collective activity was considered sacred. This was the sect of the Mourides, the only black African sect, according to Diop, which succeeded in acting independently from the rest of the Muslim world. Diop completed his bachelor's degree in Senegal and then went on to Paris in 1946 to do his graduate studies.

Proud, stubborn, independent, Diop did not take the easy road to his doctorate. Instead, he attempted something that took him straight into the mouth of the guns. He presented a lengthy and closely argued dissertation on ancient Egyptian history. The main lines of his thesis may be summarized and simplified thus: that Egypt was the node and center of a vast web linking the strands of Africa's main cultures and languages; that the light that crystallized at the center of this early world had been energized by the cultural electricity streaming from the heartland of Africa; that the creators of classical Egyptian civilization, therefore, were not the brown Mediterranean Caucasoids invented by Sergi, nor the equally mythical Hamites, nor Asiatic nomads and invaders, but indigenous, black-skinned, wooly-haired

Africans; that Greece, mother of the best in European civilization, was once a child suckled at the breast of Egypt even as Egypt had been suckled at the breast of Ethiopia, which itself evolved from the complex interior womb of the African motherland.

Of course, the jury of the University of Paris roundly rejected this thesis, labeling it "unfounded." It ran counter to all that had been taught in Europe for two centuries about the origin of civilization, although the early Greeks themselves, who knew the Egyptians of that time and studied their metaphysics and their sciences, would have agreed in the main with Diop. Diop's thesis, after all, was not entirely new. Others had stated this before. What was new was the formidable competency in many disciplines that he brought to bear to establish this thesis on solid, scientific foundations. Although it was rejected by the University, it was published under the title *Black Nations and Culture*, earning its author international recognition. It took him ten years and two more doctoral dissertations, both of which were revolutionary in perspective, before he was granted the doctorate. These dissertations were published as *The Cultural Unity of Africa* (1959) and *Pre-Colonial Black Africa* (1960).

Diop was not just a major revisionist historian. He was an extremely promising physicist. He eventually gained entry into a major nuclear research center near Paris. The establishment of this center was made possible through the influence of one of France's most distinguished scientists, Frederick Joliot-Curie, son-in-law of Marie Curie who, with her husband Pierre, won the Nobel Prize for the discovery of radium. Diop spent a lot of time working and experimenting in this laboratory. He became one of the very few Africans, as Spady notes, "with access to the most advanced body of scientific knowledge." At a time when only a handful of people in the world understood Einstein's relativity theory, Diop translated a major portion of it into Wolof, the language of his people.

His scientific background is very important in our assessment of his contribution to historical knowledge. He was able to use it to great effect to refine and develop his earlier Egyptian thesis. For example, Diop developed a chemical process for testing the level of melanin in the skin of Egyptian mummies he studied in the Museum of Man in order to establish their black African ancestry. His close examination of primary sources and his knowledge of metallurgy enabled him also to establish that the iron artifacts found in the ancient Egyptian empire were not intrusions from a higher stratum nor the accidental byproduct of another process, as Profs. Leclant and Mauny had claimed, but very strong evidence of the invention of iron-smelting by the Egyptians long before the Hittites and the Assyrians.

His greatest strength, perhaps, lay in linguistics. Assisted by the Congolese Egyptologist and linguist, Theophile Obenga, now President of the Center for Bantu Studies in Brazzaville, Diop established at the UNESCO conference on "The Peopling of Ancient Egypt" (January 1974) that the Egyptian language was African and that it was generally related to a family of African languages, including his own native Wolof. In spite of the passion and prejudice that marked some of the debates at this conference, the UNESCO report states, "the [linguistic] reports of Professors Diop and Obenga were regarded as being very constructive" and "revealed a large measure of agreement among the participants."

A summary of this conference is of interest and value to readers since it reveals the state of Egyptology at the moment and the defensive reaction to the question of "blackness" or "negroness." Professor Ghallab of the Arab Republic of Egypt declared that the human race during the paleolithic era (stone age) was more or less homogeneous and "Caucasian" and that "Negroes" only began to appear much later. A "Negro" culture, he claimed, did not appear prior to the neolithic (age of agriculture). Professor Debono of Malta spoke of a race of pyramid-builders coming into Egypt, a race with Libyco-Asiatic affinities, without even deeming it necessary to show where on this earth stands the photo-pyramid this "race" constructed before it migrated to Africa. Several participants, finding it difficult to demolish Diop, decided instead to demolish all talk about race. Professor Save-Söderberg of Sweden, while demonstrating that the majority of neolithic cultures in the Nile Valley belonged to a techno-complex of Saharan and Sudanic cultures, said the concept of race was outmoded and should now be abandoned. Professor Vercoutter of France, insisting that there was no way to tell how many of the Egyptians were white and how many were black, felt the evidence, nevertheless, showed that Egypt at least was African in its way of writing, its culture, and its way of thinking. Professor Shinnie of Canada said that Herodotus and all the Greeks and Romans who had called the Egyptians "black" were merely being subjective like Dr. Diop.

Race was not a scientific concept. Professor Mokhtar of the Arab Republic of Egypt said the problem of race was unimportant. Professor Abdallah of the Sudan, after chiding Diop for adopting an Africanist approach to this problem, went on boldly to assert that the Egyptian language belonged to a family of proto-Semitic languages and that there was abundant evidence to prove it. He had not come to the conference, however, with his "abundant evidence." This, in fact, was one of the remarkable revelations of this international conference. In its final report, UNESCO pointed out: "Although the preparatory working paper sent out by UNESCO gave particulars of what was desired, not all participants had prepared communications comparable with the painstakingly researched contributions of Professors Cheikh Anta Diop and Obenga." The Africans, at last, had done their homework, and those theses, which had once seemed formidable, now shook with the fragility of leaves in the new intellectual wind blowing from the continent.

Diop, however, was not merely fighting battles on the intellectual front. He realized that his new conception of history could provide a ground of unity and continuity on the African continent, forging new and powerful political forces to transcend the instability and fragmentation, the lack of real pride and faith and sense of a collective destiny in modern Africa. He founded the *Block of the Masses of Senegal*, a militant political party in 1960. The party was banned and he was arrested and imprisoned. He founded a second political party in 1964, the *Senegalese National Front*. This was declared illegal and he was again arrested. He founded a third political party, the *National Democratic Rally*, in 1976. Speaking of his political experience, in answer to a question posed by Larry Williams in 1985, Diop said: "I'm in the opposition party in Senegal. Senegal is perhaps one country where you can say there is a little more freedom than there is in other places. I can go from one place to another. But this is not a freedom we were given. This is a freedom we took. We paid for this freedom. For thirty years I have paid with my own self. I nearly died in prison, as you know. Things like this are no longer possible in Senegal."

His political vision was both idealistic and practical, radical and yet pragmatic and responsible. In spite of his death, it may have far-reaching consequences. As Charles Finch points out in *Further Conversations with the Pharaoh*, "He has worked out a theoretical model for the political, economic, and social reconstruction of Africa and has seen many of the programs and projects he has advocated over the last 30 years become public policy in his own country."

Diop was deeply disturbed by the grave instability of modern Africa. In a series of interviews with Carlos Moore in 1977, he spoke of the lack of national leadership that could set an example, of the swift and inevitable tumble of regimes all over the continent, of the selfish egoism of leaders running ineffectual and anachronistic mini-states. Commenting on the prospects of the newly formed Economic Community of West African States, Diop warned that all such attempts at economic regional regroupment were likely to fail unless West Africa developed "a supranational umbrella, in the form of a federal executive organ, able to make political decisions binding on all parties." Political unification is a prerequisite, he insisted, to the rational organization of African economies. "We want to create regional economic organizations from which member states can draw maximum benefits, yet we refuse to relinquish even an inch of our respective sovereignties. . . . The rational organization of African economies cannot precede the political organization of Africa. [It] must come *after* the creation of a federal political unity."

Political unity . . . a federated structure . . . these were not dreams to Diop but absolute necessities. No other African leader, including Nkrumah, set out with such energy and expertise to discover and to detail what steps should be taken to bring parts of Africa into a federation, none who examined so closely the location, distribution, and commercial value of African resources and the way in which these could most effectively be developed and deployed on an African continental basis.

He was no armchair theorist. He worked furiously to build the radiocarbon laboratory at IFAN in Dakar. This was established in 1966 for the purpose of low-energy radioactivity research and carbon-14 dating. He led the struggle for the formation of an African technology consortium. What has become of this consortium we do not yet know. Not enough information has been passed on to us. Speaking, however, as President of the World Black Researchers Association formed in 1976, Diop declared that the first objective of the association was to reverse the brain-drain. "The Association will englobe all of the scientific disciplines, both the natural and social sciences. Consequently it will comprise two permanent international secretariats, one for the natural sciences and the other for the social sciences. In both domains scholars and scientists of the black world will be asked to direct their efforts towards solving the most vital scientific and sociological problems presently confronting the black world. This will further solidify the cultural ties binding all black populations of the globe."

Some may find his vision of black global unity uncharacteristically naive for such a preeminently scientific spirit. His idealism, however, went hand-in-hand with a sound critical and commonsensical approach to both ancient and modern realities. Diop attacked the modern African tendency to establish one-party systems. "Experience has overwhelmingly shown that the one-party system has failed to build the type of Africa we desire. . . . The building of Africa must be based on freedom of choice. Only what is built on the basis of freedom is durable." Last April [1984], in a question-and-answer session with the Nile Valley Executive Committee, Diop pointed out that although ancient Egypt was elitist and had a hierarchy, it was also democratic. "It has been recorded that workers could sue ministers and governors before the law."

In terms of his vision of Africa as united territory and unifying force, Diop has been placed alongside Blyden, Garvey, and Nkrumah. There are certain refinements, however, in Diop's Pan-African philosophy that should be understood. It is not just a matter of semantics. It might be instructive to contrast his complex and dynamic view of what he calls "a cultural personality" and what Nkrumah called "The African personality" or what the poets of Negritude (Senghor and Césaire, for example) would define as "an African identity." Diop feels that an integration of three critical factors constitutes a cultural or collective personality of a people and that the emphasis on *one* can lead to flirtations with the past or an involvement in generalities. An edited version of the exchange between Carlos Moore and Diop on this point will help to explain what I mean.

MOORE: Kwame Nkrumah had opposed his concept of "African Personality" to the concept of Negritude. Are these concepts antithetical or do they converge anywhere?

DIOP: They converge in the sense that they both deal in generalities. We must get down to the facts, to the objective apprehendable realities. When we talk about personality, meaning the personality of collective groups, we can only mean a *cultural personality*. And what is the basis of the cultural personality of a people, African or otherwise, if not a historical, psychic, and linguistic self-consciousness? These three elements are the constituent elements of a people's cultural personality or identity. They are not static factors conditioned by man's social and physical environment. . . . My approach has clarified what is called the particular sensibility of the black man, or "black soul." I have tried to determine the nature of the black particularity in history and to ascertain the ways in which the "black soul" or "black sensibility" has influenced the material existence and creativity of black people by using the structures evolved by ancient black societies as a basis. . . . Rather than deal in generalities we must know what the black soul is because it is our soul. The way I saw it at the beginning was that Africa's soul had been stolen and could only be retrieved through a scientific approach.

It is this approach that has affected the new school of African-American historians. Most of us first came to know of Diop in the seventies through Mercer Cook's brilliant translation and editing of sections from *Antériorité des civilisations nègres: mythe ou vérité historique?* and *Nations nègres et culture*, which appeared under the title of *The African Origin of Civilization: Myth or Reality?* James Spady gives us the background to the scholarship on Diop's historical work. Spady has the distinction of being the first person in the English-speaking world to publish an essay on Diop. We have also been fortunate to be able to present reviews on two of Diop's major works in English and an excellent translation of the introduction and first two chapters of his last work, *Civilization or Barbarism: An Authentic Anthropology.* John Clarke and A. J. Williams-Meyers both attempt reviews of *The African Origin of Civilization.* Clarke points to Diop's predecessors, African historians like Dr. Danquah, European historians like Massey, Hereen, Volney. Clarke classes Diop among the greatest of African historians and recalls the first time he sought him out in Dakar. The anecdote tells us a lot about the Eurocentric control of African history. Clarke recalls the second meeting of the International Congress of Africanists. It was held about 300 yards from Diop's office and laboratory, yet he was not one of the participants. Reviewing the same work, Williams-Meyers expresses caution about certain aspects of Diop's methodology and terminology but he presents us with a scholarly and balanced analysis, taking account of the critics on the one hand and the body of evidence on the other.

Asa Hilliard introduces us to that difficult but central work in the Diop oeuvre, *The Cultural Unity of Black Africa*. Why this vision and dynamic of cultural unity must be used to weld a "population" into a "people" is eloquently restated by Hilliard: "No people can be liberated who are cultural neuters. 'Individuals' may survive as shooting stars with temporary spurts of speed, but with a curved path that ends in darkness. It is the group (in Diop's terms a *people* rather than a population) that survives as an eternal galaxy."

Runoko Rashidi, co-editor of *The African Presence in Early Asia*, highlights a little known aspect of Diop's work. Diop has taken a very real interest in Asia. A team of Japanese scientists visited his laboratory a few years ago to speak with him on his work. When he founded the World Black Researchers Association he placed particular emphasis on the inclusion of blacks from Australia, Fiji, New Guinea, the rest of Oceania and other parts of Asia, "a zone of the world where black populations find themselves scattered and isolated." Rashidi feels that in this area Diop has also blazed a brilliant trail.

On one point only he takes issue with Diop. That is on the question of the caste system of India. It is not the case, argues Rashidi, that in the caste system, as Diop claims, "the criteria of color has a low priority without any ethnic considerations." A fascinating addendum to Rashidi's essay comes in the form of a letter from a black untouchable sect in India, the Dalits, who have named a militant organization of Dalits, *Dalit Panther*, after the Black Panther movement in America. It is refreshing to find young historians who will provide challenges and corrections to the master's work when these are thought necessary. Diop would have welcomed the debate. As he said to me in a letter in 1979: "You must not abandon discussion out of tact. . . . There should be no concession where there is a question of establishing a scientific truth. . . . Remember we are focused on a quest for truth and not on a sacrosanct idol whom we must avoid debasing. . . ."

Diop's last work has been eagerly awaited in English translation. Several attempts have been made to do it but it is a formidable task. The unusual length of the work, the convolutions and idiosyncrasies of his style (which does not have the same directness as his speaking voice), the technical terminology growing out of his intimacy with many disciplines, daunts the prospective translator.

Fortunately, Diop gave his approval to one translation by Edward
F. Taylor of Morehouse and cabled us before his death to give the
Journal permission to publish it. Readers who would like a sense
of what the book is about in its entirety should read the excellent
summary of Leonard Jeffries in "The Legacy of Cheikh Anta Diop."
. . . What is ironic is that Diop died at the very moment that his
major thesis—that modern man proceeds from a single African ancestor—found its ultimate scientific confirmation.

We quote now from a document published on the day before
Diop's death. It is entitled "Evolutionary Relationships of Human
Populations from an Analysis of Nuclear DNA Polymorphisms." It
is the work of eleven scientists, most of them from the University
of Oxford, England, and it appears in *Nature*, vol. 319 (February
6, 1986). The team of scientists concluded: "The earliest fossils of
anatomically modern man (Homo sapiens sapiens) have been found
in Africa at Omo in Ethiopia, Border Cave in South Africa, and
at Klasies River Mouth in South Africa. The data from the last site
suggest that Homo sapiens sapiens was present in South Africa more
than 100,000 years ago, and an adult mandible from Border Cave
has been dated to about 90,000 years B.P. [before the present era].
Hence, it has been argued that the evolution of modern man took
place in Africa. Our data are consistent with such a scheme, in which
*a founder population migrated from Africa and subsequently gave
rise to all non-African populations.*"

A word or two of clarification is needed here for some of our
readers to understand the full importance of this breakthrough. What
has been in dispute is *not* whether man was born in Africa. This
has been universally accepted for some time. Those who argued against
Diop (the polygenetic theorists) for a multiple or plural origin of
man, could claim that, although man was born in Africa, he migrated
to Europe and Asia at a low-level stage (Homo erectus, say) and
then evolved into a more advanced and modern type on those continents. As more and more discoveries were made in Africa, sophisticated revisions could be made to this theory without seriously
upsetting their main thesis—of a backward African ancestor evolving
elsewhere into an advanced Homo sapiens sapiens (modern human
type). The scientific discovery above proves that this is not the case.
What it establishes is that while earlier African types might have
migrated and disappeared, the human at its most advanced stage,

at the peak of its present phase of evolution, came out of Africa to people other continents and merely underwent mutations or adaptations in other ecological zones. Perhaps, the most lucid layman discussion of this question appears in the lecture "The Beginnings of Man and Civilization" and in his interview with Listervelt Middleton, the only television interview Diop gave during his brief visit to America in April of 1985.

This visit took two years of planning. As Larry Williams says in his overview of the visit "it was the realization of a dream that had germinated in the hearts and minds of African-Americans" since the publication of his books in English. He was invited to preside over the Nile Valley Conference held in Atlanta in September of 1984. An accident with his plane, which Diop vividly describes in an interview with the Nile Valley Executive Committee, aborted a year of laborious planning. Diop finally made it, however, on a maiden flight initiated by Delta Airlines from Paris to Atlanta. His coming was like the arrival of an African president and he was received like one. Morehouse College, which had honored Presidents Kaunda and Mugabe, conferred an honorary doctorate on Diop. Mayor Young, who had issued a proclamation creating a "Cheikh Anta Diop Day" during the Nile Valley Civilizations conference in 1984, now provided him with the city's great hospitality and security. While many individuals and organizations contributed to making the visit possible, special credit should be given to Charles Finch for traveling to London with me in the winter of 1985 to finalize negotiations with Diop, to Larry Williams for his painstaking efforts to develop a valuable library of Diopiana, with the visit to America as focus (tapes, videos, translations, transcripts, slides, photographs), and Dean Lawrence Edward Carter, Sr., Dean of the Martin Luther King, Jr., International Chapel, for coordinating the visit.

It was indeed fitting that Diop should be hosted at Morehouse College, Martin Luther King's alma mater, and that he should speak in the Chapel dedicated to Dr. King.

"I have come to America to meet with those who are members of my family," he said in the Chapel, "that is to say with you all. In fact, I am convinced that my family has been divided in two and that half of it is here before me now. Just as you Americans who go to Africa feel that you are making a pilgrimage to the lands of your ancestors, I too am making a pilgrimage here in America. The most important thing that we have to do by the end of this century is to reconstruct the links that tie us as communities. I subscribe to the teachings of Martin Luther King, Jr., wholeheartedly. They are teachings that are aimed at unifying and reuniting kindred peoples. What I have to say here today is to reinforce the links that unite us and all people across the world. . . ."

Diop said and did a great deal in a very short space of time. He entered into lectures, discussions, dinners, tours, ceremonies, with the same energy that marked all his endeavors. As he looked back on his American voyage several months later in Dakar, he confided to Charles Finch: "I was very impressed by my contact with the black American community and with Americans in general. I discovered many things of which I was totally ignorant. As I said in the United States, I feel very strongly that this was a sort of pilgrimage for me. I think that all thinking Africans who go to America are, in one way or another, on a pilgrimage. I said before I left that I was going to find half of my family in America. It was just that. We are beginning to feel in a most vital way this biological kinship which ties us to America, the umbilical cord has not been cut. And this is very important. These relations must become much closer in the future. I believe that all of what lies in our common future is in this perspective. America is uniquely brought closer to Africa by historical ties. I was especially aware of this on American soil. . . ."

On this American soil, on this side or plane of time, we shall not meet again, Cheikh Anta. But we have gathered the leaves of this work together because of your presiding spirit, because of the essence and purpose of your work. It is our duty to continue what you have begun since we knew one day we would be forced to continue without your physical presence. Your spirit, after all, is the catalyst. And even if the wings, upon which your body flew, are broken, that spirit has already flown to us. It shall reside with us, it shall be enthroned in the hearts of your people always. . . .

Too soon, too soon
the banner draped for you
I would prefer a banner in the wind
not bound so tightly with a scarlet fold
not sodden, sodden, with your people's tears
but borne aloft
down and beyond this dark, dark lane of rags.

Dear Comrade,
if it must be
that I no longer speak with you
no longer walk with you
no longer march with you
then I must take a patience and a calm
for even now the greener leaf explodes
sun brightens stone
and all the river burns
Now from the mourning vanguard moving on
dear comrade, I salute you
and I say
Death shall not find us thinking that we die.[2]

NOTES

1. Ivan Van Sertima, *Ils y étaient avant Christophe Colomb* (Paris: Flammarion, 1981).
2. Excerpted from the poem "Death of a Comrade" by Martin Carter.

6

Richard Wright:
Beyond Naturalism?

Michel Fabre

That Richard Wright is a naturalist writer has generally been taken for granted by American critics. In his review of *Lawd Today,* entitled "From Dreiser to Farrell to Wright," Granville Hicks proceeded, not incorrectly, to show that

> he could scarcely have failed to be influenced by James T. Farrell who was just beginning to have a strong effect on American fiction. As Farrell had learned something about documentation from Dreiser, so Wright had learned from Farrell.

When he reviewed *The Outsider* for the *New York Times,* the same critic noted:

> if the ideas are sometimes incoherent, that does not detract from the substance and the power of the book. Wright has always been a demonic writer, and in the earliest of his stories one felt that he was saying more than he knew, that he was, in a remarkable degree, an unconscious artist.

From *American Literary Naturalism: A Reassessment.* Carl Winter Universitätsverlag, 1979. © 1979 by Michel Fabre. Reprinted by permission of the author.

Other reviewers even seemed to regret that Wright attempted to deal with ideas. In his review Orville Prescott stated that "instead of a realistic sociological document he ha[d] written a philosophical novel, its ideas dramatized by improbable coincidences and symbolical characters." And Luther P. Jackson outspokenly lamented that the

> words of Wright's angry men leap from the page and hit you between the eyes. But Wright can no more resist an argument on the Left Bank than he could a soapbox in Washington Park. The lickety-split action of his novel bogs down in a slough of dialectics.

It is clear, then, that Wright is regarded not as a novelist of ideas or as a symbolist, but as an emotionally powerful creator who writes from his guts and churns up reality in a melodramatic but effective way because he is authentic, close to nature, true to life. Conversely, the critics' displeasure at his incursions into other realms than that of social realism proves only that there are elements in his writing which cannot be reduced to their favorite image of him as a hard-boiled naturalist. The question then becomes: to what extent is he part of the naturalistic stream in American literature? Is he, in fact, sufficiently a part of it for his works to be judged, and found satisfactory or wanting, only according to that perspective? Or is his originality so strong that it cannot be adequately accounted for in terms of the Dreiser/Farrell line of succession, and does this therefore necessitate a reassessment of what is commonly held for American literary naturalism?

It is not my purpose here to reopen the long-debated question of what exactly naturalism is. In his preface to *American Literary Naturalism, A Divided Stream,* Charles C. Walcutt described it as "a beast of protean slipperiness" which, soon after it had sprung from the spring of Transcendentalism, divided into rebellious, idealistic social radicalism on one side and pessimistic determinism on the other; consequently, the assertion of the unity of nature and spirit, the equality of intuition and reason was somewhat diminished.

If we consider naturalism as a philosophy, it is clear from the start that Wright's perspective is only very partly akin to it. He had read Darwin's *Origin of Species* but he probably did not even know of Herbert Spencer, the true philosophical cornerstone of American naturalism. If he did, his Communistic leanings set him early on the side of Marx against the Spencerian view of the "survival of the fittest."

To him, the fittest were the productive workers, not the parasitic upper classes. Insofar as he was a Marxist, "the organized exercise of the social will" meant the liquidation of the bourgeoisie.

Estranged as he was from God by the oppressive religious practice of his Seventh-Day Adventist grandmother, Wright was also prone to eschew Transcendentalism as well as the very American belief that physical progress reflects spiritual progress. His childhood taught him that knowledge could indeed bring freedom, and self-education became his only means of escape from the cultural ghetto. But if knowledge can make man similar to God, he later discovered that too much knowledge can bring man beyond good and evil so that he ends, isolated from his fellowmen, in the position of a "little God" who has no right to act as one. This is the lesson in existential absurdity to be derived from *The Outsider*. Thus, at times Wright comes close to the naturalistic vision of determinism, which conceives of man as an accident, or an epiphenomenon caught in a general movement toward universal rest. This is apparent in a long (still unpublished) piece of poetry he wrote in the mid-fifties to celebrate the manifold incarnations of life. In it he deals with a force that works through man, and that inhabits him for a time, making him the vessel of a principle he cannot control. This force, though, does not tend toward static, cosmic rest; rather, it aims at self-fulfillment and unlimited expansion, it gropes toward a kind of pantheistic harmony in which matter and spirit are one. If this is transcendentalism of a kind, it represents only a transitory stage in Wright's thinking. On the whole, he is a humanist who retains the Marxist perspective as an ideological tool, and who believes in ethical responsibility, and a certain degree of free will in a world whose values are not created by a transcendental entity but by the common workings of mankind.

Insofar as naturalism is opposed to romanticism as a philosophy, it attacks the unscientific values of tradition and evinces a distrust of those natural forces that man cannot control; it thus corresponds to one facet of Wright's personality. If we look at an early short story, "Superstition," and at a later one, "Man, God Ain't Like That," we find that both denounce the obscene power that such beliefs—and Wright deliberately makes no difference between religion and superstition—can wield over the spirit of man. There, Wright is largely a rationalist. Similarly, when he advocates the cultural liberation of African nations, he still upholds the idea that what was good for Europe, insofar as rationalism and technology are concerned, should be good for the Third World: colonialism has unwittingly given Africa the tools for her own liberation from her religion-ridden ancestral past, and the new African leaders should seize that opportunity to step boldly into the twentieth century. Such is Wright's contention—an opinion which encountered strong opposition on the part of many African intellectuals at the 1956 Congress of Black Artists and Writers in Paris.

Where America was concerned, however, Wright held somewhat different views; he often regretted that his country had no past, and no traditions (however unscientific or irrational they might be).

Like many naturalists before him, Wright feared the forces that reason cannot control, forces that lie within the darkest recesses of man's soul, and his descriptions of Africa evoke at times Conrad's sense of horror in *Heart of Darkness*. Mostly he fears the forces man has unleashed and can no longer subdue, like the overpowering social systems that stifle the development of individuality.

A brief survey of Wright's many-faceted *weltanschauung* shows him to be inconclusively close to or remote from what passes for the common denominators of the various American naturalists. His position oscillates between Marxism and humanistic Existentialism.

We ought to remember that he is not primarily a thinker but a novelist, and therefore, that whatever may be characteristically naturalistic in his fiction is more likely to have resulted from his personal experience as a poor black American, or from his early readings and stands as an embattled writer. Although naturalism is as protean as a set of literary forms and techniques as it is as a philosophical view, it is, nevertheless, on these forms that the brunt of our analysis must rest.

In the often quoted episode from *Black Boy* in which he relates how he was spiritually saved by reading a few American novelists to whom he had been introduced by Mencken's *Book of Prefaces,* Wright mentions Sinclair Lewis's *Main Street,* Dreiser's *Jennie Gerhardt* and *Sister Carrie* as well as Stephen Crane:

> I was overwhelmed, I grew silent, wondering about the life around me. It would have been impossible for me to have told anyone what I derived from these novels for it was nothing less than a sense of life itself. All my life had shaped me for the realism, the naturalism of the modern novel, and I could not read enough of them.

Two things are important in this statement. First, the experiential basis of Wright's literary outlook ("all my life had shaped me for the realism, the naturalism of the modern novel"); second, the apparent lack of distinction between realism and naturalism; he seems to consider the two terms practically interchangeable. In this piece, written in 1943 after he had established his reputation as a novelist, Wright considers naturalism loosely, as simply another version of American realism; he is mostly interested in it because it provokes an authentic sense of life and an understanding of the American scene:

> *Main Street* . . . made me see my boss, Mr. Gerald, and identify him as an American type [. . .] I felt closer to him though still distant, I felt that now I knew him, that I could feel the very limits of his narrow life.

Such naturalistic novels convinced Wright that his life, hemmed in by poverty and racism, was not the only life to be circumscribed. Even the lives of the powerful whites that he had pictured as glamorous were restricted by uncontrollable circumstances. All men were encompassed by the same definition of the human condition. In a sense, Wright is relieved to see that white people don't escape man's common destiny; the racial gap artifically established by them tends to disappear, yielding at the same time to a more social perspective of rich versus poor, and to a universal humanistic view. Realistic/naturalistic fiction is thus defined, through Wright's own experience, as an eye-opener, in opposition to the romantic tales, the dime novels, the detective stories, the blood and thunder episodes he relished primarily because they provided him with an escape from everyday life. Romantic fiction became for him a synonym of evasion and vicarious revenge, wholly artificial because it precluded meaningful action. Naturalistic fiction provided him with a means of liberation through understanding. Although he sometimes read it, he contritely admits, as he would take a drug or dope, he generally derived from it a new social perspective.

> The plots and stories in the novel did not interest me so much as the point of view revealed. [. . .] I could not conquer my sense of guilt, the feeling that the white men around me knew that I was changing, that I had begun to regard them differently.

That early impact upon his sensibilities was to last. Throughout his life, he considered Dreiser, his favorite American master, a literary giant nearly on the par with Dostoyevski. Nothing indicates that he had read such early naturalists as Harold Frederic, Hamlin Garland, or even Frank Norris. Yet he knew the works of Gorki, Hauptmann, George Moore, London, Stephen Crane, and Sherwood Anderson. Anderson appealed to him because of his revolt against small-town life in *Winesburg, Ohio* and because of the essentially instinctive realism of his portrayals of domestic revolt. Anderson, like Wright, neither apologized for himself nor submitted to naturalistic despair; rather he tended to make of personal freedom a sort of mystic quest, and to consider fiction as a substitute for religion—a thing in which Wright also characteristically indulged.

Later, the discovery of James T. Farrell's works and his personal acquaintance with him in the mid-thirties had some impact on his own writing, as is apparent in *Lawd Today*. True, Wright certainly derived more from Conrad or Poe with regard to the expression of moods; from Henry James and Hemingway with regard to the use of symbols; from Gertrude Stein with regard to speech rhythms; and he learned from Joyce, T. S. Eliot, and above all Dostoyevski. Yet the impact of the American realists was important because it came first, and because it closely corresponded to Wright's own experience. There is a kinship between the lives of Dreiser and Wright that goes beyond literary theories. From the first, Dreiser was hard-pressed by suffering, and the destitution of the existence to which he was born suggested to him a vision of men struggling aimlessly in a society which excluded them. American life he could thus identify as a figure of distant, capricious destiny. He grew up hating the narrow-mindedness and helplessness of his family, and was so overpowered by suffering that he came to see it as a universal principle, to the point that he considered only the hand of fate where others saw the political and economic evils of capitalism.

Isn't that largely what happened to Wright? The suffering due to poverty and family disruption, the narrow-minded religion practiced at home, the subservient attitudes of the family figures of authority caused him to question and to rebel against the order of things. He, too, hated the threadbare woof of his spiritually deprived childhood so strongly that he tended to generalize it in his oft-criticized declaration about black life.

I used to mull over the strange absence of real kindness in Negroes, how unstable was our tenderness, how lacking in genuine passion we were, how void of great hope, how timid our joy, how bare our traditions, how hollow our memories, how lacking we were in those intangible sentiments that bind man to man, and how shallow even was our despair . . . what had been taken for our emotional strength was our negative confusion, our flights, our fears, our frenzy under pressure.

He, too, disliked his father who had relinquished his responsibilities; he, too, deplored his mother's inefficacy; he, too, had a brooding boyhood and the lonely joys of wallowing in books. He, too, came to experience destiny as an unexpected dispensation of fate, particularly brutal in the case of his mother's stroke, and he started to build up the precariousness of his own life into a philosophy. At twelve, he held

a notion as to what life meant that no education could ever alter, a conviction that the meaning of living came only when [he] was struggling to wring a meaning out of meaningless suffering.

He concluded:

It made me want to drive coldly to the heart of every question and lay it open . . . love burrowing into psychology, into realistic and naturalistic fiction and art, into those whirlpools of politics that had the power to claim the whole of men's souls. It directed my loyalties to the side of men in rebellion; it made me love talk that sought answers to questions that could help nobody, that could only keep alive in me that enthralling sense of wonder and awe in the face of the drama of human feelings which is hidden by the external drama of life.

If Wright followed Dreiser along the road of pessimistic determinism and stressed the helplessness of man, it also appears that the racial oppression he suffered enabled him to find the cause for his own, and his people's, sufferings in the hatred of the surrounding white world. Severed from knowledge and from the mainstream of American culture, he tried to join it. A victim of oppression, he directed his efforts toward rebellion. Thus he partly escaped Dreiser's deep pessimism while his reverence for the invisible helped him maintain a sense of wonder and awe in front of his existential dilemma.

The fact that Wright came of age, in a literary sense, under the aegis of the Communist party and during the depression largely accounts for the special tenor of his naturalism. The revival of naturalism in the thirties corresponded to Wright's efforts to adapt his writing to a style he could achieve relatively easily. Among the John Reeders he found for the first time a milieu akin to, and favorable to, his preoccupations. That was the time when America was being educated by shock, and the impact of the crisis on the values of American culture was probably stronger than the repercussions of the economic crash upon the capitalist system. The rational character of the social structure seemed to disintegrate, and its existential components were revealed through the alienation of the individual from a society which did not care for him. Wright had experienced this since his childhood in Mississippi, and could thus translate his own experience into general terms. His desire to use words as weapons, after the fashion of Mencken, in order to achieve some kind of liberation, had also become a nearly general tenet. The novelists of the thirties seemed heir to new obligations, and were called upon to leave their ivory towers and become politically relevant. Authenticity, which had always been Wright's criterion, was rehabilitated to stand against artiness. A comparable movement had already taken place at the turn of the century, when Frank Norris supposedly declared, as he embraced naturalism out of hatred for so-called pure literature, "Who cares for fine style, we don't want literature, give us life." And in Europe, the social studies of Émile Zola had developed in opposition to the stylistic achievements of Flaubert's realism. Yet, in the thirties, a new sense of urgency was added, and Wright felt strongly confirmed in what he believed his mission as a writer to be.

> In their efforts to recruit masses [the Communists] had missed the meaning of the lives of the masses, had conceived of people in too abstract a manner. I would try to put some of that meaning back. I would tell Communists how common people felt, and I would tell common people of the self-sacrifice of Communists who strove for unity among them.

There was indeed a deep convergence between Wright's idiosyncratic attraction to violence (or compulsive counterviolence), and protest and, on the other hand, the social attitude of the committed writers of the times as Alfred Kazin has analyzed it with perspicacity. Of course, there did not remain much of the original philosophy of naturalism in that attitude. It was taken for granted that the writer should be a tough guy. In fact, most of the so-called proletarian writers were the sons of the bourgeoisie, but they considered themselves as starting from scratch and rejected literary traditions. On the contrary, Wright came from the lower classes, was largely self-educated, and had been kept from a literary tradition; he tried to invent one for himself, and this explains why he could endorse writers in the thirties who, like T. S. Eliot, were often attacked by the Left as "decadents."

Also, the hardness of naturalism was more or less instinctive to those writers who tended to see life as oppression. Wright had really suffered oppression, so he could be vehement about what he repudiated. They all shared a common belief in social determinism, not the biological determinism of Spencer or even Dreiser, but the conviction that man is made and crushed by his social background and environment.

As Kazin further emphasizes, proletarian naturalism generally had narrow categories and ready-made prescriptions. It was assumed that the embattled novel ought to be relatively fast-paced so that the reader could be stimulated into active sympathy with the right cause; accordingly, thought was often subordinate to action, and the characters developed in a predetermined way toward class-consciousness. The novelists did not pose psychological problems whose refined variations constituted the novel proper. The strategy, Kazin argues, consisted in beginning with a state of fear or doubt which action dissipated. One always found a great deal of facts and documentation which answered for documentary realism.

This enumeration of the characteristics of the proletarian novel nearly amounts to a description of Wright's outstanding success of the period, i.e., *Native Son.*

Above all, Wright is conspicuous by his use and abuse of violence. This theme of violence was revived in fiction where it tended to become a demonstration of economic and social dislocation, and a reflection of the state of the American system. Wright's own inclination to violence in fiction (in life he abhorred physical violence) could mirror the violence inflicted by American society, pass for the counterviolence of the oppressed Negro, and prefigure revolutionary violence. This was also the case for Erskine Caldwell and, to a degree, for James T. Farrell, both of whom displayed real excitement in reporting capitalistic decay. One may wonder, indeed, whether those novelists—in spite of their different political affiliations, temperaments, and styles—were not united by this coming of age in a time of catastrophe, a time which corresponded to their deep need for terror. Such terror, in Wright, hardly finds release except in a kind of obsession with details of utter brutality; the endings of his novels are not cathartic. Although Bigger discovers that he is what he killed for, this does not really free him from his alienation. On the contrary it fills Max with horror at the thought of his own (and the Communists') failure. *Native Son* differs noticeably from the standard proletarian novel in that the protagonist does not achieve real social and political consciousness; as a piece of propaganda, it is much weaker than "Fire and Cloud" and "Bright and Morning Star," in spite of the opinions of the reviewers and critics of the time. The writing of violent novels thus appears, above all, to be a search for emotional catharsis, and maybe for vicarious fulfillment; this is what Wright meant when he said that writing "drain[ed] all the poison out of [him]."

Brutality is also, at times, deliberate, and calculated to shock the reader. Because bankers' daughters had wept when reading *Uncle Tom's Children* and thereby found relief, Wright says in "How Bigger Was Born" that he wanted *Native Son* to be so taut, so hard that they would have to face it without the relief of tears. This cultivation of violence often brings him closer to Dostoyevski who excels in depicting characters under extreme stress—think of Raskolnikov or Karamazov before and after the murder—than to the American naturalists. The naturalists' supposed contempt for style and their refusal of sensationalism do not apply to Wright, and is certainly better exemplified by James T. Farrell's literalness of description. Farrell renounces effects to such a degree that this becomes an attribute of his writing (his writing is far more barren and clinical than Dreiser's, whose epic imagination took him, like Zola, into wild and beautiful flights). By accumulating details with detachment and also with some cruelty to his characters, Farrell achieves a sort of stone-like solidity which is a monument in itself. Not so with Wright. There is in him a great attention to detail, but he depends much more for his effects upon the sweep and the suspense of narrative rather than upon the accumulation of revealing evidence—with the exception of *Lawd Today*.

At times, Wright's realism is quite naturalistic. He does not attempt to create simply the illusion of reality; after a careful study of life, he sometimes resorts with evident relish to nearly photographic verisimilitude. This, of course, is true mainly for descriptions and details, and is best documented by *Lawd Today*. This is also true for reactions and attitudes. For instance, while Wright was writing *Native Son*—in which he depicts in deterministic terms, "the story of a boy born amid poverty and conditions of fear which eventually stopped his will and control and made him a reluctant killer"—the Thomas Nixon case broke out in Chicago, and the novelist was quite happy to copy verbatim some of the *Chicago Tribune*'s descriptions of the murderer and to use the brief prepared by attorney Ulysses Keys. Wright also resorted to authentic sources in order to present a view of the racist reactions of the white reporters—perhaps he did so to forestall any possible challenge by his critics. Why did he desire such literalness? One may surmise that he wanted to emulate Dreiser who had based *An American Tragedy* on the Grace Brown/Chester Gillette case. In several other instances, however, Wright goes beyond that need for undebatable proof and documentation. As I have tried to show elsewhere, even in a novella as surrealistic and existentialist as "The Man Who Lived Underground" Wright did not use Dostoyevski's *Notes from Underground* as a source, but used instead a glaring account of the subterranean adventures of a Hollywood delinquent he had lifted from *True Detective Magazine*. Likewise, we have to go back to actual events in order to find the origin of his humorous and imaginative "Man of All Work." "The Man Who Killed a Shadow" actually comes from the Julius Fischer case which attorney Charles E. Houston had related to Wright shortly before his departure for France. Wright secured a transcript and nearly contented himself with narrating it: describing, for instance, the way the defendant had strangled and clubbed with a stick a librarian, Catherine Cooper Reardon, because she had complained about his work, Wright went as far as lifting whole sentences from the court record; even details which one could think came from his imagination and zest for horror, such as the use of the victims' pink panties to wipe her blood from the floor, are borrowed from the official transcript. Again and again, whether for details or plot episodes, Wright goes back to actual occurrences. Of course there is in this something of the painstaking search for documentary proof that he greatly admired in Émile Zola. An interview he gave to a Swedish newspaper in the late fifties shows how much he wanted to imitate the French naturalist master. Just as Zola, notebook in hand, jotted down information about prostitutes when he wanted to write *Nana,* we discover that Wright, not satisfied with copying real letters from American sailors to Spanish prostitutes in *Pagan Spain,* also tried to buy similar letters from French prostitutes when gathering documentation on GI's in France for the last volume of his Fishbelly trilogy.

To Wright, the document, designed as proof, is nearly sacred. His industrious research into the facts can sometimes be ascribed to the necessity to check actual details because of a lack of personal experience: for instance, apropos of the arraignment of Tyree in *The Long Dream,* he had to learn the details of Mississippi court procedure. In other instances his journalistic zeal seems to be a carryover from his beginnings as a correspondent for the Harlem Bureau of the *Daily Worker.* As was the case with Crane, Norris, London, Dreiser, and many muckrakers, Wright's schooling in the writing profession began partly in a newspaper office, hence his reverence for the document as objective record. Yet, contrary to Sinclair Lewis, he never turns the novel into a sort of higher journalism, and it might be truer to say that his best journalism—articles like *Twelve Million Black Voices* or "Joe Louis Discovers Dynamite"—derives its power from a nonjournalistic interest in time, locale, and dramatic sequence.

Among the many reasons for the importance of the authentic record in Wright's fiction, two seem to prevail: first, the obligation of a black writer to substantiate his most trifling indictments of the white system; second, but not least, Wright's naive pleasure in discovering that reality is often more fiction-like than fiction itself and in persuading the reader of this.

As far as form is concerned, a commonly held opinion is that the naturalists did not really care for the niceties of style. This may be true of a few proletarian novelists who disguised their ignorance in literary matters as a deliberate contempt for refined "bourgeois" estheticism. This may be true of Farrell; and it may even be partly true of Dreiser, though his clumsier attempts at elegance are the result of a failure rather than a lack of care. This is never true of Wright, who always evinced a deep interest in style. His best-known pronouncement about writing, "Blueprint for Negro Writing," stresses the balance between content and expression. Indeed he takes writing seriously, sometimes awfully so; for him it is no gratuitous game but a weapon, a vital, self-justifying activity, a means to change the world.

In his eyes, to write well was not sufficient. He did, for instance, censure Zora Neale Hurston because the "sensory sweep of her novel [*Their Eyes Were Watching God*] carries no theme, no message, no thought." And he praised Carl Von Unruh because his comprehension of the problems of fascism in *The End Is Not Yet* "lifts him, at one stroke, out of the class of fictionneers and onto the plane of writers who, through the prophetic power of their vision, legislate new values for mankind." For Wright, the ideal for people "writing from the Left," as he does, should be to "create in the minds of other people a picture that would impel them to meaningful activity." This quest for the meaningful even leads Wright to assert that Stephen Crane's *Maggie: A Girl of the Streets* is simply a coldly materialistic picture of poverty while Jack Conroy's *The Disinherited* is the picture of men and women groping their way to a new concept of human dignity and to find Arna Bontemps's or Langston Hughes's novels more relevant, though not better, than *Sister Carrie* because their characters are "haunted with the desire to make their lives meaningful."

The strength of true fiction comes above all from the nature of the writing itself which must achieve a nice balance between form and content; "the limitations of the craft constitute its greatest virtues. If the sensory vehicle of imaginative writing is required to carry too great a load of didactic material, the artistic sense is submerged," Wright states in "Blueprint for Negro Writing." This explains why he did not hesitate to fight the attempts of CP leaders who wanted him to propagandize. He did so in the name of personal freedom, and also for the validity of an art defined by intrinsic criteria; in reply to the Jewish liberal critic David Cohn, he says:

> Mr. Cohn implies that as a writer I should look at the state of the Negro through the lens of relativity and not judge his plight in an absolute sense. This is precisely what, as an artist, I try NOT to do. My character, Bigger Thomas, lives and suffers in the real world. Feeling and perception are absolute, and if I dodged my responsibility

as an artist and depicted them otherwise, I'd be a traitor not to my race alone but to humanity.

Art certainly requires a "point of objectivity in the handling of the subject matter" yet Wright will never define it through extrinsic criteria: "In the last analysis," he answers engraver Antonio Frasconi in a beautiful letter dated November 1944, "the artist must bow to the monitor of his own imagination; must be led by the sovereignty of his own impressions and perceptions; must be guided by the tyranny of what troubles and concerns him personally. There is no other true path."

Wright himself spent hour upon hour trying to master the craft of fiction, experimenting with words, with sentences, with scenes; and with the help of other novels or prefaces after he had found grammar books and style manuals quite useless, he tried patiently to make his writing jell, harden, and coalesce into a meaningful whole. When he was successful, stories such as "Big Boy Leaves Home" or "Down by the Riverside" are proof that he was able to blend and to fuse elements and techniques borrowed from Joyce, Hemingway, Gertrude Stein, Conrad, and even James. His single-mindedness can, at times, be reminiscent of the efforts of Flaubert, whom he greatly admired. Proust's *Remembrance of Things Past* also filled him with boundless admiration, and equal despair because he felt unable to do as well. In one of the most revealing chapters of his autobiography, Wright confesses:

> My purpose was to capture a physical state or movement that carried strong subjective impressions, an accomplishment which seemed supremely worth struggling for. If I could fasten the mind of the reader upon words so firmly that he would forget words and be conscious only of his response, I felt that I would be in sight of knowing how to write narrative. I strove to master words, to make them disappear, to make them important by making them new, to make them melt into a rising spiral of emotional climax that would drench the reader with a sense of a new world. This was the single end of my living.

Here we are far indeed from the supposed naturalistic/proletarian distrust for fine writing!

The major difference between Wright's view of how fiction should depict the lives of the common people and what the believers in scientific determinism tried to achieve in fiction can be found in Wright's opinion of Nelson Algren's *Never Come Morning*. The preface he wrote for that novel considers a few of the literary strategies which could have been used for the treatment of Bruno Bicek and his friends: some writers would have resorted to satire or humor, others would have "assumed an aloof 'social worker' attitude toward it, prescribing 'pink pills' for social ills, piling up a mountain of naturalistic detail." Wright, by the way, did *not* go in for such techniques and he believed that Algren's perspective excelled all of those because he "depicts the intensity of feeling, the tawdry but potent dreams, the crude but forceful poetry and the frustrating longing for humanity residing in the lives of the Poles of Chicago's North West Side."

Here, the importance attributed to intensity of feeling over naturalistic detail, the insistence on the forceful poetry of commonplace lives is somewhat unexpected; yet, is this not what Wright attempted when he depicted Bigger Thomas's or Jake Jackson's frustrated longings for a movie-like world? And, at the same time, is not such a statement in the very vein of a Frank Norris who considers naturalism, as incarnated by Zola, as another kind of romanticism?

In "Blueprint for Negro Writing," Wright seems to be responding to Norris's desire that ordinary characters "must be twisted from the ordinary" when he prescribes:

> The presentation of their lives should be simple, yes; but all the complexity, the strangeness, the magic, the wonder of life that lays like a bright sheen over the most sordid existence should be there. To borrow a phrase from the Russians, it should have a *complex simplicity*.

This is a way of claiming equal treatment for all in the field of literature, hence a political statement. At the same time, Wright is convinced that no literature exists without romance, without "the bright sheen" of illusion—he dedicated *Native Son* to his mother who taught him as "a child at her knee, to revere the fanciful and the imaginative." He was convinced that art had little to do with scientific objectivity (not to be mistaken for authenticity and honesty), and that:

> An artist deals with aspects of reality different from those which a scientist uses. My task is not to abstract reality but to enhance its

value. In the process of identifying emotional experience in words, paint, stone or tone, an artist uses his feelings in an immediate and absolute sense.

Literature is thus less the depiction of the actual world than the representation of emotional experience through words. The world interests Wright only insofar as it affects the individual, as it is perceived, experienced, acted upon or reacted against. He places the emphasis on emotion, the emotional potential of the material, the emotion to be aroused in the reader, the emotion of the creator at work. It may be in that last domain that his intimate convictions about literary creation bring him the farthest from the theoreticians of the experimental novel and "laboratory creation." He does not view writing as a conscious production in which intellect and critical sense are unceasingly called upon to regulate fancy. His conception is rather dangerously close to the romanticists' definition of inspiration. Being a rationalist and an agnostic, if not an atheist, he confesses there is something paradoxical in such a view, and he honestly admits this contradiction:

> I abhor the very notion of mysticism; yet, in trying to grasp this [creative] process in me, I encounter a reality that recedes and hides itself in another reality and, when hunted too openly, it alters its own aspect, chameleon-like, thereby escaping introspectional observation. I sigh, shrug, leave it alone, but still trust it, welcoming it when it comes again.

Doesn't this half-reluctant admission amount to a recognition of the contingency of visitations of quasi-divine inspiration? Further on, Wright recalls that, preceding the writing of all his books, not only fiction but even travel narratives, he had been invaded by a feeling of estrangement from his surroundings, a sense of "being possessed by a slow stirring of the emotions, a sort of haunting incitation as though . . . vainly seeking to recall something long forgotten." He owns that he had no power over these creative moods, that they came when they wanted, and that no distraction could dislodge them until the writing of the piece had actually drained them off. Such a perspective defines the writer as the instrument of a power which inhabits him temporarily, coerces him to express it, and then leaves him after these strange visitations. This is strongly reminiscent of Wright's description of the working of the life force in a poem of his that was mentioned previously. It corresponds to a fatalistic creation, because it becomes, in this view, a process which takes place without much actual effort on the part of the writer:

> I was aware of subjective movements . . . finally being strung out in time, of events spelling a sequence, that of interlocking images shedding that kind of meaning we associate with a "story" [. . . .] Such moods . . . suck themselves into events, long past and forgotten, declaring them their personal property; then to my amazed delight they telescope alien and disparate images into organic wholes [. . . .] A crime story in a newspaper evokes a sense of excitement far beyond the meaning of the banal crime described, a meaning which, in turn, conjures up for some inexplicable reasons its emotional equivalent in a totally different setting and possessing a completely different meaning.

Even more significant than his conception of inspiration is the definition Wright provides of a "story": it is not so much an organized plot carried out through narrative, as it is a "sequence of interlocking images shedding [a] kind of meaning." "Meaning" here is emotional rather than intellectual, and the image-pattern stands for the essential element. A close reading of Wright's symbolic, often dream-like fiction reveals that the crudely apparent three-to-five-act dramatic structure is only an external frameworld which supports a finely woven symbolical texture. The dramatic frameworld is mainly a means of prodding the narrative onwards at the hectic pace required by the narrow time limits of the classical tragedy (these time limits are actually narrow in *Lawd Today, Savage Holiday,* and even *Native Son;* they are made to seem narrow in *The Outsider* and *The Long Dream* by the selection of important scenes and by glossing over several months in a few sentences). As a result, Wright's narrative derives its emotional unity not so much from the plot or even the breathless rhythm with which he carries the reader forward, as from the "complex simplicity" of its associational imagery. Again, this brings Wright closer to the expressionists (or the impressionists, for that purpose) than to the naturalists. But does not the power and beauty of *Sister Carrie* derive less from Dreiser's objective presentation or see-saw-like structure than from its weird and emotionally-laden images? Isn't this true also of the glittering world of *Nana* or Flaubert's *Madame Bovary*?

In the last resort, can't the best naturalists be declared great *because of,* not in spite of, their diffuse romanticism or epic vision? It may well be that the tendency to weave emotion and passion into documentation and reportorial accuracy is the secret of successful naturalistic writing, and that naturalism should be reassessed in that light. Rather than sheer reaction against romantic exaggeration, it would appear to be a semi-conscious attempt to rationalize the sense of doom which was so keenly felt by the romantics. Scientific theories were introduced into the naturalists' critical and conceptual views of literary creation, but did they ever turn the novel into a scientific process? On the contrary, they tended to subordinate and assimilate science to the imagination. What they considered slice-of-life authenticity, what Wright believed to be real and authentic in his novels because it rested upon documentary proof, was often only a starting point, as he admitted toward the end of his career.

> A crime story in a newspaper evokes a sense of excitement far beyond the meaning of the banal crime described, a meaning which, in turn, conjures up, for inexplicable reasons, its emotional equivalent in a totally different setting and possessing a completely contrary meaning.

If the setting and meaning are thus totally "contrary" can the original reports still be considered as relevant proof of authenticity?

Wright's conception of the artistic aim is, in the final analysis, that of a technique directed at bringing the reader, through poetic ecstasy or shock treatment, to acceptance of a new consciousness. A sort of alchemistic strategy (he actually uses and abuses the terms "to blend" and "to fuse") must be devised in order to drench the reader with the sense of something unheard, a result which could not be achieved by demonstrative logic or philosophizing. It is not surprising, then, that Wright should compliment Fritz Von Unruh because his novel is:

> a marvelous nightmare which has the power to shed light upon your waking hours. It depends for its continuity not upon the logic of two plus two equals four but upon the blooming of opposite images, upon the linking of widely disparate symbols and events, upon the associational magic of passion.

"The linking of widely disparate symbols" was the touchstone of "good" surrealistic imagery in the eyes of the French surrealists; they considered the image more successful as the symbols were more distant and unrelated. At the root of Wright's fondness for what he calls surrealism one finds not a reading of the French surrealists (although Wright liked Dali's paintings and wrote a poem in homage to Aargon) but rather the influence of his grandmother whose Seventh-Day Adventism connected in his eyes ordinary reality with remote beliefs and, even more, the influence of the blues with their typical ability to bring together seemingly unrelated elements of the American Negro's existence and blend them into a new, meaningful whole.

Another, more obvious, trend of Wright's fiction which, at times, differentiates him from the naturalists is his sensationalism. True, such sensationalism could pass for an answer to Norris's demand that a naturalistic tale must possess "a violent and energetic greatness," that the characters must be "wrenched from the quiet, uneventful round of ordinary life and flung into the throes of a vast and terrible drama that works itself out in unleashed passions, in blood and sudden death." Certainly, if the naturalists thrive on the appearance of power and gross effects (which might be defined as expressionistic), then Wright is very much of a naturalist because he retains a great deal of the awareness of American naturalism. Visceral writing is his forte; critics generally agree that he is "a born story teller" with all the implications of such a definition. Yet, if he willingly resorts to suspense, melodrama, coincidence, and subjection of character analysis to plot and story telling, does not Wright do so mostly because of his early schooling in the stock techniques of popular fiction? In his mind rawness and brutality are associated with fantasy and the gothic, i.e., another kind of romanticism. Here, the influence of Edgar Allan Poe is prevalent; in the most gruesome episodes of *Native Son,* for example, Wright blends two such apparently irreconcilable trends as gothic horror and sadism and, on the other hand, matter-of-fact, slice-of-life reporting. Perhaps he was able to do so because of his early ability to live simultaneously on the level of everyday destitution and that of evasion through popular fiction. The tenets of naturalism would impose upon Bigger a passive character, one subject to the workings of determinism and fate; we are made to share in his subordinate behavior through a quasi-reportorial rendition of his physical and psychosomatic reactions, sensations, and half-formulated thoughts. At the same time he evolves, by implication, in a world which is more that of Dostoyevski's *Crime and Punishment* than that of Dreiser's *An American Tragedy,* and by indirection he is enlarged into a King-Kong stereotype (quite consistent with the Rue Morgue murderer)—all without losing any of his humanity, because the reader is compelled to see the whole scene from his eyes.

Wright's conception of fiction as a magic telescoping of disparate elements is certainly linked to his childhood discovery of the power of the written word. He read with the feeling that he was performing a forbidden act, and, indeed he was, given the reactions of his grandmother, who saw fiction as a creation of the devil, and the attitude of the Deep South, which banned Negroes from public libraries. As much as the educational power of fiction, its capacity to arouse wonder was always important to him. As a Communist, he emphasized the former without renouncing the latter. He made ready use of the naturalistic and proletarian perspective, but only among other possible ones. Only in the late twenties did the philosophy of social determinism answer his questions concerning the restrictions which had been imposed upon him: universal determinism posited the equality of the oppressed Negro and his white oppressor under the common sway of human destiny. Wright could then consider the absurdity of the world through the eyes of Dreiser who, he wrote, "tried to rationalize and justify the defeat of the individual in biological terms; with him it was a law of the universe." Yet he could no more accept subjection and powerlessness as a universal law, since subjection amounted to his own slow death in a racist setting, than he could his grandmother's attempt to explain his mother's illness in terms of his own impiety and God's ensuing wrath. Determinism provided him, at best, with only a transitional belief, soon superseded by the optimistic social revolutionism of the Marxist faith. When he could no longer believe in the irreversible progress of history in communism, Wright had to face again the absurdity and precariousness of the human predicament but he did so in terms that were closer to Russian, German, or even French existentialism. Existentialism left a way open for the creation of values by man, for individualism, and for solidarity, in a fashion that even the optimistic Spencerian brand of determinism could not. At the same time, existentialism satisfied Wright's tragic sense of life. The novel which best illustrates this shift in his philosophy (or rather the different emphasis he placed on different philosophies at different times) is undoubtedly *The Outsider.* Its first section, derived as it is from the then unpublished *Lawd Today,* is strongly naturalistic, not only in the piling up of documentary detail but in the fashion in which economic, family, and sexual ties determine both Cross Damon's and Jake Jackson's life. That Wright has to resort to violent circumstances and largely coincidental plot in order to break off with this materialistic setting and deterministic definition of Damon's life is irrelevant here. The break is significant because it represents a jump into existential freedom and into an absurd world beyond the laws of "normal" causation. Cross will lie, kill, burn a church, drive to suicide the woman who loves him, act like one of those "little gods" he so vehemently condemned for their ruthless use of power, only to discover finally the necessity of human solidarity and some kind of moral law. The break in the style is itself a significant transition from naturalistic reportage in didactic, philosophical prose, somewhat in the fashion of Sartre's *Les chemins de la liberté.* Although Wright's contribution to that type of fiction is of historical importance, we must confess that he is not at his best as a stylist when he resorts to such long-winded arguments, and that the jump from naturalism to the philosophical novel does not always suit his talents.

He, on the contrary, effected the change from naturalism into what he would call surrealism quite successfully in "The Man Who Lived Underground." It is revealing that the piece was begun as a novel, in whose naturalistic first part the protagonist was a victim of circumstances: the police arrested him and beat him up on suspicion of a crime he had not committed. This part (which was suppressed from the published novella) ended with Fred Daniels's literal jump outside reality into the underground world of the sewer. Chance allowed him to escape in the way Cross Damon later did, but necessity and a search for an emotional relationship also drove him back above ground and into the hands of his torturers. In the same way, Damon owns on his deathbed that man cannot bear absolute solitude, that he must establish a bridge with other men, that the necessity of man's determinism must, in some way, be acknowledged. As a change from naturalism into another kind of literary strategy "The Man Who Lived Underground" is a success because surrealism, as we tried to show, better suits Wright's passion for gothic detail and violence than philosophical didacticism. It appears that Wright functions best as an artist whenever, in his own words, he is able to

> fuse and articulate the experiences of man, because his writing possesses the potential cunning to steal into the inmost recesses of human hearts, because he can create the myths and symbols that inspire a faith in life.

To that end, American naturalism, both as a philosophy and as a literary technique in the line of Dreiser and James Farrell, provided him only with a starting point; then either, as we suggested, a larger definition of naturalism must be given—if it is to encompass the many facets of Wright's writing—or it must be recognized that he often overstepped its boundaries. Wright's attraction to the fanciful, the mysterious, the irrational always proved too strong for him to remain attached to his self-declared rationalism and deliberate objectivity. His heavy reliance upon visceral and violent emotions may account for this inability. Far from being a limitation, it turns out to be one of the major resources of his narrative power, in the same way that his obstinate refusal to submit to authority and his insatiable curiosity concerning everything human certainly led him to ask some of the most relevant questions of our time.

Part Two

Essays by
African-American Humanists

7

"Appendix" to
Narrative of the Life of Frederick Douglass: An American Slave

Frederick Douglass

I find, since reading over the foregoing Narrative, that I have, in several instances, spoken in such a tone and manner, respecting religion, as may possibly lead those unacquainted with my religious views to suppose me an opponent of all religion. To remove the liability of such misapprehension, I deem it proper to append the following brief explanation. What I have said respecting and against religion, I mean strictly to apply to the *slaveholding religion* of this land, and with no possible reference to Christianity proper; for, between the Christianity of this land, and the Christianity of Christ, I recognize the widest possible difference—so wide, that to receive the one as good, pure, and holy, is of necessity to reject the other as bad, corrupt, and wicked. To be the friend of the one, is of necessity to be the enemy of the other. I love the pure, peaceable, and impartial Christianity of Christ: I therefore hate the corrupt, slavehold-

Reprinted by permission of the publishers from *Narrative of the Life of Frederick Douglass, an American Slave, Written by Himself,* Benjamin Quarles, editor, Cambridge, Mass.: Harvard University Press, copyright © 1960 by the President and Fellows of Harvard College.

ing, women-whipping, cradle-plundering, partial and hypocritical Christianity of this land. Indeed, I can see no reason, but the most deceitful one, for calling the religion of this land Christianity. I look upon it as the climax of all misnomers, the boldest of all frauds, and the grossest of all libels. Never was there a clearer case of "stealing the livery of the court of heaven to serve the devil in." I am filled with unutterable loathing when I contemplate the religious pomp and show, together with the horrible inconsistencies, which everywhere surround me. We have men-stealers for ministers, women-worshippers for missionaries, and cradle-plunderers for church members. The man who wields the blood-clotted cowskin during the week fills the pulpit on Sunday, and claims to be a minister of the meek and lowly Jesus. The man who robs me of my earnings at the end of each week meets me as a class-leader on Sunday morning, to show me the way of life, and the path of salvation. He who sells my sister, for purposes of prostitution, stands forth as the pious advocate of purity. He who proclaims it a religious duty to read the Bible denies me the right of learning to read the name of the God who made me. He who is the religious advocate of marriage robs whole millions of its sacred influence, and leaves them to the ravages of wholesale pollution. The warm defender of the sacredness of the family relation is the same that scatters whole families,—sundering husbands and wives, parents and children, sisters and brothers,—leaving the hut vacant, and the hearth desolate. We see the thief preaching against theft, and the adulterer against adultery. We have men sold to build churches, women sold to support the gospel, and babes sold to purchase Bibles for the *poor heathen! all for the glory of God and the good of souls!* The slave auctioneer's bell and the church-going bell chime in with each other, and the bitter cries of the heart-broken slave are drowned in the religious shouts of his pious master. Revivals of religion and revivals in the slave-trade go hand in hand together. The slave prison and the church stand near each other. The clanking of fetters and the rattling of chains in the prison, and the pious psalm and solemn prayer in the church, may be heard at the same time. The dealers in the bodies and souls of men erect their stand in the presence of the pulpit, and they mutually help each other. The dealer gives his blood-stained gold to support the pulpit, and the pulpit, in return, covers his infernal business with the garb of Christianity. Here we have religion and robbery the allies of each other—devils dressed in angels' robes, and hell presenting the semblance of paradise.

> Just God! and these are they,
>   Who minister at thine altar, God of right!
> Men who their hands, with prayer and blessing, lay
>   On Israel's ark of light.
>
> What! preach, and kidnap men?
>   Give thanks, and rob thy own afflicted poor?
> Talk of thy glorious liberty, and then
>   Bolt hard the captive's door?
>
> What! servants of thy own
>   Merciful Son, who came to seek and save
> The homeless and the outcast, fettering down
>   The tasked and plundered slave!
>
> Pilate and Herod friends!
>   Chief priests and rulers, as of old, combine!
> Just God and holy! is that church which lends
>   Strength to the spoiler thine?

The Christianity of America is a Christianity, of whose votaries it may be as truly said, as it was of the ancient scribes and Pharisees, "They bind heavy burdens, and grievous to be borne, and lay them on men's shoulders, but they themselves will not move them with one of their fingers. All their works they do for to be seen of men.—They love the uppermost rooms at feasts, and the chief seats in the synagogues, . . . and to be called of men, Rabbi, Rabbi.—But woe unto you, scribes and Pharisees, hypocrites! For ye shut up the kingdom of heaven against men; for ye neither go in yourselves, neither suffer ye them that are entering to go in. Ye devour widows' houses, and for a pretense make long prayers; therefore you shall receive the greater damnation. Ye compass sea and land to make one proselyte, and when he is made, ye make him twofold more the child of hell than yourselves.—Woe unto you, scribes and Pharisees, hypocrites! For ye pay tithe of mint, and anise, and cumin, and have omitted the weightier matters of the law, judgment, mercy, and faith;

these ought ye to have done, and not to leave the other undone. Ye blind guides! which strain at a gnat, and swallow a camel. Woe unto you, scribes and Pharisees, hypocrites! For ye make clean the outside of the cup and of the platter; but within, they are full of extortion and excess.—Woe unto you, scribes and Pharisees, hypocrites! For ye are like unto whited sepulchers, which indeed appear beautiful outward, but are within full of dead men's bones, and of all uncleanness. Even so ye also unwardly appear righteous unto men, but within ye are full of hypocrisy and iniquity."

Dark and terrible as is this picture, I hold it to be strictly true of the overwhelming mass of professed Christians in America. They strain at a gnat, and swallow a camel. Could anything be more true of our churches? They would be shocked at the proposition of fellowshiping a *sheep*-stealer; and at the same time they hug to their communion a *man*-stealer, and brand me with being an infidel, if I find fault with them for it. They attend with pharisaical strictness to the outward forms of religion, and at the same time neglect the weightier matters of the law, judgment, mercy, and faith. They are always ready to sacrifice, but seldom to show mercy. They are they who are represented as professing to love God whom they have not seen, whilst they hate their brother whom they have seen. They love the heathen on the other side of the globe. They can pray for him, pay money to have the Bible put into his hand, and missionaries to instruct him; while they despise and totally neglect the heathen at their own doors.

Such is, very briefly, my view of the religion of this land; and to avoid any misunderstanding, growing out of the use of general terms, I mean, by the religion of this land, that which is revealed in the words, deeds, and actions of those bodies, north and south, calling themselves Christian churches, and yet in union with slaveholders. It is against religion, as presented by these bodies, that I have felt it is my duty to testify.

I conclude these remarks by copying the following portrait of the religion of the south (which is, by communion and fellowship, the religion of the north), which I soberly affirm is "true to the life," and without caricature or the slightest exaggeration. It is said to have been drawn, several years before the present antislavery agitation began, by a northern Methodist preacher, who, while residing at the south, had an opportunity to see slaveholding morals, manners, and piety with his own eyes. "Shall I not visit for these things? saith the Lord. Shall not my soul be avenged on such a nation as this?"

A PARODY

Come, saints and sinners, hear me tell
How pious priests whip Jack and Nell,
And women buy and children sell,
And preach all sinners down to hell,
 And sing of heavenly union.

They'll bleat and baa, [go on] like goats,
Gorge down black sheep, and strain at motes,
Array their backs in fine black coats,
Then seize their negroes by their throats,
 And choke for heavenly union.

They'll church you if you sip a dram,
And damn you if you steal a lamb;
Ye rob old Tony, Doll, and Sam,
Of human rights, and bread and ham;
 Kidnapper's heavenly union.

They'll loudly talk of Christ's reward,
And bind his image with a cord,
And scold, and swing the lash abhorred,
And sell their brother in the Lord
 To handcuffed heavenly union.

They'll read and sing a sacred song,
And make a prayer both loud and long,
And teach the right and do the wrong,
Hailing the brother, sister throng,
 With words of heavenly union.

We wonder how such saints can sing,
Or praise the Lord upon the wing,
Who roar, and scold, and whip, and sting,
And to their slaves and mammon cling,
 In guilty conscience union.

They'll raise tobacco, corn, and rye,
And drive, and thieve, and cheat, and lie,
And lay up treasures in the sky,
By making switch and cowskin fly,
    In hope of heavenly union.

They'll crack old Tony on the skull,
And preach and roar like Bashan bull,
Or braying ass, of mischief full,
Then seize old Jacob by the wool,
    And pull for heavenly union.

A roaring, ranting, sleek man-thief,
Who lived on mutton, veal, and beef,
Yet never would afford relief
To needy, sable sons of grief,
    Was big with heavenly union.

"Love not the world," the preacher said,
And winked his eye, and shook his head;
He seized on Tom, and Dick, and Ned,
Cut short their meat, and clothes, and bread,
    Yet still loved heavenly union.

Another preacher whining spoke
Of One whose heart for sinners broke:
He tied old Nanny to an oak,
And drew the blood at every stroke,
    And prayed for heavenly union.

Two others oped their iron jaws,
And waved their children-stealing paws;
There sat their children in gewgaws;
By stinting negroes' backs and maws,
    They kept up heavenly union.

All good from Jack another takes,
And entertains with flirts and rakes,
Who dress as sleek as glossy snakes,
And cram their mouths with sweetened cakes;
    And this goes down for union.

Sincerely and earnestly hoping that this little book may do something toward throwing light on the American slave system, and hastening the glad day of deliverance to the millions of my brethren in bonds—faithfully relying upon the power of truth, love and justice, for success in my humble efforts—and solemnly pledging myself anew to the sacred cause,—I subscribe myself,

Frederick Douglass

Lynn, Mass., April 28, 1845.

8

On Christianity

W. E. B. Du Bois

It is painfully true that white Christianity has in the twentieth century been curiously discredited. First, it is faced by the fact of the [First] World War. Here in the twentieth century of the Prince of Peace the leading nations representing His religion have been murdering, maiming, and hurting each other on a scale unprecedented in the history of mankind. Again, into the white Church of Christ race prejudice has crept to such an extent it is openly recognized and in the United States at least it is considered the natural and normal thing that white and colored people should belong mostly to different organizations and almost entirely to different congregations. Finally in the white church an obvious and open segregation has taken place so that a poor man in some of the great churches of the north would be as great an anomaly as a black man in the Methodist Church South. These facts do not impugn Christianity but they do make terrible comment upon the failure of its white followers.

On the other hand, the colored church of Christ has certain things of which it may rightfully boast. It is a democratic church; a church

Reprinted from *Against Racism: Unpublished Essays, Papers, Addresses, 1887–1961,* by W. E. B. Du Bois, ed. Herbert Aptheker (Amherst: University of Massachusetts Press, 1985), copyright © 1985 by the University of Massachusetts Press.

where the governing power is largely in the hands of the mass of membership, where everybody is courteously welcomed even if the application of a white person might cause astonishment, and where the attempts to organize aristocrat and exclusive congregations have been curiously unsuccessful as compared with the enormous success of the great churches of the [white] people.

This success of the colored Christian church calls, however, for no "Holier than thou" attitude. As colored people we have not yet been faced by the kind of temptation that has led white people astray. We have no human beings in our power to despise. We have little wealth to tempt us to aristocracy, and we have so near to us the example of what prejudice and hatred can do that most of us have been well warned.

On the other hand, there are many faults and dangers: First of all the kind of sermon which is preached in most colored churches is not today attractive to even fairly intelligent men; we have gotten into the widespread habit of letting preachers talk to us without giving them any attention because we assume that most of the things they say are not worth attention.

The theology of the average colored church is basing itself far too much upon "Hell and Damnation"—upon an attempt to scare people into being decent and threatening them with the terrors of death and punishment. We are still trained to believe a good deal that is simply childish in theology. The outward and visible punishment of every wrong deed that men do, the repeated declaration that anything can be gotten by anyone at any time by prayer. Especially is the colored church failing by its dogmatic hypocrisy in relation to amusements:—While church members and nearly all decent people dance and play cards and go to the theater under certain circumstances, the church continues to pretend that these things are always absolutely and eternally wrong. At the same time it seldom punishes or seeks to punish those of its members who indulge in them. Lastly, the colored church finds itself continually in the treadmill of its economic lack of vision: It builds a church edifice, works hard to pay the mortgage interest, follows this by a series of tremendous rallies to pay off the principal and burns the mortgage. By that time the church is old and either needs repairs or a new church. When the new church is built the same circle is gone over again.

In the first of these dangers what must the new Negro Church do? It must make its sermons a regular source of real information. It must give the people knowledge. It must inspire them with high ideals of good deeds, and not simply entertain them or scare them or merely yell at them. Especially must the new Negro Church take a consistent stand on amusements. It must discourage excesses and immorality, but it must cease to condemn every person who dances under any circumstances, every person who sees a play of Shakespeare and every person who sits down with his friends for a game of eucre. It is absolutely impossible to class all dancing, entertainment, and the playing of games with debauchery and lewdness; all attempts to do this are bound to be flat failures.

Again, the method of recruiting persons to church membership should be changed. It is not necessary to carry on our present method of periodical revival with the hiring of professional and loud-mouthed evangelists and reducing people to a state of frenzy or unconsciousness in order to get them into the church. A regular campaign carried on every month in the year, quietly and seriously among reasonable people, will bring to the aid of the church a much better class of membership than present methods attract.

Above all, the business activities of the new Negro Church must be more systematic. The same methods that procured and paid for the church home can buy and pay for homes of the church members. Buying clubs and cooperative effort can reduce the cost of living for the church members and for the church neighborhood. More systematic effort can be made for obtaining employment for colored folk and for encouraging enterprises that will employ them. The burden of educating its children even through high school and college should rest upon every Negro church.

Above all, the church must take an unbending stand on the matter of character. It seems almost inconceivable that today so many churches and ministers and so many good church members actually sneer at good men and good deads and honest action. They seem to want the world to believe that dipping a man into a pool of water is more important in the sight of God than inducing him to keep his body clean and pay his honest debts and refuse to spread malicious gossip. Clean straightforward character, honest unbending unselfishness must be the product of the Negro Church if it is to survive; and this coupled with a helpful business program and a sane attitude toward amusements will characterize the New Negro Church.

9

Salvation

Langston Hughes

I was saved from sin when I was going on thirteen. But not really
saved. It happened like this. There was a big revival at my Auntie
Reed's church. Every night for weeks there had been much preaching, singing, praying, and shouting, and some very hardened sinners
had been brought to Christ, and the membership of the church had
grown by leaps and bounds. Then just before the revival ended, they
held a special meeting for children, "to bring the young lambs to
the fold." My aunt spoke of it for days ahead. That night I was
escorted to the front row and placed on the mourners' bench with
all the other young sinners, who had not yet been brought to Jesus.

My aunt told me that when you were saved you saw a light,
and something happened to you inside! And Jesus came into your
life! And God was with you from then on! She said you could see
and hear and feel Jesus in your soul. I believed her. I had heard
a great many old people say the same thing and it seemed to me
they ought to know. So I sat there calmly in the hot, crowded church,
waiting for Jesus to come to me.

The preacher preached a wonderful rhythmical sermon, all moans and shouts and lonely cries and dire pictures of hell, and then he sang a song about the ninety and nine safe in the fold, but one little lamb was left out in the cold. Then he said: "Won't you come? Won't you come to Jesus? Young lambs, won't you come?" And he held out his arms to all us young sinners there on the mourners' bench. And the little girls cried. And some of them jumped up and went to Jesus right away. But most of us just sat there.

A great many old people came and knelt around us and prayed, old women with jet-black faces and braided hair, old men with work-gnarled hands. And the church sang a song about the lower lights are burning, some poor sinners to be saved. And the whole building rocked with prayer and song.

Still I kept waiting to *see* Jesus.

Finally all the young people had gone to the altar and were saved, but one boy and me. He was a rounder's son named Westley. Westley and I were surrounded by sisters and deacons praying. It was very hot in the church, and getting late now. Finally Westley said to me in a whisper: "God damn! I'm tired o' sitting here. Let's get up and be saved." So he got up and was saved.

Then I was left all alone on the mourners' bench. My aunt came and knelt at my knees and cried, while prayers and songs swirled all around me in the little church. The whole congregation prayed for me alone, in a mighty wail of moans and voices. And I kept waiting serenely for Jesus, waiting, waiting—but he didn't come. I wanted to see him, but nothing happened to me. Nothing! I wanted something to happen to me, but nothing happened.

I heard the songs and the minister saying: "Why don't you come? My dear child, why don't you come to Jesus? Jesus is waiting for you. He wants you. Why don't you come? Sister Reed, what is this child's name?'"

"Langston," my aunt sobbed.

"Langston, why don't you come? Why don't you come and be saved? Oh, Lamb of God! Why don't you come?"

Now it was really getting late. I began to be ashamed of myself, holding everything up so long. I began to wonder what God thought about Westley, who certainly hadn't seen Jesus either, but who was now sitting proudly on the platform, swinging his knickerbockered legs and grinning down at me, surrounded by deacons and old women on their knees praying. God had not struck Westley dead for taking his name in vain or for lying in the temple. So I decided that maybe to save further trouble, I'd better lie, too, and say that Jesus had come, and get up and be saved.

So I got up.

Suddenly the whole room broke into a sea of shouting, as they saw me rise. Waves of rejoicing swept the place. Women leaped in the air. My aunt threw her arms around me. The minister shook my hand and led me to the platform.

When things quieted down, in a hushed silence, punctuated by a few ecstatic "Amens," all the new young lambs were blessed in the name of God. Then joyous singing filled the room.

That night, for the last time in my life but one—for I was a big boy twelve years old—I cried. I cried, in bed alone, and couldn't stop. I buried my head under the quilts, but my aunt heard me. She woke up and told my uncle I was crying because the Holy Ghost had come into my life, and because I had seen Jesus. But I was really crying because I couldn't bear to tell her that I had lied, that I had deceived everybody in the church, that I hadn't seen Jesus, and that now I didn't believe there was a Jesus any more, since he didn't come to help me.

10

A Rationalist Examines
Some Crucial Issues of His Time

Melvin B. Tolson

THE DEATH OF AN INFIDEL (APRIL 2, 1938)

It seems that I am always in the objective case. But the records show
that Aristotle, Columbus, Pasteur, Socrates, and Jesus were in the
same classification. So I'm in good company. I am not a yes-man
nor an amen-brother. In fact, the only reason I can endure this worst
of all possible worlds is this: I have a supply of brickbats and there
are plenty of glass houses to throw at. The Big Boys have tried to
buy me off and some of them have tried to cut off my meal ticket
in this Christian country, but I go on my way hurling my rocks
at superstitions and prejudices and cruelties. If I think a thing is
right, I'm ready to debate any man, anywhere, and at any time. I
let Joe Louis fight all my physical battles, but I myself meet all comers
in the arena of argumentation. A.B.s, A.M.s, and Ph.D.s are not
barred. I admit I do have some fear of D.D.s, for they may call
upon me the wrath of an angry God. I am the son of a preacher,

From *Caviar and Cabbage: Selected Columns by Melvin B. Tolson from the
Washington Tribune, 1937–1944,* ed. Robert M. Farnsworth (Columbia, Mo.:
University of Missouri Press). These columns appeared originally in the *Washington
Tribune.*

who was the son of a preacher, who was the son of a preacher. One time I spent four months eating and sleeping with about 500 white preachers. I shall tell you about that.

Mouth-Christians

I want to say a few words about an infidel, the late Clarence Darrow. He did not live the way an infidel is supposed to live; he did not die the way an infidel is supposed to die. He was a thorn in the side of the good Christians. His life of unselfishness was an ever-lasting challenge to the Christianity-talking followers of Jesus. All they could do was condemn old Clarence Darrow for the things he said. You see, the Christians talked about the Golden Rule and the brotherhood of man, while this old infidel practiced the Golden Rule and the Ten Commandments. The question is: Who will get to heaven first—the man who talks or the man who acts?

By their fruits shall ye know them! Anybody who is scared to die can cry, "Lord! Lord!" It's easy to love God. It's easy to love Jesus. It's easy to pray for the heathen African 10,000 miles from the house where you live. It's hard to call a lousy tramp your brother and set him down at your table. It's hard to keep from feeling superior to Aunt Dinah and Uncle Tom in the one-room shack on Misery Alley. The only test of a Christian is this: How does he treat the poor? How does he treat the lame, the halt, and the blind?

People who believe in a black aristocracy, in capitalism, in jim-crow churches, in exclusive fraternities and sororities, in the perpetual ignorance of the masses, in the I-thank-God-that-I-am-not-like-other-men theory—these persons are no more followers of the poverty-stricken Jesus than a cannibal in the equatorial jungles. Such a person is a mouth-Christian. If Jesus were here today, he'd be calling the lowly Nazarene a Red; and Jesus would be calling him a viper and hypocrite. It's easy to love a man who lived in Jerusalem 2,000 years ago. It's respectable to be a mouth-Christian.

An Infidel Champions the Underdog

With death closing in on him—and if a man is ever serious, it is when he must meet the grim reaper alone—old Clarence Darrow said that the greatest satisfaction of his life had been spurred from his efforts in behalf of the underdog, and that his hardest task had been trying his hardest to overcome the cruelties of the world. That's greatness talking.

Once I censured a student for making an error in grammar. The student told me that Shakespeare made mistakes. I told him that when he was able to write a masterpiece like Shakespeare's *Hamlet*, I would say nothing about the errors he made in his themes.

Darrow doubtless made mistakes, like you and me. But his virtues towered above his weaknesses like the Rocky Mountains above a molehill. The evil that men do lives after them, but the good is not interred with their bones.

Darrow defended Eugene V. Debs, the Socialist leader who had been accused of conspiracy in the railway strike of 1894. I wish I could have been there when old Darrow and Debs met beyond the grave, two defenders of orphans and broken-down workers shaking hands and talking things over. If you have a spark of humanity in you, read the life of Debs; then see if you are worthy to unlace the shoes of a Debs. A daily newspaper informs me that the last recorded act of this infidel was to go to Joliet state penitentiary to secure the parole of Jesse Binga, 71-year-old Negro ex-banker serving a term of ten years for embezzlement. Race meant nothing to Clarence Darrow—only human suffering.

An Infidel and the Song "America"

Clarence Darrow believed in practical democracy. He believed that society is responsible for most of our crimes. He studied hard and got the facts. Nobody answered the facts. Instead of attacking the facts, ignoramuses, as usual, attacked the man. You can't destroy an idea by attacking a man. It took Americans, intelligent Americans, fifty years to discover that the old lawyer was right.

Once Darrow said publicy that if a Negro sang "My Country 'Tis of Thee," he was either a fool or a crook. Some of the big Negroes were shocked. Big Negroes are always being shocked by the truth. It's a wonder that more of them don't die of heart failure —so the race can move ahead. Death solves more problems than logicians. God knew what He was doing when He let death roam up and down creation.

How can a black man honestly sing "My Country 'Tis of Thee"

when he doesn't own enough of his country in which to bury a cockroach? How can a black man honestly sing "Sweet Land of Liberty" when, if a white man heard him whisper that he wanted to vote in thousands of Southern towns, it would cost him his life? Black men were afraid to say that; so old Darrow told the truth for them. No wonder the good white folk and the "yessah" Negroes thought him a dangerous man!

Darrow is gone. I'm sorry. He was a fighter. He loved the lame, the halt, and the blind. He loved the lousy underdog. I'm sorry that every Negro newspaper and preacher and teacher didn't say something to black America and white America about this great man's life. I'm sorry they didn't mention his death. But I'm always in the objective case.

A Warning to Black Men

The case of Clarence Darrow points a lesson. Black folk are too easily deluded by superficial facts. Call a man an infidel or a radical and you can hoodwink us to death. Why should a black man fear a radical? The abolitionists were radicals in their day. At one time it was radical in America to say "I believe the black man has a soul; I believe a black man can be educated." If it had not been for the radicals, every black man would be in a cotton patch with a white man standing over him with a forty-four and a horsewhip three yards long.

And whenever you hear anybody denounce radicals, remember this: persecuted races get their rights only through the agitation of radicals. The man who denies the truth of this is as dumb as Balaam's jackass. Amen!

PORTRAIT OF JESUS, THE YOUNG RADICAL
(JUNE 4, 1938)

I have read a lot, heard a lot, and thought a lot about Jesus. I am the son of a preacher who was the son of a preacher who was the son of a preacher.

A sermon is a word-picture painted by an artist-preacher to be hung in the gallery of memories. A good sermon thrills me as I am thrilled by Peter Paul Ruben's *Landscape with the Rainbow* or Leonardo da Vinci's *Mona Lisa.*

But so many third-rate painters have attempted to do the word-picture of Jesus that it's hard to tell just what He looked like. You've seen those cheap snapshots that rookie cameramen make of you for ten cents at the circus. Well, in thousands of cases, bad photographs have messed up the likeness of Jesus.

On Mother's Day I attended the chapel services at Wiley College and got a marvelous portrait of Jesus the young radical. The word-picture was done with that imaginative quality that possesses the amazing accuracy of truth, just as Shakespeare's Julius Caesar in *Julius Caesar* is more real, more lifelike than the historical Julius Caesar who walked the streets of ancient Rome.

I was thrilled by this vivid picture of Jesus the young rebel. My soul was uplifted all day. I found myself in Nazareth. I was standing in the presence of the young man Jesus—Jesus the only radical in a village that time and progress had forgot.

Dr. James L. Farmer, the Artist-Preacher

A great preacher is a great artist. Words are his tubes of paint. Verse, his brush. The souls of men the canvas on which he portrays the truths caught in moments of inspiration. The God-man is a man of imagination.

No two painters see an object through the same eyes. No two artists give the same interpretation of a scene. Jan Van Goyen's pictures of the sea are not like those of S. van Ruisdael. Franz Hals's portraits of women reveal moods and nuances in the subtler sex not found in the pictures of Van Dyck. But both are fine artists.

Likewise, no two preachers derive the same thoughts from the same text; no two pulpit orators give identical pictures of the world-character that came out of the village-rut that was Nazareth.

Why is this? Well, a man sees Jesus through the eyes of his experiences, through his native imagination, through his moral and intellectual training; and the picture that he gives us of Jesus is determined by his ability to use words.

Dr. James Leonard Farmer's personality is the product of an interesting career. When you enter his study and look around at the massive rows of books reaching to the ceiling, you realize that the gates of scholarship didn't close in his face when he received his Ph.D. degree from Boston University in 1918. As a liberal scholar, his researches have carried him into many fields, giving his intellect a catholicity of taste and interest.

As dean of Rust College, registrar of Samuel Houston College, professor of the Old Testament at Gammon Seminary, dean of the Gulfside summer school and professor of philosophy at Wiley College, he has made noteworthy contributions to the field of education. His sociological and philosophical articles in some of the leading magazines of the country have created a favorable reaction among outstanding scholars in these spheres. He emphatically represents modern scholarship in the church, as typified by Dr. Harry Emerson Fosdick and Rabbi Jonah Bondi Wise and Professor William David Schermerhorn.

Jesus, the Friend of the Masses

In a few striking sentences on the subject "The Young Man Jesus and His Parents," Dr. Farmer etched in the social background of Nazareth and placed against it Jesus.

Said Dr. Farmer: "Jesus was teaching contrary to the social and religious traditions of his people. . . . They thought one thing, but practiced another. As a consequence, wherever He went He made many enemies for himself among the social and religious leaders."

Yes, the Big Boys were against Jesus, and if He should return today the Big Boys would be against Him. They would call Him an infidel, an atheist, a radical, a red.

In one clean sentence, Dr. Farmer pointed out the dilemma of a man like Jesus—a man who wants to help the people: "The more popular He became with the masses, the more hostile these leaders became towards Him, and the more determined to destroy Him."

Martin Luther would sanction that and John Wesley, and Frederick Douglass, and Abe Lincoln, and Oliver Cromwell, and Franklin Roosevelt!

If you become a defender of labor, you become an enemy of capital. If you are a lover of the masses of people, you may expect the Big Boys and their flunkies to get on your trail like a pack of hungry wolves. Jesus found that out.

Jesus' Mother Tried to Save Him!

Dr. Farmer painted one of the finest pictures of a loving mother and her son that I have ever seen. When Jesus broke away from the moss-back teachings of His parents and community, He gave himself a very bad reputation. The gossipers in Nazareth said he was crazy, criminal, wayward. The priests and respectables denounced Him. His mother was grieved as any other mother would have been. Youth has vision! Old age, dreams.

It's easy to be a Christian today. It puts you in the best society. But I wonder how many of us would have had the guts to follow Jesus when the mob was on His trail! It's easy to love Him now since He's been dead some 2,000 years.

Jesus was a radical, as Dr. Farmer pointed out in his striking analysis. He didn't knuckle to the old folk. He wasn't considered a model boy, by any means. He loved His parents but He loved His duty more. Truth was His pole-star. He was a God-man. The greatest God-man working for the ages.

Christian Youth and Parents

I don't have space to reproduce this sermon masterpiece. It's like trying to put Samuel Taylor Coleridge's unforgettable "Kubla Khan" in stammering prose.

But, I suppose the core of the sermon was the conflict between the hypocrisy of parents and the frankness of youth, the mouth-Christianity of parents and the demands of youth for the everyday practice of the teachings of Jesus.

It's refreshing to find a preacher who faces the challenge of youth with intelligence and poise. It's wonderful to find a parent who does not call a questioning youngster a smart guy. Parents say that "under our present competitive system we cannot successfully practice the ideals of Jesus," and youth replies, "Why not change the system?"

Dr. Farmer sees clearly the dilemma in which an honest man finds himself in a dishonest world. "You must neither practice what you preach nor preach what you practice." I've never seen that put better. Again: "You must say that you believe the right, but you must not do it. And you must do what you believe not to be right; but you must not say it!"

And then the eminent doctor of philosophy takes his stand with old Martin Luther and John Wesley when he says, "If ever there was an occasion for radicalism, I declare it is amply provided here. Not an axe to fell the tree, but a spade to undermine its roots, is the urgent need of the times."

Parents say, "Take the world as it comes, and make the best of it." Christian youth says, according to Dr. Farmer, "Change the world and make it what it ought to be."

I'll take my stand with American youth and Dr. Farmer and Jesus, the young radical.

PAUL ROBESON REBELS AGAINST HOLLYWOOD'S DOLLARS (MARCH 12, 1939)

It was years and years ago on the gridiron at Lincoln University. A magnificent bronze god was helping Fritz Pollard get the Lions ready for their attack on the Bisons. The brown god was scrimmaging against the varsity. I saw him pick up bodily our All-American tackle, hurl him into the advancing backfield, and break up an off-tackle play. The bronze god was Paul Robeson, the All-American of all time. Yes, if old Walt Whitman, America's greatest poet, had seen that, he would have included Paul Robeson in America's greatest epic, *Leaves of Grass*.

Football and boxing are my favorite sports. They require guts. Great white players who encountered Robeson in his days as a collegiate and professional athlete admired the youth's intestinal fortitude. But a man can be physically courageous and morally craven. You see that in politics, religion, and education. Paul Robeson's moral courage equals the physical fortitude of his magnificent body. He is a MAN.

And it takes a man to turn down Hollywood's dollars. In fact, you can tell a man by his attitude toward the dollar. Listen to a man when he gushes about his love of humanity and Jesus and God. But you'll learn more about him when you see how he acts toward a dollar!

I say that to say this—Mr. J. Danvers Williams, the international columnist, writes from London, home of monkey-faced Chamberlain's sell-out gang, that "Paul Robeson has broken with the big commercial film industry."

That's news for dark America. But it hasn't been discovered by the copies I've seen of the Negro press. Robeson refuses to be what my friend, Langston Hughes, calls "the international Uncle Tom." Black boy, I feel like jumping up and cracking my African heels together! But I have to get out this article before the deadline.

Robeson has met the big shots of the white world. You know what Woolcott, the big-time critic, said about Paul in that best-seller, *Where Rome Burns*. You know what Gertrude Stein, the famous American patron of the arts and literature, said about Paul in her celebrated *Autobiography of Alice B. Toklas*. Yet Paul Robeson said: "I never felt that I was a man until I visited Russia."

Now, Robeson wants to return to Moscow to make a picture under Eisenstein, the world's greatest producer. Like Marian Anderson, he received a tremendous ovation in Russia. There is no American DAR* there to jim-crow black artists and windjam about democracy —the mockery.

Robeson wants to make a picture of that heroic Chicago Negro, Oliver Law, who died leading white soldiers in the International Brigade of Spain against the Ratzis.

Listen to what Robeson says about Hollywood: "I shall not attempt to make my picture about Oliver Law for any of the big companies, for I know only too well that the directors of the industry wouldn't consider it 'policy' to depict a Negro leading white men into battle."

And yet didn't I hear, over the radio, the President and the Chief Justice of the Supreme Court, commemorating our 150 years of liberty under the Constitution? Didn't I hear an opera singer hymning in the House of Representatives:

> My country 'tis of thee,
> Sweet land of liberty?

Black boy, maybe I'm wrong. Maybe Paul Robeson is wrong, but that makes me think of a bad-smelling Diogenes, who hasn't had a bath for many years, trying to sell you and me a bottle of exquisite perfume.

Robeson takes a slam at the atrocious lies of the Hollywood industry. These films picture rich young men who fall in love with

---

*Daughters of the American Revolution—Ed.

girls in the five-and-ten-cent stores, or heiresses who marry the family chauffeur—once in a million years. The musical comedies play up half-naked girls wriggling like Minnie the Moocher, to arouse the desires of adolescents and bald-headed husbands yearning for a last fling before seeking oblivion.

Robeson is the New Negro in action. He is not a rugged individualist. He is not a snob. He does not scorn the masses. He is not concerned in rising from the ranks, but in rising with the ranks. Negroes have to learn that. He wants life in the arts; not sentimental romanticism. Robeson believes in ours for us; not mine for me. Robeson wants the films to show actual people; factory workers, farmers, shipbuilders, longshoremen, cottonpickers. We've had enough of the top hats, evening gowns, and limousines. Robeson wants the films to show real people with real problems, with the masses aspiring and militant as masses. Robeson wants Mr. Average Man and Miss Average Woman put on the screen!

MARIAN ANDERSON, A SOUTHERN PAPER, AND A NEGRO DRUNK (APRIL 15, 1939)

It is Easter, goodwill to men. A study in contrasts. The famous contralto, barred from singing in the concert hall of the un-American Daughters of the American Revolution, makes her debut in a free, open recital on the steps of Lincoln Memorial before a crowd of 75,000.

At the feet of the Great Emancipator whose likeness is preserved in marble within the classic memorial, the magnificent voice of the Negro singer rings across a continent.

> My country 'tis of thee,
> Sweet land of liberty . . .

One thousand and five hundred miles away, sitting pressed against my radio, I try to visualize the Negro singer. I try to imagine what she is thinking as she utters the ironical words, "Sweet land of liberty." I try to figure out what is running through the minds of the white listeners. What does Secretary Ickes think? In his fine address did he say all that was in his heart?

Beyond Constitution Hall, from which women have banned her—women who would be honored by her genius and character—the dark angel's voice sweeps the profound theme of "Ave Maria" into millions of homes.

A thousand years from now, when the 1939 un-American Daughters of the American Revolution shall have been forgotten in scattered dust, the name and voice of Marian Anderson shall be known at the fireside of American womanhood.

An item for future historians: Easter, 1939. The *Shreveport Times* gives Marian Anderson's recital 4 words; the editor gives Abraham Bell, a Negro drunk, 49 words in the same paper.

Easter at Medicine Park, Oklahoma (April 15, 1939)

Medicine Park, Okla., is a small mountain village. This morning 175,000 people are gathered to see the spectacle of the crucified and risen Christ. Men and women and children sit on the sloping mountain. They have come afoot, on horseback, in cars to witness this thirteenth production.

As Jesus dies between the two thieves, some of the people burst into tears. As the sun comes up over Fort Scott and Jesus rises from the dead, thousands cry hallelujahs.

The only road from the scene, according to E. C. Wallis, who reports the dramatic happening, is a graveled road just wide enough for two cars. And there are 50,000 cars that must wind around mountains and cross streams to get back home with their pilgrims.

But all the scores of thousands of good white citizens are happy this Easter morning. They have been deeply moved by the crucifixion and resurrection of Christ.

A few Indians look on at the mighty biblical drama. Also a few Negroes. But the white spectators, while sitting on the Indians' mountain, do not think about how their paleface ancestors stole the Indians' rich oil lands in Oklahoma and killed off the Indians. And the pious white spectators, of course, do not see the crucifixion of the Negro race in the crucifixion of Jesus.

So this Easter morning the white citizens leave Medicine Park with their souls uplifted, and go back to their jim-crow schools and jim-crow churches and jim-crow politics. The Indians go back to their gloomy reservations. The Negroes go back to their daily crosses. Next Easter, Medicine Park will give its fourteenth presentation of the crucified and risen Christ.

Easter in Europe! (April 15, 1939)

A mighty array of Italian infantry, motorized units, tanks, and bombing planes roll into Albania, and again that freedom-loving country finds itself the slave of a foreign power.

Four Italian warships blast the town of Durazzo. King Zog and his wife, with a baby three days old, flee before the onrushing hordes of fascists. Four hundred planes thunder over the little country, every whir of four hundred motors proclaiming death on earth, ill will to men.

Italian heavy guns face each other across the narrow neck of the Adriatic, and the famous six-foot Grenadiers push on across the mountains to the borders of Yugoslavia.

Today is Easter. Peace on earth! Yet in London, old Chamberlain cuts short his holiday and hurries to call a meeting of the cabinet, "fearful of a lightning attack by Germany without a declaration of war."

In Paris, it is Easter. Good will to men. Yet Premier Daladier calls hastily his military, naval, and air chiefs to map out plans to counter the vast army movements on the other side of the Rhine.

And now Pope Pius XII raises his voice in his first Easter message from the throne of St. Peter's in an eloquent appeal for peace and charity. His scholarly address is delivered in Latin.

That is just as well. Hitler and Mussolini don't know anything about Latin: so they won't know what the pope is talking about. Hitler and Mussolini understand only the language of bombing planes and machine guns. Hitler and Mussolini don't fear the pope as long as he talks in Latin.

1,900 Years after the Resurrection of Jesus! (April 15, 1939)

It is Easter. Centuries and centuries ago the Lowly Nazarene walked and talked among men. Never a man spoke like Jesus, the friend of the lame, the halt, and the blind. He came into a world torn with political strife, domestic disharmony, racial animosities, and the greed for gold.

He preached a straight doctrine. He didn't beat around the bush. He was an agitator. His enemies said: "He stirreth up the people."

Here on my wall hangs a picture of Him talking to the rich

young man. I look at that picture a great deal. I showed it to a big white merchant who came to talk to me about Jesus. The sweat popped out on his forehead as he read the words of Jesus:

"Take what thou hast and give it to the poor."

It is Easter. Spring is here. Life is flowing into bud and leaf and flower. In the grand cathedrals of the earth mighty organs thunder the messsage of the Christ. In a hundred lands millions of mouth-Christians sing hosannas. The Risen Master! What does He see? What does He hear? What does He feel?

He did not build a church of brick and mortar. He built His church in the hearts of men. He was not interested in isms. He wanted to make a better world. He lived to rid men of envy, jealousy, the lust of power, and the lust for gold.

He said to His followers: "Take nothing for your journey, neither staves, nor scrip, neither bread, neither money: neither two coats apiece."

Jesus looks down upon His followers this Easter. What are they taking on their Christian journey? Some of them are taking Cadillacs, ten-room houses, trunks of fine clothes, delicious foods, and all the money they can get out of other folks' pockets.

What does Jesus think about these people as He looks at them this morning? Jesus was humble; these mouth-Christians are proud. Jesus was poor; these mouth-Christians are rich, or breaking their necks trying to get rich. Jesus stood for His principles, died for His principles; these mouth-Christians are "practical" and "diplomatic" and "expedient." Jesus loved the poor; these mouth-Christians scorn the lousy and ignorant. Jesus said that only the pure in heart shall see God; these mouth-Christians have explained things so that anybody can see God. Jesus denounced the hypocrisies and exploitation of the Big Boys; these mouth-Christians worship high positions and material success. Jesus whipped the money-lenders out of the temple; these mouth-Christians take in anybody who has a dollar.

Jesus said some straight things. The man who says he loves God and hates his brother is a liar and the truth isn't in him. You can't serve God and Mammon. By their fruit you shall know them. He who is without sin, let him cast the first stone. Judge not that ye be not judged.

One thousand and nine hundred years after His resurrection, Jesus is still holding up His principles. Jesus doesn't want words; Jesus wants deeds. Jesus wants Christians; Jesus doesn't want mouth-

Christians. Fears and superstitions and traditions make mouth-Christians. Everybody who is scared to die or lose his job will make a good mouth-Christian.

Jesus didn't believe in jim-crow churches, jim-crow cars, child labor, snobbery, exploitation, slums, Uncle Tomism, big society. If you believe in these things you are not a Christian. You can't hold on to these things and hold on to Jesus. Let that sink in! Jesus is all wrong. Why are things in such a mess after 1,900 years of talking about Jesus? Perhaps there's been too much talk!

THE NEGRO AND RADICALISM (AUGUST 12, 1939)

Radicalism is spread in the United States. Every Negro who knows anything about Negro history is glad of this. Radicalism is the great Emancipator of Negroes. When I see a Negro kicking off radicals, I know he is either dumb or crooked.

Conservatism is the Negro's worst enemy. The South is the most conservative part of the country, and therefore it is the graveyard of Negro rights. In our most radical cities, Negroes enjoy the widest freedom. Your biggest Negro haters are the most conservative people. That is true in Boston, Dallas, Tucson, Washington, and Waycross, Georgia. Conservatism breeds every kind of prejudice.

I've heard educated Negroes in the South say that they like to live in "a wide-open town"; that is, a town where anything goes. Of course, such a town is not conservative. It is a place for a good time. These Negroes I refer to are respectable citizens. But they have observed that in "a wide-open town" the cops don't beat up Negroes for pastime. Then, too, the white citizens don't spend the day and night keeping Negroes in their place.

A conservative is a man who is opposed to change. Since he is all right, he imagines that everything is all right. God deliver me from a conservative Negro!

I realize that there are some places in the Land of the Free where there is no freedom of speech. But even in such hellholes a Negro can give the radicals a silent Amen. The Devil himself cannot keep a man from thinking. Then, too, if you are scared to be radical, you can cheer the man who has the guts to speak out for human rights. You can write him a letter of appreciation and tell him to burn it up.

Escape from Chattel Slavery

The Negro would not have escaped from chattel slavery if it had not been for radicals of all classes, isms, ologies, and sects. Don't forget that. For 150 years before the Civil War, radicals kept up a continuous fight for Negro freedom. Many of them were lynched.

Conservatives have stood for prostitution, blood-letting, polygamy, illiteracy, ignorance, witch-burning, voodooism, piracy, plagues, child labor, social diseases, and cannibalism. Why? Conservatives have always opposed change at all times and in all places.

Conservatives have always believed: "Whatever is, is right."

Conservatives have always laid the blame for everything on either God or human nature. When the filth in London produced the Black Plague that killed unnumbered thousands, conservatives called the Black Plague "an act of God." When a man dies because he is ignorant of the laws of health, the conservative says: "Too bad. But his time had come."

The conservative is a peculiar bird. He always has a hundred good reasons for doing nothing. If you pull on the oars, he declares you're trying to upset the boat. If you want to organize the Negroes, he sees a massacre of the Negro race. If Negroes picket a white man's store, he sees 12,000,000 Negroes losing their jobs. Anytime you want to make a change, the conservative sees the collapse of the universe.

The conservative is always talking about the eternal truths he has discovered. This is whistling in the dark near a graveyard. A new idea gives a conservative a spasm of fear. Thus all conservatives die of heart failure.

Yes, if the Negro had waited for the conservatives to free him, he would still be in chattel slavery. It took radicals like Douglas, Garrison, Lovejoy, Greeley, and John Brown to arouse the conscience of a nation to the brutalities of slavery. Economic materialism plus radical propaganda turned the trick.

A favorite excuse of the conservative is this: "The time is not ripe."

This statement is a feather bed in which the conservative sleeps from the cradle to the grave unless he is rudely awakened by a strike, a revolution, or war.

Radicalism Comes to the Defense

When I was in college, the Negro was the victim of vicious propaganda in all the sciences. He was described as unintellectual, unintelligent, immoral, irresponsible, childish, brutal, lustful, undependable, and criminal.

Conservative sociologists, historians, educators, statesmen, anthropologists, and novelists filled thousands of pages with Uncle Toms, Aunt Dinahs, Sambos, black rapists, black Al Capones, and grinning crapshooters.

After the World War, white radicals came to the defense of the Negro in larger and larger numbers. Negro art, music, and literature flourished. The Harlem Renaissance seems now a long way off. But it took place in the 20s. It is quite recently that the Negro has been considered a human being in American life and literature with the virtues and vices of human beings.

Can you remember when Dr. Du Bois and the late Dr. James Weldon Johnson were making their valiant pleas for the Talented Tenth?* It seems like a far-off dream. What professor would dare write a book now on contemporary American literature without including Negro poets and novelists?

I may say here that no race is civilized until it produces a literature. A great work of literature is a race's ticket to immortality. Races do not live in history because they have produced Henry Fords. Some so-called educated Negroes haven't discovered that well-known fact yet!

Rome owned a great material civilization, but Rome will be but a name to antiquarians when future generations will still be studying and admiring the great thinkers and writers of Greece.

Science, literature, and art have been the tireless defenders of Negroes. These three fields are renowned for their production of radicals.

The Most Powerful Thing

Propaganda is the most powerful thing in the world. It controls the destinies of men and nations. Every dictator knows that.

---

*The Talented Tenth. Du Bois at one time believed that the most talented ten percent of the African-American population (i.e., scholars, intellectuals, business persons, and others), working in concert, could serve as role models and lead African Americans to freedom, justice, and equality—Ed.

"Seize the press," says the dictator when he gives his first command to his flunkies.

The Negro didn't have a chance to be a man as long as conservative writers were depicting him either as a clown or a rapist. The seeds of racial prejudice were sown in the minds of millions of innocent schoolchildren and college students. This had gone on for generations.

Then came the radicals. With them came a proletarian literature and art dealing with the masses. These radicals said that a man was the product of social and economic forces. These radicals proved that a man is not the master of his fate and the captain of his soul.

This social philosophy marked the second emancipation of the Negro. No longer could the enemies of the Negro condemn him for being ignorant, illiterate, immoral, and criminal. The radicals said if you want to change the Negro, change his environment. Nurture changes nature.

In intellectual circles, you don't hear intellectuals arguing now about heredity and environment. Of course, we still have a few Negro snobs boasting about their heredity. But they are not geniuses like Richard Wright, Langston Hughes, and Paul Robeson.

I am glad to see radicals raising hell. The more hell they raise, the better it is for my people. Minority groups escape into the Promised Land only when radicals are raising hell.

RADIO NEWS FLASH: "JESUS LYNCHED IN AMERICA, 1939!" (DECEMBER 16, 1939)

This is the Age of Hypocrisy. As Dr. Leonard Farmer has said, "You must neither practice what you preach nor preach what you practice." As long as you talk and write about Heaven, the Garden of Allah, the Promised Land, Sodom and Gomorrah, the Hebrew Children in the Fiery Furnace, Abe Lincoln, the Constitution, Hitler, Stalin, Mussolini, the Reds, David and Goliath, Beauty, Patriotism, Jesus, Virtue, the Book of the Seven Seals—as long as you write and talk about somebody or something way off, the 2×4 respectables will give you the big hand.

A preacher may preach about David's stealing Uriah's wife: but he'd better not breathe a word about Deacon John Doe who stole Deacon Littlejohn's wife.

It's okay to describe Jesus driving the moneylenders out of the

Temple 1,900 years ago, but you'd better not talk about the 1939 racketeers in the Temple.

Quacks Rake in the Money

No wonder that great scholar, Samuel D. Schmalhausen, in the *Modern Quarterly*, dubbed this period "The Age of Lies."

Everybody knows we are rotten with hypocrisy. Everybody knows we tell lies by direction and indirection—black lies and white lies. Everybody knows that while we mouth Christian platitudes we practice devilish vices. Everybody knows that while we talk about heaven we're on our way to hell with a one-way ticket. Yet most of us are scared to face the truth. We're like a guy with the syphilis who is scared to see the doctor; therefore, he visits a quack.

Our society and its institutions are diseased. So we call in quacks of all sorts. Dale Carnegie comes along with *How to Win Friends and Influence People*. So we buy a million copies containing his bunk. A dusky mulatto with showbutton eyes and straight hair puts on an Oriental costume and we pay four bits when he tells us how to win success and love. Somebody starts a chain letter that ends in the outhouse.

In spite of the iron fact that Big Business has ruined the white man, simpleminded Negroes and college professors shout: "Business is the salvation of the Negro." Now and then some big Negro, with his belly stuffed with roast chicken, comes along and tells the little Negroes "to think on higher things."

Dr. Flunky of the famous Pow-wow University shoots craps with some statistics and writes: "Business is on the upgrade. Prosperity is just around the corner. All you need is faith. All you need is hope. Fellow citizens, the dirty radicals tell you the Old Ship of State has hit a rock. Beware. Beware of such hasty generalizations! The Old Ship of State has just sprung a leak. That's all."

Condemnation of the Rich; Exaltation of the Poor

Nothing is more beautiful than genuine service. The early Christians had it. Taking neither two coats nor scrip, neither gold nor silver, they went about doing good. They were the first Communists: that is, they held everything in common. They were not social climbers. They did not cater to the selfishness of the Big Boys. If Luke had a loaf of bread, he shared it with Mark. They had Christianity: they didn't know anything about modern Churchianity.

The early Christians rendered a great service. I think V. F. Calverton has summed it up best in his recent best-seller, *The Awakening of America*: "It elevated the concept of man as man, regardless of his position in society, his wealth, his office in the state. It made all men equal in the eyes of the Lord. It condemned the rich and exalted the poor."

Why did Christianity grow? Well, the early Christians practiced what they preached. Its revolutionary democratic ideal in a world of human slavery and poverty appealed to the masses. That's the reason Christianity made a vigorous appeal to the black slaves.

How Jesus Differed from Other Christs of His Day

Why was Jesus lynched? Why were the ancient Christians burned at the stake? Mr. Calverton gives us the answer: "The Roman emperor did not attempt to suppress Christianity because of its religious content, but because of its political and economic threat. Roman civilization was full of too many Christs, too many messiahs of all kinds—Mithraic, Zoroastrian, Manichean—to be alarmed about another Savior born of the Jews."

Then why did the Big Boys in Rome get scared of Jesus? Why did they single out Jesus? Why did the Unholy Three of ancient times —the Pharisees, the Sadducees, and the Sanhedrin—plot the downfall of Jesus?

Mr. Calverton tells us: "It was the revolutionary doctrine of this particular Christ, who associated with fishermen, carpenters, tradesmen, whores, that terrified the Romans and made them drive his followers to the hills and the catacombs and finally to the lions when they were captured."

This stern fact is overlooked by 9,999 persons out of every 10,000 who go to church every Sunday.

If Jesus Came to America in 1939?

The essence of the teachings of Jesus is democracy, as contained in the Golden Rule. He who says he loves God and hates his brother is a liar and the truth isn't in him.

The disciples of Jesus were poor. His followers were the riff-raff, the down-and-outers, the scum of society. The fox has a hole, the bird has a nest; but the lowly Jesus didn't have a place to lay his head.

You recall the high tragedy of the rich young man who came to Jesus. He had kept all the commandments from his youth up. But that was not enough. Needless to say, that rich young man could have joined any church in America. By our low standards, he would have been okay. But not by Jesus'.

Jesus said: "Take what thou hast and give it to the poor."

The rich young man did just what most of us would do today. He told Jesus good-bye.

Let us quote one of those ole-time Christians of the seventeenth century, Winstanley by name: "At this day the poor people are forced to work for 4d. and corn is dear. And the tithing-priest stops their mouth and tells them what 'inward satisfaction of mind' was meant by the declaration, 'the poor shall inherit the earth.' I tell you the scripture is to be really and materially fulfilled."

Doesn't that priest sound just like some of these mouth-Christians who say: "You'll eat pie, in the sky, bye and bye"?

And when grand old Winstanley told the Big Boys about piling up goods on earth and building up classes, doesn't he sound just like a soapbox radical? Jesus came to level things. Great men were to be servants; not exploiters. Jesus didn't believe in economic, racial, and social distinctions.

We look upon servants—the scrubwoman and the street sweeper—with contempt. Am I telling the truth? Amen! You talk about Karl Marx, the Communist! Why, don't you know Jesus was preaching about leveling society 1,800 years before the Jewish Red was born?

Listen to old Winstanley: "You jeer at the name of the Leveller. I tell you Jesus Christ is the Head Leveller. The day of Judgment is begun . . . the poor people you oppress shall be the saviours of the land . . . and break to pieces the bands of property." Then come the English Revolution, the American Revolution, the French Revolution, the Russian Revolution!

Jesus Is Lynched in America in 1939!

That's what you would see in your newspaper if Jesus returned to America in 1939. Why? What did Jesus do to get lynched?

Well, Jesus did some radical things. Because of his un-Americanism, the Dies Committee called him in. Jesus had white Christians and black Christians meeting together at Okay, Arkansas, thereby violating the State Jim Crow Law in that Christian State. Jesus said He wasn't going to have any jim-crow churches. So the whites and blacks got together for the first time and ran Jesus across the state line.

Then Jesus wanted the rich Christians to take what they had and give it to the poor. Henry Ford and the Supreme Court and the Big Negroes asked Jesus: "What you trying to put over, you Red?"

Then Jesus said He wasn't going to have any more preachers knifing other preachers in the back to get bigger churches and positions. Jesus started abolishing fraternities and sororities; that caused the Alphas and Omegas and Kappas to gang Jesus. Then Jesus ran around with bums: He didn't know how to pick the right company. Jesus went into the colleges and universities and started the students thinking. Then Jesus walked into Wall Street and started breaking up the rackets He found there. That's the reason they lynched Jesus!

AN EASTER SERMON—WITHOUT A PREACHER
(MARCH 30, 1940)

It is Easter. Before me lies the greatest Easter sermon. It is not the work of a preacher. Thousands of sermons will be delivered today, but not one will equal this. It is a sermon without a preacher. I'm not joking, either.

Before me lies a huge metropolitan newspaper. I wish every man in the world could read it, as I shall read it. Now, the owner and editor of this newspaper didn't intend to put out a sermon this morning. This Easter edition was simply a business proposition.

At the top of the page is the word *Easter* in large, Old English type. In the center is a fine-looking church. To the right and to the left, handsome boys are singing in a choir. Then, there are beautiful doves flying above serene meadows.

Christians and the Battlefield!

I read an article from the Associated Press. It says: "Christians turn from battlefield to church for day of rejoicing. Holy City is a Mecca for thousands."

Do you see the contradiction, my friend? Do Christians, battlefield, and church go together harmoniously? You would think that the Devil himself wrote that sentence. Yet it is the truth. We are a race of hypocrites. We hate and shoot each other down like dogs; then go to church!

The article continues: "The eyes of the Roman Catholic world turned to Vatican City, where Pope Pius XII personally arranged to celebrate Mass in historic St. Peter's."

Read that quotation again. We are told that the message of the pope will be a vigorous appeal for peace. And yet the pope is having a bomb-proof room built in the Vatican! I take these facts from the magazine *News-Week*.

Easter Parade in a Thousand Cities

This morning, in a thousand cities, ladies of refinement and culture are on parade in their Easter dresses. Before me lies a full-page picture of four ladies smiling among beautiful flowers. When I was a young man in Atlantic City, I used to see ladies in $10,000 fur coats taking a stroll along the famous Boardwalk. Our civilization is very kind to—some ladies.

This morning, in a thousand cities, overworked, poverty-stricken mothers and daughters get out of filthy beds in man-made tenements. Millions of poor women didn't have the new dress to wear to church.

This morning, in Waco, Texas, Bob Crowder, 50, killed his sister-in-law and wounded his wife and killed himself. He used a 12-gauge pump shotgun. The husband of his sister-in-law lost his job and the murdered woman came to live with her sister.

Then Bob Crowder lost his job. Despondent for weeks, Crowder decided to fix things so that they wouldn't have to worry any more about jobs. Ten million men in America woke up this Easter morning—without jobs. Jobs for husbands and fathers would help a great deal in bringing "peace on earth; good will to men."

A Picture of the Risen Lord

Here before me lies a beautiful picture of the Resurrection. It was painted by that genius, Fra Angelico, about the middle of the fifteenth century.

To the left of this masterpiece is an article on the political and economic situation in Old Mexico. The Mexicans are having trouble, with Big American Business, over oil properties. Mexico is about to hold a presidential election. The issues revolve around these oil properties. Dollars are making a mess out of things—as usual. The greatest enemy of Jesus is the dollar.

The article says a revolution is expected, because guns and ammunition are being smuggled into Mexico from the United States. American Business started the trouble by blackjacking the Mexicans out of their oil wells; now American Business sells guns to the Mexicans so they can murder each other over the oil wells. Many "Christians" won't see anything wrong with this on Easter morning.

Across from the picture of the risen Lord is a picture of children called "The Junior Red Cross." The children have a truck loaded with provisions. I wonder if the Junior Red Cross is getting ready to send aid to the Mexicans who will kill each other with the guns produced in our "Christian" country. And I bet those Big Businessmen are sitting in church this morning with their wives and children! Are the gunmakers also in church, singing: "Peace on earth; good will to men"?

What Is the Title of This Sermon?

Now, the title of this newspaper sermon is "Hypocrisy." For 1,900 years we have preached one thing and practiced another. We are so hypocritical that we don't know why we are hypocritical. A white American can denounce Hitler for persecuting 500,000 Jews, and at the same time see nothing wrong in persecuting 12,000,000 Negroes.

We are so downright dirty that we can take sacrament and plot the destruction of another human being. We can say we love God—whom we have not seen—and hate our neighbor next door. We can give to the Red Cross, and sell guns to murder other men. We can say God hates a liar, and lie faster than the Broadway Limited can run. We can say the truth will make you free, and then do our best to destroy any man who has guts enough to tell the truth.

We are a race of vipers and hypocrites! If Jesus returned, we'd lynch Him before a cat could sneeze. We put on our fine clothes and talk about Jesus. Jesus wouldn't have a thing to do with us. Jesus was interested in bums. The lame, the halt, and the blind followed Jesus. If the dirty mobs that walked after Jesus came into one of our fine churches, the good "Christians" would turn up their noses and call the police!

All that Jesus said can be summed up in the Golden Rule. When I hear anybody talking about God or Jesus, I simply look to see if he's practicing the Golden Rule. If he isn't practicing the Golden Rule, he's as far from Jesus as the earth is from Jupiter.

Only radicals can be Christians.

11

Religion

Zora Neale Hurston

You wouldn't think that a person who was born with God in the house would ever have any questions to ask on the subject.

But as early as I can remember, I was questing and seeking. It was not that I did not hear. I tumbled right into the Missionary Baptist Church when I was born. I saw the preachers and the pulpits, the people and the pews. Both at home and from the pulpit, I heard my father, known to thousands as "Reverend Jno" (an abbreviation for John) explain all about God's habits, His heaven, His ways and means. Everything was known and settled.

From the pews I heard a ready acceptance of all that Papa said. Feet beneath the pews beat out a rhythm as he pictured the scenery of heaven. Heads nodded with conviction in time to Papa's words. Tense snatches of tune broke out and some shouted until they fell into a trance at the recognition of what they heard from the pulpit. Come "love feast"* some of the congregation told of getting close

---

"Religion" from *Dust Tracks on a Road* by Zora Neale Hurston. Copyright 1942 by Zora Neale Hurston. Copyright renewed 1970 by John C. Hurston. Reprinted by permission of Harper-Collins Publishers.

*The "Love Feast" or "Experience Meeting" is a meeting held either the Friday night or the Sunday morning before Communion. Since no one is supposed to take Communion unless he or she is in harmony with all other members, there

enough to peep into God's sitting-room windows. Some went further. They had been inside the place and looked all around. They spoke of sights and scenes around God's throne.

That should have been enough for me. But somehow it left a lack in my mind. They should have looked and acted differently from other people after experiences like that. But these people looked and acted like everybody else—or so it seemed to me. They plowed, chopped wood, went possum hunting, washed clothes, raked up back yards, and cooked collard greens like anybody else. No more ornaments and nothing. It mystified me. There were so many things they neglected to look after while they were right there in the presence of All-Power. I made up my mind to do better than that if ever I made the trip.

I wanted to know, for instance, why didn't God make grown babies instead of those little measly things that messed up didies and cried all the time? What was the sense in making babies with no teeth? He knew that they had to have teeth, didn't He? So why not give babies their teeth in the beginning instead of hiding the toothless things in hollow stumps and logs for grannies and doctors to find and give to people? He could see all the trouble people had with babies, rubbing their gums and putting wood-lice around their necks to get them to cut teeth. Why did God hate for children to play on Sundays? If Christ, God's son, hated to die, and God hated for Him to die and have everybody grieving over it ever since, why did He have to do it? Why did people die anyway?

It was explained to me that Christ died to save the world from sin and then, too, so that folks did not have to die any more. That was a simple, clear-cut explanation. But then I heard my father and other preachers accusing people of sin. They went so far as to say that people were so prone to sin, that they sinned with every breath they drew. You couldn't even breathe without sinning! How could that happen if we had already been saved from it? So far as the dying part was concerned, I saw enough funerals to know that somebody was dying. It seemed to me that somebody had been fooled and I so stated to my father and two of his colleagues. When they got through with me, I knew better than to say that out loud again, but their shocked and angry tirades did nothing for my bewilderment. My head was full of misty fumes of doubt.

---

are great protestations of love and friendship. It is an opportunity to reaffirm faith plus anything the imagination might dictate.

Neither could I understand the passionate declarations of love for a being that nobody could see. Your family, your puppy and the new bull-calf, yes. But a spirit away off who found fault with everybody all the time, that was more than I could fathom. When I was asked if I loved God, I always said yes because I knew that that was the thing I was supposed to say. It was a guilty secret with me for a long time. I did not dare ask even my chums if they meant it when they said they loved God with all their souls and minds and hearts, and would be glad to die if He wanted them to. Maybe they had found out how to do it, and I was afraid of what they might say if they found out I hadn't. Maybe they wouldn't even play with me any more.

As I grew, the questions went to sleep in me. I just said the words, made the motions and went on. My father being a preacher, and my mother superintendent of the Sunday School, I naturally was always having to do with religious ceremonies. I even enjoyed participation at times; I was moved, not by the spirit, but by action, more or less dramatic.

I liked revival meetings particularly. During these meetings the preacher let himself go. God was called by all of His praise-giving names. The scenery of heaven was described in detail. Hallelujah Avenue and Amen Street were paved with gold so fine that you couldn't drop a pea on them but what they rang like chimes. Hallelujah Avenue ran north and south across heaven, and was tuned to sound alto and bass. Amen Street ran east and west and was tuned to "treble" and tenor. These streets crossed each other right in front of the throne and made harmony all the time. Yes, and right there on that corner was where all the loved ones who had gone on before would be waiting for those left behind.

Oh yes! They were all there in their white robes with the glittering crowns on their heads, golden girdles clasped about their waists and shoes of jeweled gold on their feet, singing the hallelujah song and waiting. And as they walked up and down the golden streets, their shoes would sing, "sol me, sol do" at every step.

Hell was described in dramatic fury. Flames of fire leaped up a thousand miles from the furnaces of Hell, and raised blisters on a sinning man's back before he hardly got started downward. Hell-hounds pursued their ever-dying souls. Everybody under the sound of the preacher's voice was warned, while yet they were on pleading terms with mercy, to take steps to be sure that they would not be a brand in that eternal burning.

Sinners lined the mourner's bench from the opening night of the revival. Before the week was over, several or all of them would be "under conviction." People, solemn of face, crept off to the woods to "praying ground" to seek religion. Every church member worked on them hard, and there was great clamor and rejoicing when any of them "come through" religion.

The pressure on the unconverted was stepped up by music and high drama. For instance I have seen my father stop preaching suddenly and walk down to the front edge of the pulpit and breathe into a whispered song. One of his most effective ones was:

> Run! Run! Run to the City of Refuge, children!
> Run! Oh, run! Or else you'll be consumed.

The congregation working like a Greek chorus behind him would take up the song and the mood and hold it over for a while even after he had gone back into the sermon at high altitude:

> Are you ready-ee? Hah!
> For that great day, hah!
> When the moon shall drape her face in mourning, hah!
> And the sun drip down in blood, hah!
> When the stars, hah!
> Shall burst forth from their diamond sockets, hah!
> And the mountains shall skip like lambs, hah!
> Havoc will be there, my friends, hah!
> With her jaws wide open, hah!
> And the sinner-man, hah!
> He will run to the rocks, hah!
> And cry, Oh rocks! Hah!
> Hide me! Hah!
> Hide me from the face of an angry God, hah!
> Hide me, Ohhhhhh!
> But the rocks shall cry, hah!
> Git away! Sinner man git away, hah!

(Tense harmonic chant seeps over the audience.)

<pre>
                   You run to de rocks,
CHORUS: You can't hide
SOLOIST: Oh, you run to de rocks
CHORUS: Can't hide
SOLOIST: Oh, run to de mountain, you can't hide
ALL: Can't hide sinner, you can't hide.
                   Rocks cry " 'I'm burning too, hah!
                   In the eternal burning, hah!
                   Sinner man! Hah
                   Where will you stand? Hah!
                   In that great gittin'-up morning? Hah!
</pre>

The congregation would be right in there at the right moment bearing Papa up and heightening the effect of the fearsome picture a hundredfold. The more susceptible would be swept away on the tide and "come through" shouting, and the most reluctant would begin to waver. Seldom would there be anybody left at the mourners' bench when the revival meeting was over. I have seen my father "bring through" as many as seventy-five in one two-week period of revival. Then a day would be set to begin the induction into the regular congregation. The first thing was to hear their testimony or Christian experience, and thus the congregation could judge whether they had really "got religion" or whether they were faking and needed to be sent back to "lick de calf over" again.

It was exciting to hear them tell their "visions." This was known as admitting people to the church on "Christian experience." This was an exciting time.

These visions are traditional. I knew them by heart as did the rest of the congregation, but still it was exciting to see how the converts would handle them. Some of them made up new details. Some of them would forget a part and improvise clumsily or fill up the gap with shouting. The audience knew, but everybody acted as if every word of it was new.

First they told of suddenly becoming conscious that they had to die. They became conscious of their sins. They were Godly sorry. But somehow, they could not believe. They started to pray. They prayed and they prayed to have their sins forgiven and their souls converted. While they laid under conviction, the hell-hounds pursued them as they ran for salvation. They hung over Hell by one strand of hair. Outside of the meeting, any of the listeners would have laughed at the idea of anybody with hair as close to their heads as ninety-nine is to a hundred hanging over Hell or anywhere else by a strand of that hair. But it was part of the vision and the congregation shuddered and groaned at the picture in a fervent manner. The vision must go on. While the seeker hung there, flames of fire leaped up and all but destroyed their ever-dying souls. But they called on the name of Jesus and immediately that dilemma was over. They then found themselves walking over Hell on a foot-log so narrow that they had to put one foot right in front of the other while the howling hell-hounds pursued them relentlessly. Lord! They saw no way of rescue. But they looked on the other side and saw a little white man and he called to them to come there. So they called the name of Jesus and suddenly they were on the other side. He poured the oil of salvation into their souls and, hallelujah! They never expect to turn back. But still they wouldn't believe. So they asked God, if he had saved their souls, to give them a sign. If their sins were forgiven and their souls set free, please move that big star in the west over to the east. The star moved over. But still they wouldn't believe. If they were really saved, please move that big oak tree across the road. The tree skipped across the road and kept on growing just like it had always been there. Still they didn't believe. So they asked God for one more sign. Would He please make the sun shout so they could be sure. At that God got mad and said He had shown them all the signs He intended to. If they still didn't believe, He would send their bodies to the grave, where the worm never dies, and their souls to Hell, where the fire is never quenched. So then they cried out "I believe! I believe!" Then the dungeon shook and their chains fell off. "Glory! I know I got religion! I know I been converted and my soul set free! I never will forget that day when the morning star bust in my soul. I never expect to turn back!"

The convert shouted. Ecstatic cries, snatches of chants, old converts shouting in frenzy with the new. When the tumult finally died down, the pastor asks if the candidate is acceptable and there is unanimous consent. He or she is given the right hand of fellowship, and the next candidate takes the floor. And so on to the end.

I know now that I liked that part because it was high drama. I liked the baptisms in the lake, too, and the funerals for the same reason. But of the inner thing, I was right where I was when I first began to seek answers.

Away from the church after the emotional fire had died down, there were little jokes about some of the testimony. For instance a deacon said in my hearing, "Sister Seeny ought to know better than to be worrying God about moving the sun for her. She asked Him to move de tree to convince her, and He done it. Then she took and asked Him to move a star for her and He done it. But when she kept on worrying Him about moving the sun, He took and told her, says, 'I don't mind moving that tree for you, and I don't mind moving a star just to pacify your mind, because I got plenty of *them*. I ain't got but one sun, Seeny, and I aint going to be shoving it around to please you and nobody else. I'd like mighty much for you to believe, but if you can't believe without me moving my sun for you, you can just go right on to Hell.' "

The thing slept on in me until my college years without any real decision. I made the necessary motions and forgot to think. But when I studied both history and philosophy, the struggle began again.

When I studied the history of the great religions of the world, I saw that even in his religion man carried himself along. His worship of strength was there. God was made to look that way, too. We see the Emperor Constantine, as pagan as he could lay in his hide, having his famous vision of the cross with the injunction: *"In Hoc Signo Vinces,"* and arising next day not only to win a great battle, but to start out on his missionary journey with his sword. He could not sing like Peter, and he could not preach like Paul. He probably did not even have a good straining voice like my father to win converts and influence people. But he had his good points—one of them being a sword—and a seasoned army. And the way he brought sinners to repentance was nothing short of miraculous. Whole tribes and nations fell under conviction just as soon as they heard he was on the way. They did not wait for any stars to move, nor trees to jump the road. By the time he crossed the border, they knew they had been converted. Their testimony was in on Christian experience and they were all ready for the right hand of fellowship and baptism. It seems that Reverend Brother Emperor Constantine carried the gospel up and down Europe with his revival meetings to such an extent that Christianity really took on. In Rome where Christians had been looked upon as rather indifferent lion-bait at best, and among other things as keepers of virgins in their homes for no real good to the virgins, Christianity mounted. Where before, emperors could scarcely find enough of them to keep the spectacles going, now they were everywhere, in places high and low. The arrow had left the bow. Christianity was on its way to world power that would last. That was only the beginning. Military power was to be called in time and time again to carry forward the gospel of peace. There is not apt to be any difference of opinion between you and a dead man.

It was obvious that two men, both outsiders, had given my religion its chances of success. First the Apostle Paul, who had been Saul, the erudite Pharisee, had arisen with a vision when he fell off of his horse on the way to Damascus. He not only formulated the religion, but exerted his brilliant mind to carry it to the most civilized nations of his time. Then Constantine took up with force where Paul left off with persuasion.

I saw the same thing with different details, happen in all the other great religions, and seeing these things, I went to thinking and questing again. I have achieved a certain peace within myself, but perhaps the seeking after the inner heart of truth will never cease in me. All sorts of interesting speculations arise.

So, having looked at the subject from many sides, studied beliefs by word of mouth and then as they fit into great rigid forms, I find I know a great deal about form, but little or nothing about the mysteries I sought as a child. As the ancient tent-maker said, I have come out of the same door wherein I went.

But certain things have seemed to me to be true as I heard the tongues of those who had speech, and listened at the lips of books. It seems to me to be true that heavens are placed in the sky because it is the unreachable. The unreachable and therefore the unknowable always seems divine—hence, religion. People need religion because the great masses fear life and its consequences. Its responsibilities weigh heavy. Feeling a weakness in the face of great forces, men seek an alliance with omnipotence to bolster up their feeling of weakness, even though the omnipotence they rely upon is a creature of their own minds. It gives them a feeling of security. Strong, self-determining men are notorious for their lack of reverence. Constantine, having converted millions to Christianity by the sword, himself refused the consolation of Christ until his last hour. Some say not even then.

As for me, I do not pretend to read God's mind. If He has

a plan of the universe worked out to the smallest detail, it would be folly for me to presume to get down on my knees and attempt to revise it. That, to me, seems the highest form of sacrilege. So I do not pray. I accept the means at my disposal for working out my destiny. It seems to me that I have been given a mind and will-power for that very purpose. I do not expect God to single me out and grant me advantages over my fellow men. Prayer is for those who need it. Prayer seems to me a cry of weakness, and an attempt to avoid, by trickery, the rules of the game as laid down. I do not choose to admit weakness. I accept the challenge of responsibility. Life, as it is, does not frighten me, since I have made my peace with the universe as I find it, and bow to its laws. The ever-sleepless sea in its bed, crying out "How long?" to Time; million-formed and never motionless flame; the contemplation of these two aspects alone, affords me sufficient food for ten spans of my expected lifetime. It seems to me that organized creeds are collections of words around a wish. I feel no need for such. However, I would not, by word or deed, attempt to deprive another of the consolation it affords. It is simply not for me. Somebody else may have my rapturous glance at the archangels. The springing of the yellow line of morning out of the misty deep of dawn, is glory enough for me. I know that nothing is destructible; things merely change forms. When the consciousness we know as life ceases, I know that I shall still be part and parcel of the world. I was a part before the sun rolled into shape and burst forth in the glory of change. I was, when the earth was hurled out from its fiery rim. I shall return with the earth to Father Sun, and still exist in substance when the sun has lost its fire, and disintegrated in infinity to perhaps become a part of the whirling rubble in space. Why fear? The stuff of my being is matter, ever changing, ever moving, but never lost; so what need of denominations and creeds to deny myself the comfort of all my fellow men? The wide belt of the universe has no need for finger-rings. I am one with the infinite and need no other assurance.

12

Poems from a Progressive Freethinker

Claude McKay

The White City

I will not toy with it nor bend an inch.
Deep in the secret chambers of my heart
I muse my life-long hate, and without flinch
I bear it nobly as I live my part.
My being would be a skeleton, a shell,
If this dark Passion that fills my every mood,
And makes my heaven in the white world's hell,
did not forever feed me vital blood.
I see the mighty city through a mist—
The strident trains that speed the goaded mass,
The poles and spires and towers vapor-kissed,
The fortressed port through which the great ships pass,
The tides, the wharves, the dens I contemplate,
Are sweet like wanton loves because I hate.

Enslaved

Oh when I think of my long-suffering race,
For weary centuries, despised, oppressed
Enslaved and lynched, denied a human place
In the great life line of the Christian West;
And in the Black Land disinherited,
Robbed in the ancient country of its birth,
My heart grows sick with hate, becomes as lead,
For this my race that has no home on earth.
Then from the dark depth of my soul I cry
To the avenging angel to consume
The white man's world of wonders utterly:
Let it be swallowed up in earth's vast womb,
Or upward roll as sacrificial smoke
To liberate my people from its yoke!

Tiger

The white man is a tiger at my throat,
Drinking my blood as my life ebbs away,
And muttering that his terrible striped coat
Is Freedom's and portends the Light of Day.
Oh white man, you may suck up all my blood
And throw my carcass into potter's field,
But never will I say with you that mud
Is bread for Negroes! Never will I yield.

Europe and Africa and Asia wait
The touted New Deal of the New World's hand!
New systems will be built on race and hate,
The eagle and the Dollar will command.
Oh Lord! My body, and my heart too, break—
The tiger in his strength his thirst must slake!

If We Must Die

If we must die, let it not be like hogs
Hunted and penned in an inglorious spot,
White round us bark the mad and hungry gods,
Making their mock at our accursed lot.
If we must die, O let us nobly die,
So that our precious blood may not be shed
In vain; then even the monsters we defy
Shall be constrained to honor us though dead!
O kinsmen! we must meet the common foe!
Though far outnumbered let us show us brave,
And for their thousand blows deal one deathblow!
What though before us lies the open grave?
Like men we'll face the murderous, cowardly pack,
Pressed to the wall, dying, but fighting back!

The Negro's Tragedy

It is the Negro's tragedy I feel
Which binds me like a heavy iron chain,
It is the Negro's wounds I want to heal
Because I know the keenness of his pain.
Only a thorn-crowned Negro and no white
Can penetrate into the Negro's ken,
Or feel the thickness of the shroud of night
Which hides and buries him from other men.

So what I write is urged out of my blood.
There is no white man who could write my book,
Though many think their story should be told
Of what the Negro people ought to brook.
Our statesmen roam the world to set things right.
This Negro laughs and prays to God for Light!

13

Catholic Justice

Bruce Wright

Aunt Catherine, in the large fullness of her flesh,
nightly blocked my bedroom door
with God's vigilance;
never agile in my kneeling, I nevertheless
made the posture she enjoined,
closed my eyes and sought in vain
to clasp a vision to my mind.
I was programmed in my bedtime repetitions,
compelled by loving oppression
to address her triple icons,
all certified by priest and pope.
thus bent to reluctant duty,
I alerted God to bless my aunt
and ease her smiting
in the passion of belief
and see in me at least some virtues of The Good Thief.

—Bruce Wright
"Catherine's Wheel"

From *Once A Catholic*, by Peter Occhiogrosso. Copyright © 1987 by Peter Occhiogrosso. Reprinted by permission of Houghton Mifflin Co. and Sterling Lord Literistic, Inc.

Dressed in striped tie, pale yellow button-down Oxford shirt, khaki trousers, and brown loafers, Bruce McMarion Wright looks pretty much like any other graying prep school grad capping a respectable legal and juridical career with a tenure as state supreme court justice. So much so, in fact, that it's hard to visualize the whitecaps of outrage that have swirled around him for the past fifteen years as he sailed the high seas of the New York courts. Could it have something to do with the fact that he's black—or merely that he won't let anyone forget it?

For Justice Wright, notoriety began in 1970 with his appointment to the criminal court by New York Mayor John Lindsay, but the storms had arisen long before that. Wright was born sixty-eight years ago in Princeton, New Jersey, which he refers to with only a trace of sarcasm as "a Southern plantation town in those days." He was awarded a four-year scholarship to Princeton University but once he arrived was emphatically discouraged from attending by the dean, as he explains in the interview. Wright then suffered a similar contretemps at Notre Dame. He wound up attending Lincoln University, a predominantly black school in Pennsylvania and, after graduating in 1942, entered the army. A career with a law firm that wouldn't make him a partner "because clients weren't ready for it" and then in private practice led to work as legal counsel for the Human Resources Administration and to the criminal court appointment. During his career as a lawyer, Bruce Wright represented some of the greatest American musicians of the day, including John Coltrane, Miles Davis, Max Roach, and Charles Mingus, and the estate of Billie Holiday.

Following hard upon his appointment to the bench, Judge Wright attracted the attention of the press and the indignation of the Patrolmen's Benevolent Association through his policy of setting low bail where he felt it was justified. Wright's contention is that bail should be imposed only to ensure the defendant's presence at trial and ought to be based on the defendant's character, employment, finances, and roots in the community, as well as his previous record. Although the law appeared to back him in theory, bail was not customarily handled that way, according to Wright, because in New York City defendants tend to be black and most judges are white. "Bail is not a game of money," he said, "to be won only by the rich. It is to ensure the appearance in court of the accused. If he has roots in the community, there is no [high] bail." Wright once defined excessive bail this way: "If you come into my court and you have one penny, and my bail is two cents, that's excessive." The judge soon put his theory to the test, setting bail at five hundred dollars for a man accused of shooting a policeman. Even though Wright's percentage of no-shows wasn't any worse than that of other judges, the police quickly labeled him "Turn 'Em Loose Bruce," and the battle was joined.

In 1975, Wright was reassigned from criminal to civil court through political pressure brought by the PBA* but was eventually reinstated after threatening to sue. The case that brought him national head-lines occurred in 1979, when a thirty-year-old black man named Je-rome Singleton was accused of slashing the neck of a decoy cop dis-guised as a Bowery bum. The defendant was married with two children, held a job, and had no criminal record, prompting Wright to release him without bail, on his own recognizance. Famed wordsmith Mayor Ed Koch immediately pronounced the decision "bizarre," and the PBA resuscitated its "Turn 'Em Loose" sobriquet. This time civil rights or-ganizations supported Judge Wright. Singleton showed up for trial and was aquitted by a jury of the attempted murder charge.

Wright's experience of social injustice was not limited to univer-sity entrance policies and the court system. He met it in the army (where he served in the infantry from 1942 to 1946, winning a Bronze Star and other decorations), and he encountered it in the Catholic Church. The witty and often whimsical manner of his comments and anecdotes—the judge is an inveterate punster, a composer of doggerel, and a published poet—tends to camouflage, but not conceal, some of his indignation. The child of an Irish Catholic mother and a West Indian agnostic father, Bruce Wright may, after all, have been raised a reluctant communicant. But to hear him tell it, the Church did little to quicken his belief.

My mother was Irish—in fact, five of her brothers became police officers, including her twin brother. No clergy in the family, we're all too sensible for that—too sensual, also. My mother was born here in New York, as her father was, on West Eighteenth Street. But their people came over from Ireland in the eighteen forties. My father came to this country in 1917 from Montserrat, which is located about forty miles off the coast of Antigua and still pays allegiance to the Queen. My father was a baker. He was a bitter man because,

---

*Patrolmen's Benevolent Association—Ed.

being black, he couldn't join the craft unions in those days. He was a baker, a short-order cook, and he learned how to look under the hoods of automobiles, though he was much better at putting gas in the tank—it was easier. He was a nice guy. He was not a Catholic, good Lord, no—that's how I got my name. He saw that my mother was looking through the dictionary of saints' names to get a proper name when I was born, and he didn't like that at all. So she named me Bruce, after him, with the middle name McMarion. It was a year when they were venerating the Virgin Mary, called the Marian Year, and so I became McMarion, the son of the Virgin—guess it fooled the old man a little bit.

My father was not violently opposed to the Church, but he was certainly not a member of any religious group. He was a semi-free thinker, I suppose. I say "semi" because he was illiterate—he certainly wasn't educated, and he wouldn't have known what a free thinker is. He was a phonetic writer, though he wouldn't have known what *that* is either. But he was a nice guy, a very gentle soul. That's why I am a pacifist, I assume.

I was in law school when my father died, after World War II. He was only fifty-nine, but he died of cancer, unfortunately. The last two years of his life were very painful. Although I never knew his parents, I was fortunate enough to know my father very well. However, I was pretty much reared by my Aunt Catherine, one of my mother's sisters, who thought I was cute. Her sole exercise, other than driving one of a series of Oldsmobiles, was crossing herself and praying to Saint Jude, the patron saint of hopeless cases, for Bruce Wright. It didn't do much good. She thought I was a hopeless case because I wasn't religious enough, because when serving as an altar boy I was a truant half the time, because I spent my Sunday school money on Tootsie Rolls, and because I was a *naughty* boy. She would make notes on those cold, winter days when I was naughty. Then, on the days when the sun was shining and I could hear the guys out in the street playing, she would say, "Bruce, do you remember this and that?" And she would literally tie me to the bed and make me read the Bible.

My sister said that my Aunt Catherine also beat me, but I don't remember that. I was just a kid, about ten or eleven. I suppose she was a good Irish Catholic, and there was an attempt at Catholic training at home. I did attend parochial school, the Church of the

Ressurection on 152nd Street between Macombs Place and Eighth Avenue. They have a black priest there now, Father Lawrence Lucas. In fact, he wrote a book called *Black Priest in a White Church*. It's his protest against the Church rampant, which he allowed was not rampant enough, especially in catering to the special needs of its black members and those whom it recruited under the Society for the Propagation of the Faith. He's rather angry—on account of which he is no doubt guaranteed to remain nothing more than a parish priest for the rest of his life. In the nineteen thirties, when I attended the Church of the Resurrection, they did not have a black pastor; there wasn't one black priest to be found in Harlem at that time. We did have nuns who beat the hell out of you, though. They heard me say, "Hail Mary, full of grapes, Shirley goodness and Murphy," etc., etc. But everybody said that. It was just that my voice seemed to carry. I have the marks on me to this day.

I was a true believer for a while, I suppose, until I discovered the truth about mythology and pious fictions. That was when I was fifteen. I had received a four-year scholarship to Princeton and had the chutzpah to turn up to register, trunk and all, only to be taken out of the registration line and told by Dean Radcliffe Heermance, who had the girth of Sir John Falstaff: "Professor Weiss did not say you were colored when he arranged your scholarship." He looked down upon me as though I happened to be a disgusting specimen under a microscope. He said I wouldn't be happy at Princeton, that there were too many Southerners there. Then I was immediately referred to the dean of the chapel, Robert Russel Wickes, and after talking to him I never thereafter trusted people with three names. He told me that he had had close intercourse with God, and he pointed to his bookshelf where there were several books he had written on the subject—presumably they were diaries. He said the race problem was beyond solution and did I come to Princeton to make a problem? And did I want to be like a certain citizen of Princeton named McCormick, who was a Communist and who wanted to be places where he was not wanted? And, he added, I must stop my agitation because the race problem is beyond solution in this country.

He may be right, of course. Obviously, he thought I was a precursor of the civil rights movement and I was going to do a sit-in at Princeton. Radcliffe Heermance told me that he had no animosity toward my race and that his colored cook lived under the same roof with his family and that, indeed, in World War I he had had a colored orderly, I think he called it. His patriotism was beyond dispute. Well, at fifteen, to have that kind of dream shattered, and to be a long way from home, was shocking to me. I didn't cry until later. My mother, very sensibly calling upon her totems, said to my father, "Bruce, we should have sent him to Notre Dame." Of course, the priests were rallied around, and we tried to make arrangements for Notre Dame. But Notre Dame wrote a letter to me, which of course will be a footnote in my book. They were pretty much the same as Princeton, saying that the Church had done enough work in the South, that there were many Southerners at Notre Dame, and they had to accept the situation as it was. The only difference in their letter was that they added a line that read, "But you will be happy to know that our first President freed his slaves before taking up his duties at South Bend." So I thought I should attend a Mass of celebration for that little item.

Notre Dame really dismayed me. And then *after* the war to be so *pious* about having blacks there on the football team and saying that they were very happy. I've got *that* letter they wrote to me, too. They said, "We have three Negroes in attendance and they all seem very happy." I must tell you that the first black person to attend Notre Dame was a guy who weighed two ninety and was a football player, but he wasn't too keen *up here*. Do you know what his name was? It was Entes Shine—a very unfortunate name.

So that really did it for me with the Church. Before I even knew the term, there were "bare ruined choirs," before I had ever heard of Garry Wills—I assume I am much older than he is. In any case, that's what did it, changed my whole attitude. Indeed, it almost estranged me from my mother and my Aunt Catherine. But my Aunt Catherine had a new Oldsmobile each year so it didn't estrange me too far.

The Church is not liberal. They issue epistles promoting social justice every so often, but it's easy to say that. Who would be against that, Atilla the Hun? The thinking of the Church goes up to a certain point, but beyond that it is all faith and belief and trust and strict allegiance. I've been down to the chancery twice when Cardinal Spellman was the head of the archdiocese here. On the first occasion, a group of alleged intellectuals was summoned and the inquiry was "Why aren't more Roman Catholics winning the Nobel Prize in one category or another?" Some of us made bold to suggest that if you were going to be a good Catholic, your thought processes have to stop at a certain point. To win a Nobel Prize, generally, you have to give your thoughts free rein, be creative and original. Look what they did to John Rock [the Roman Catholic scientist and author of *The Time Has Come*], who was inventing a contraceptive pill. He's on the Index of Forbidden Books. Look what they do to women who marry divorced men. My second wife, whom I love dearly— a wonderful woman; indeed, she practiced law with me for several years—had to sneak around to various churches because I was a divorced man when she married me.

The other time, Cardinal Spellman called me down to the church because he had been told that I was a Catholic poet. Jimmy Dumpson, who used to be the commissioner of Human Resources in New York City, among other things, told him that. He was a convert, naturally more zealous than people who were reared in the faith. Cardinal Manning, Cardinal Newman, they all shot up to the red hat in a hurry over people who were born into the faith. On this occasion, Spellman decided that there were not enough black Catholics in New York. So he got twelve black intellectuals to come down, and he wanted us to go throughout Harlem and the South Bronx and Bedford-Stuyvesant to help convert *other* black intellectuals to the true faith. I thought that was rather funny. I had a good time there. I can drink tea and eat cookies with the best of them. Nothing came of that meeting, of course. He made a terrible mistake. Spellman was a lousy poet, by the way—like somebody in the fourth grade.

The Church's attitude toward black Catholics? Condescending, paternalistic, superior. We were treated as what the French call *évolués*, those who are evolving. That's the way they treated their African intellectuals. They did not realize that the rituals of the Church are as barbaric and filled with superstition and images as any African jungle voodoo belief. The pottery may be more refined; the chalice may be silver. You know the poem?

> There was a young woman named Alice,
> Who pissed in the archbishop's chalice,
>   'Twas common belief
>   She peed for relief
> And not out of Protestant malice.

Well, you've got it now—feel free to copy Wright. But I thought the Church's attitude was entirely paternalistic. They looked down upon us as being of an inferior intellectual status and quality, and I found that to be true when I was at Fordham Law School. In those days the law school was in the Woolworth Building on the twenty-eighth floor, and there was a crucifix over the desk of each professor. They don't have that now because when the law school moved to public property near Lincoln Center, they had to agree that they would be open to everybody. That's why they keep Rose Hill in the Bronx, so they can indulge their Jesuit fantasies there.

When I got to high school there was one black woman teacher— *one* black on the faculty—who taught me more in one semester than I ever learned from the Church in all the years of my life. She was a woman who was a Catholic, but she taught me about Denmark Vesey [the black American insurrectionist]. I knew about Marcus Garvey from my father. I learned more black history from that woman—she opened up secrets and I *learned* how suppressed black history has been. If you want to deprive a people—make them nothing—you make them believe they have no history, and that's what has been done to blacks in this country. The Catholic Church has *not* done as much as it could. It is certainly the richest church in the world, as far as I'm concerned. At least my paltry little library on the wealth of the Church and the papacy and so forth leads me to believe that. After all, it is the *Vatican* that owns the water works and electricity works that supply Rome. No, I don't think I learned anything very exalting from the Church.

The Church is superstition to me. I'm a lawyer, and I look for evidence: haven't seen a Holy Ghost, haven't seen a God or anything of that sort. And I read the Bible and I instruct my children to know something about biblical history—either as literature or as fiction, as they wish. I think they *should* know something about it, especially when you have a season such as Christmas and they might be strangers or babes in the woods.

I have no religion. I am what probably would be called an atheist. Probably, by other people, yes, I often am. But that's their problem, that's not my problem. I have given my body to Columbia University's College of Physicians and Surgeons—to pick it apart, do whatever they wish with it. And if any friends of mine wish to have a memorial service to remember me, which is unlikely, I have insisted that they play a certain tape that I have prepared, which is my funeral oration. There is some music on it, and they are admonished to obey the lyrics of that tune, which start: "Do nothing till you hear from me." It's the old Duke Ellington tune, played by Randy Weston, one of my former clients.

One of my closest friends is Father Louis Gioia, a Jesuit. He teaches medieval history and classics at Baruch College. I think his salary is about thirty-seven thousand dollars a year, and Bishop Mugavero in Brooklyn wants that money. He says, "*I* will distribute it to the poor. You took a vow of poverty." And Lou says, "Screw you, I've a poor, black, and Hispanic parish, and I pay their rent, I buy their food." And he *does*. If Lou didn't have parents who live in Bay Ridge, he wouldn't make it. He gives his money away. He doesn't even give it to tax-deductible units. So we have to go to his mother's house sometimes to eat. I don't think they let him perform marriages anymore. He and I had projects where we tried to get prisoners out and rehabilitate them, all over the country, not just here in New York. He's wonderful at that.

Phil Berrigan, I think, clings to the vestige of the Catholic faith just to spite the Church. I don't think he is a devout Roman Catholic in the true sense of the word. He's too sensible, and yet his poetry is certainly Roman Catholic. It represents the theology of liberation. I spent till three A.M. with him one night when we were both on the same speaking program. So we meet now and then. He is very impressive as a human being. And I vote for him for pope—exept I guess I'd have to make him a cardinal first, wouldn't I? We can buy a red hat.

The pope is not concerned about the theology of liberation any more than he is about the American theologians. He squelches those people. The pope is a dictator, an *absolute* dictator. I don't think anybody can quarrel with that. Not even the Conference of Bishops, talking about the Holy Father—he is our universe and that sort of thing. Of *course* he's a dictator. He's also an actor, a consummate actor. He is to the Church what Ronald Regan is to the Republican party. The Great Communicator . . . the Great Tourist, that's what he is. You have to give him credit, though—he's brave enough not to care about being shot. But I don't know what he wants to do or what he's worried about. He wouldn't have very much trouble,

I shouldn't think, converting Africans, for example, or Haitians in the jungle, because there's very little difference between voodoo and the formal Catholic Church—little images of worship and so forth. The Jews have it right: no big altar, no images, certainly no idols. Have you been to the marvelous Greco-Roman imitation in Paris, the Madeleine? You must go in there sometime, it's full of images and statues.

The other thing that made me distrust the Church happened when I was in the army. I was in the infantry, and as we pushed our way around Munich, going through the woods, we would be frightened to death. Those goddamn Nazis had statues all over the place, all kinds of bloody saints in the woods, and so forth—scare the hell out of you, especially at night. Look at the Nazi—look at the Ku Klux Klan in *this* country—they're all deeply religious. Now they're welcoming *Catholics*. We're done for.

My parents were married at a time when Jack Johnson was catching hell for fooling around with white women. But you must understand one thing I learned from my mother's father. Keep in mind that he was born in 1857, the year of the Dred Scott decision. The Irish were known here in New York City as the white niggers. They shared, with blacks, the dirtiest, filthiest jobs they had—the "night soil" job, for example, before plumbing was universal. They called it "night soil" because they had outhouses, and you did your dookie into the soil and, because of the danger to the water supply, they had to be emptied. The Irish and the blacks did that.

If you were Irish, when my grandfather was a boy, you couldn't go to Macy's unless you went with the lady who employed you, who was generally a white Protestant. When the potato famine drove millions of the Irish here and to Boston, the first thing they saw were police officers dressed as London bobbies—as they were in those days—and this symbol of British authority offended them. The Irish bully boys used to travel in gangs and beat the hell out of the police. Finally, the man in charge of the police, who was not a commissioner, allowed them to dress in mufti and wear a shield. Not only did they beat them up, but they called them "coppers" because the shield was made of copper. Now that's been shortened to "cops" and they still call them cops, although the shield is no longer made of copper. The Irish couldn't go to certain bars; they couldn't go to Delmonico's, that's for sure. And they went into the police force finally because the mayor decided, "We can't have these fellows beating up our police—if we can't beat them, let them join us." And they folded them all in without the benefit of a civil service examination, and they brought their cousins, their uncles, and everybody else over to join the police force. And so we've had the Irish mafia for a number of years. That's disappearing; the Italians are coming into prominence on the force now.

The fire department is pretty much the same. Everything was volunteer in the old days, and the Irish formed volunteer fire brigades and relied upon the generosity of whoever owned the building they were trying to save. But unfortunately, many of them competed. They'd both get to the same fire at the same time and fight each other for the honor of putting out the fire—meanwhile, the fire wasn't waiting. You could tell those who had money because they had a horse pulling their wagon. Those who didn't have money had Negroes pulling their water wagons.

And it was very interesting to hear my grandfather tell about those early days, with a pipe in his mouth and a smile which was rather tolerant. But today there are no more shanty Irish, I think—they're all lace curtain. And now the Catholics in Belfast sing the same songs that we sang in the civil rights movement here; they have adopted "We Shall Overcome."

The animosity between blacks and the Irish police built up in those early days. Look at the so-called Second Rebellion during the Civil War, when if you had three hundred dollars, you could buy freedom from service. And the Irish said, "We don't have three hundred dollars, but we're not going to fight to free the niggers." And they burned down the Colored Orphan Home, which used to be right where Bryant Park is now, where the Public Library is at Forty-second Street and Fifth Avenue. And they killed the blacks. It was an Irish serving-girl who spread the story that black slaves were trying to take over the city in 1741 when they had the so-called Negro Plot, and they almost wiped out the entire black population of the city of New York.

Many people thought that judgeships were bought. In fact, we had a Seabury investigation in the thirties and a book written on that subject called *The Tin Cup*. When Lindsay called me over to city hall and asked me how I'd like to be a judge, I was shocked. I said I didn't have any money to buy a judgeship. And he blanched, properly and innocently, and said that I needed no money. I said, "I'll think about it," because I didn't think it was realistic. I didn't even belong to a party, and I certainly had never been in politics. But there are many people—as a matter of fact, a black guy who is now a judge stopped me and asked me how much I paid. He said, "I was supposed to be the next black judge. How did you do that?" Anyway, he's a schmuck, I never cared for him. I think it's reality but I have no proof. Sure, I don't know why people want to be a judge. If you see the work I have to do around here—it's well-paid slavery. Not well paid enough, however, for a man who has been married four times.

I've never been married in a church. I've never even had a ring for any of my wives. It's a symbol: "The endless circle of love, the oneness." The Church loves that sort of thing. Now guys wear rings. Never had a ring on my finger—had one through my nose, I guess.

I majored in philosophy, so I suppose some humanitarian instinct was bound to rub off. When I was at Fordham, I liked the natural law. It almost got me in jail. The natural law says that if something is evil and wicked, you're supposed to resist it. So I prepared a little speech when I went to my draft board, and it went this way: "This country has examined me and found me fit to fight for it. I've examined the country and found it not fit to be fought for." And the guy says, "Whaddaya say, young fella?" And I said, "Aw, shit, what do I have to do?" And I went into the bloody army. That's not the only time I said "shit." I said "shit" in front of a priest once. It was the third time I got wounded. They left me lying in the snow for almost eighteen hours. I was a mess. Sometimes I was conscious and sometimes I wasn't, and once I came to and I saw a cross, and I said, "Oh, shit." Then I heard *"Et spiritus sanctus. . . . "* The priest was giving me the last rites, and I said, "Father, I *will* be the last Wright, unless you get me out of here." But he had no sense of humor.

Yes, I spent some time as an altar boy—doesn't everybody? But there was a priest who kept chasing me, so I complained to my Aunt Catherine to get out of going to church anymore. He liked little boys. You know what happens when you renounce sex and take to whiskey and things like that: chasing lads. Well, it happens. All I can say is that it's something that happens. But I was not that fond of ritual at all, pomp and ceremony was a waste of my time when I could have been much more fruitful out in the streets. I was never fond of the Church.

Being an altar boy, of course, is something that's bestowed on males—women didn't have a chance. That didn't offend me till later. I thought it was normal, and it was, that's the way things were. It took me until fifteen to start protesting against "things as they were" and to realize that they didn't have to be that way. And perhaps should not be that way. It took some time to see the hypocrisy of the Church and the timidity of the Church. I thought the Church could get away with anything, that no one would call them Communists. People would respect them because they were clergy, because they did have a Roman collar on. And then I learned that if you're a black priest, you're going to be a parish priest the rest of your life, especially if you're militant. What's the black bishop's name in Harlem? Emerson Moore—he knows how to kiss the proper ass. Where did the pope stop when he came to Harlem? Emerson Moore's church.

I was an absolutist. I would never vote for Roosevelt because he went to Hot Springs, Georgia. Blacks couldn't go to Georgia and be human beings. I didn't speak to my friends who went to Florida on vacation and who pretended they didn't see the signs: "Colored" this, "Colored" that. You had to sit in the back of the bus, that sort of thing. They pretended they didn't see those things. They were not my friends. Yes, I was an absolutist about it. I was furious. And I have been furious to this day that whites with Southern accents can come to New York and be big shots.

14

A Psychiatrist Views Humanism, Racism, and Religion

Charles W. Faulkner

THE MISUSE OF RELIGION*

Jim and Tammy Bakker are not the only people who abuse religion. At the trial of Oliver North, an interesting, though not unusual, abuse of religion was made.

Here is the situation. The trial, which was held in Washington, D.C., had a jury of twelve African-American men and women. At the end of the trial, when the prosecuting attorney and the defense attorney made their final arguments, both attorneys began their arguments with an unusual emotional appeal to the jury. *They quoted words from the Bible.* When the trial was completed and the verdict was in, the jury foreman said that she knew the two attorneys, both white, were trying to manipulate the jurors by appealing to their emotional feelings about God. The attorneys seem to believe that the black jurors were "brainwashed" by religion.

The attorneys obviously believed that the religiously inspired jurors would find a guilty man *innocent* simply because the jurors believed deeply in religion—even if he was guilty. The fact is that this tactic actually works, often. Advertisers regularly use a biblical symbol, such as a cross, to convince people to buy a certain product. If a

---

*From "Coping," *Capital Spotlight* (November 6, 1989): 6. Reprinted by permission of the author.

milk company puts the picture of a cross on its milk cartons, it will sell far more cartons of milk than will the company that does not use the symbol of the cross in its advertisements.

Religion, like other similar endeavors, has the capability of brainwashing people and causing them to sometimes make irrational decisions. They might think, "if it has God's approval, it must be O.K." The symbol of the cross implies that God approves of the product or, even, *wants* people to buy it. Thus, Blacks are often "used" simply because of their deep feelings for religion.

"God will make a way, somehow." This very popular expression is often interpreted to mean that God is like a super-parent who protects his children no matter what troubles they encounter. The relationship of most people to God is parent-child. With the individual being the child.

On the surface, this relationship seems O.K. However, in practice, it tends to make people become dependent upon a supernatural spirit. A child-like adult is not likely to make it in this tough society. Some people even plan, in advance, to commit a sin "knowing" that they can ask the Lord for forgiveness, later.

When people expect God to plan their lives for them, and protect them, they tend to lose their motivation to guide and control their own lives.

A friend once said, "what goes around, comes around," God will punish the evil-doers. I said to him, "Don't hold your breath and expect someone else to do your dirty work. If you want someone to be punished, you had better do it yourself."

ESP*

"Dear Dr. Faulkner:

I think that I have ESP (extra-sensory perception) and can know in advance when something is going to happen. How can I improve my great ability.

Mr. V.,
Toronto"

---

*From "Coping," *Capital Spotlight* (November 23, 1989): 6. Reprinted by permission of the author.

Dear Mr. V.:

I think that what you refer to as extra-sensory perception is actually your ability to reason things out, *logically.*

By definition, ESP is the ability to sense things that other people cannot sense. Extra-sensory means "extra-sense." All normal human beings have five senses. They have the ability to *see, feel* (through touch), *smell, hear,* and *taste.* These are our *senses* and they let us know that the world exists. If we could not see, feel, smell, hear or taste, we would be "vegetables." We would not be alive mentally, emotionally, or physically.

A person who even loses the ability to taste, cannot enjoy his food. A blind person cannot see and, thus, has lost an important capability. The same is true of all of the senses which are needed in order for us to live "normal" lives.

If you feel that you have an *extra* sense, then you can know a new dimension of our world. You can perceive of things that others cannot. Some people think that they can "see" into the future; or, can "know" what other people are doing in another part of the world. Some people think that they can predict death, fortune, and other events.

Now for the *bad* news. There is no documented, scientific evidence that anyone has an "extra-sense." Many people say or think that they have an extra-sense. Yet, no one has *consistently* proven his/her ability to look into the future. Some people (palmists, fortune tellers) have made huge sums of money by convincing others of their great ability to see into the future. Many of us refer to this as "con." If these people *could* see into the future, they would have guessed the correct lottery numbers and would be multimillionaires. They wouldn't have to work.

Now for the *good* news. Some people are extremely logical and can *reason* what *probably* will happen in the future. For instance, one might think that a relative is going to die. Then, tomorrow, the relative actually dies, and you actually think that you knew about it *before* it happened.

The fact is that everyone is going to die, eventually. So, if you think that it will happen, you are correct because it will, at some point, but this is logic. Not ESP. If you have an older relative whom you love dearly, you probably *think about* or *fear* the possibility that he/she will die every day. When it actually happens you think that you "guessed" right. You actually simply used reason. *You forgot about the hundreds of times that you thought it would* happen and it didn't. If you want to "improve" your ESP, improve your ability to *reason,* first.

TELL CHILDREN THE TRUTH*

"Dear Dr. Faulkner:

Christmas was a wonderful time of the year, but I am worried about the effect that it had on my four-year-old son. All of the little children who go to his school believed in Santa Claus. The children thought Santa Claus rode through the sky on a sleigh, pulled by reindeer that flew through the air. They thought Santa was able to read their minds and knew what they were thinking. They thought he could climb down chimneys and put presents under their trees. They thought Santa was so supernatural that he could deliver presents to millions of children in every country in the world, on the same night. The worst part of this fantasy is that parents and school teachers actually encouraged these children to leave food and gifts for Santa Claus. On Christmas day they told their children that Santa Claus had eaten the food they left. Is it healthy for a parent to brainwash a child into believing these supernatural, unreal things? What should I tell my own child about Christmas?

Mrs. T.
Dallas, TX."

Dear Mrs. T.:

You are very wise to be concerned about the effect that the belief in Santa Claus could have upon your child. Here are some important points:

Young children are very impressionable. What you tell them *now,* will remain in their subconscious, *forever.* If you tell them that ghosts exist, they will believe it, forever. If you tell them that Santa Claus can do supernatural things that no other being can do, they are likely to believe in superstition, astrology, fortune-telling, mind-reading and

*From "Coping," *Capital Spotlight* (January 7, 1991): 6. Reprinted by permission of the author.

a host of other very questionable phenomena. The wise parent will explain to the child why people celebrate Christmas. You can tell the child the Santa Claus story. You should, also, tell the child the truth. It is fine to give presents, but the child must be told that no person can defy the laws of physics and do what they are told Santa does. So, let the child enjoy Christmas parties with his classmates, but also educate him about *reality*.

Now is the time to develop the child's trust in you. If the parent lies to the child *now,* eventually he will discover that Santa Claus doesn't exist, but he will also know that the parent lied to him, and actually used tricks to make him believe the lie. (Tricks such as having him leave food for a nonexistent Santa.) If the parent lied previously, what's to stop the parent from lying again? The child, as an adult, might prefer to confide in his/her friends rather than in the parents.

Some people will think the Santa Claus myth is harmless, and that children soon forget about it. The fact is, children eventually *do* accept Santa as a myth. However, later in life, as adults, they might believe, for the rest of their lives, that certain people can do things that are actually impossible, such as read minds, tell fortunes, read palms, and predict the future.

CLARIFYING MY POSITION ABOUT RELIGION*

"Dear Dr. Faulkner:

I read your recent article on religion, and it is obvious to me that you are *against* religion. You need to find Jesus.

"Dear Dr. Faulkner:

How can you say some of the bad things that you say about religion? Where did you go wrong? If people did not have religion in their lives, they would be in the street killing each other. You obviously have no morality."

---

*From "Coping," *Capital Spotlight* (April 5, 1990): 6. Reprinted by permission of the author.

The excerpts from these two letters represent the attitude of a number of readers who have taken issue with my ideas about religion. Let me clarify my position about religion, so that I will not be misunderstood.

(1) I think of religion as the belief that a being exists that has far more power than man. This being is called "God" and is believed by many to be the "Father" of mankind.

(2) The belief in a supreme being has given stability to the lives of many and has given them hope; especially as people identify with the story of Jesus of Nazareth who died for the sins of man, and was born again.

(3) If you find this belief inspirational, I am happy that you are able to find something in this difficult life that is inspirational.

(4) If you expect "God" or any supreme being to take you by the hand and guide you along the *right road,* I am not so happy for you. Inspiration is just the start, the actual trip along the right road is entirely in your hands.

(5) Millions of nonbelievers are not guided by scripture. Nevertheless, they treat their fellow humans the same way they would like to be treated. They have a morality that is produced by their own common sense.

(6) Many people who profess to accept "God" abuse others, nonetheless. Their support for religious principle is primarily verbal, and is applicable mainly on Sunday mornings.

(7) Many people who say that they accept the Savior as their "Father," actually expect to be guided, protected, and counseled by the heavenly "Father." Before doing many important things, they wait for "guidance." In the absence of guidance, they may do nothing.

(9) Many (most?) people who believe in "God" tend to mercifully chastise those individuals who have not, as yet, made up their minds about whether to accept the belief in a supreme being. Even a simple question about the powers of the supreme being may draw a harsh rebuke or criticism.

To be sure, there are some tolerant Christians who would be "Godly" in their behavior even if they were not Christians. My major problem with religion is that it has not found a way to confront the realities that we face daily, such as drug sales, drug murders and drug rehabilitation, AIDS, homosexuality, and the right of people to believe or disbelieve in religion and still be respected as "right thinking" individuals.

THE PSYCHOLOGICAL EFFECTS OF RELIGION ON THE MASSES*

It is virtually impossible to name ten famous black men without naming at least five clergymen. Religion has been the catalyst that has motivated black people to take part in the social and political process that controls their lives.

The church has traditionally provided a gathering place for blacks to meet, discuss their problems with people of common philosophies, and to release their frustrations. The church has for centuries been the place to go to "lay your burdens down" and feel good about life again.

The black churchgoer can find a loving and understanding "Father" in the church, which provides an escape from fear and trouble. It is a way to get back at the evil world or at least to insure that the evildoer, white or black, will be punished—if not in this world at least in the hereafter. Retribution will surely take place and the "weak shall inherit the earth." The Bible promises it.

In his book, *Dark Ghetto,* Kenneth B. Clark states: "Within the church a Negro porter or maid can assume responsibilities and authority not available to him [or her] elsewhere. Only there can they engage in political intrigue and participate in financial decisions open to whites in many other aspects of their lives. Here the Negro domestic exchanges her uniform for 'high-fashion' dress and enjoys the admiration and envy of other friends."

He feels that the church can provide self-esteem for blacks that will permit them to tolerate almost any degree of personal, theological, or educational inadequacy on the part of their minister, so long as he holds the church together as a successful social and financial institution.

The imposing effect of religion in the black community is traditional and well-known. Since the days of slavery, blacks have

---

*From *Dollars and Sense* 7, no. 2 (June/July 1981): 27–30.

been so greatly influenced by the promises of redemption and retribution that slaves were able to endure the worst, most tortuous aspects of their plight for the promise of a "better life" in the hereafter.

The significance and influence of the promise of a better life cannot be underemphasized nor can it be adequately measured. Slaves were provided a psychological crutch. They could always lean on their belief that they would, themselves, be rewarded for maintaining their faith and that their tormentors would eventually "burn in hell" for their transgressions. Slaves could finally achieve equality—at least in the eyes of the Lord.

Slave holders were careful to allow their "property" the right to practice their religious philosophies as a means of partially civilizing them and hopefully pacifying them. Slaves were allowed sacrament although, just as today, they were not allowed to attain priesthood in some churches.

The fact that slaves later revolted supports the thesis that slaves used church meetings as opportunities to plan social movements that led, ultimately, to their freedom. The characterization of the church as the place were kindred spirits of social change met to revamp a troubled and unfair society is historically accurate.

As Lyndrey A. Niles states in his position paper, "In the days of slavery, a sense of humor and religion allowed slaves to release suppressed emotions in ways that did not offend. The functions of the black church and its preaching include providing adult education, creating social roles, being a news medium, and offering a place to develop leadership. Black sermons, often not written in manuscript form, tend to be based on the hereafter and begin by touching the deep emotions of the audience. They often include an extended description or recreation of a Bible story, and have an emotional climax that may be tearful or ecstatic." He feels, in addition, that black preachers usually use contemporary black language, utilize cadence, including occasional intonation or chants, receive responses from the audience during their preaching, and make the service a psychologically moving and emotionally cleansing experience.

Today, this atmosphere drains the body of stress, relaxes the mind, and heightens one's suggestibility to such a degree that the individual often becomes much like a human robot that responds almost automatically.

In the black church, energies are redirected and one becomes conditioned to the good feeling produced by the church service. The anticipation of the good feeling that is felt at the Sunday service, at which one can pour out stress and tension, is similar to the anticipation of a "hit" that a narcotic addict gets. It tends to heighten the feelings when the service actually takes place. Many blacks become regular attendees in order to attain the relaxation therapy that is presented. Interestingly, many churchgoers are not consciously aware of this benefit that they obtain in church. They would, however, feel disappointed if they had as much stress at the end of the church service as they had at the start. This is one of the reasons that black clergymen can easily assume the role of counselors and advise church members on various aspects of their private lives.

This role of family counselor soon develops into that of "psychological" counselor. The point is made by Calvin Sutter in his book, *Religion and Psychiatry.* He says: "A large segment of the grown-up man's life is in fact in the same condition as the child's. Does not the soldier give over his mind entirely to his superior officer? We do not sail a ship by the opinion of a sailor, nor do we run a war by the opinion of a soldier. All is executed by the minds of the top men. In government we have the laws and statutes limiting, guiding, and directing the conduct of its citizens. The principle, then, is at work in every field of endeavor."

He thinks that in many religions the pious worshipper takes the mind and will of the priest and minister as a substitute for his own and, in the most essential questions of his internal life, there is complete submission.

In *Love and Will*, by Rollo May, there is a detailed statement about the linking by man of religious symbols to the most powerful impulses in life, both the destructive and the creative ones. Prayer, a powerful religious symbol, is often viewed suspiciously by psychotherapists who think that the aspect of someone talking to an unseen and alleged "other" is caught up in an illusion that tends to regress the individual to previous dependent stages in the development of the personality. Some neo-Freudians see prayer for "better things" as obsessive or even neurotic behavior. The symbolic character of marches, prayer vigils, and discussion groups are good for the spirit and the conscience. Their pragmatic value for black people is determined by the actual positive changes that they bring about in the society-at-large.

Clemont Vontress, in his paper "Self-Hatred in Americans of African Descent," presented at the annual meeting of The American Psychological Association, says: "In spite of attempts to destigmatize themselves with the 'Black is Beautiful' rhetoric, efforts by Americans of African descent to disavow their imputed inferiority have not been successful. The black is reacted to as a handicapped person by the white American. The most direct way to remove self-hatred in black Americans is to excise racism in the society at large." The absence of a well-defined national social movement tends to nullify the prescription of Vontress. The effect of these negative, rejective responses on the self-concept of the rejected black person is, Vontress feels, self-hatred, because consciously and unconsciously the dominant person's acceptance means so much to him. So, the black person has one more reason to seek out the church.

It might be said that as frustration increases, so does church attendance. Does a session at the Sunday church service bolster one's resolve and send him or her out into society with new determination and motivation to change a socially unjust society? The absence of a major social movement among blacks suggests that the activist spirit is not enhanced in church.

Indeed, the psychological pressures of society indicate that the church provides the black person with just enough strength to survive the day-to-day pressures caused by the job, family bills, inflation, and racism. The psychological escape provided by the black church seems to result in social inactivity or, even, passivity. Interviews with many black churchgoers elicited the following responses: "He (the cause of social injustice) will be punished by the Almighty." "What goes around, comes around; the white man will get what is coming to him." "God is the final judge." "The Lord is going to punish the evildoer." "We need a leader like Martin Luther King."

The "what goes around, comes around" school of thought, which is currently popular, vests its confidence in a cyclical metaphysical apparatus of poetic justice that it presumes will counter rather than support evil. Historical evidence does not seem to support this theory.

The "let Him do it" statements suggest that quite a few black people have given up the personal struggle and are waiting for God or some other unseen force to punish the doer of evil deeds. Or, they are waiting for a new black leader to appear on the horizon and lead the masses to the promised land of equal justice under the law. In either case blacks seem to be "on hold" and waiting for something to happen.

Blacks seem to anticipate that God will punish the perpetrators and perpetuators of this unjust society. No leader, from the human race, is expected to appear any time soon.

Church leaders who were traditionally social leaders seem dedicated to solidifying their political positions within the church, increasing church membership, enlarging the physical church structure, and separating the religious aspect of life from the political.

Did Martin Luther King describe the condition accurately when he wrote in his letter from the Birmingham city jail, "There was a time when the church was very powerful. It was that period when the early Christians rejoiced when they were deemed worthy to suffer for what they believed.

"Things are different now. The contemporary church is often a weak, ineffectual voice with an uncertain sound. It is so often the arch supporter of the status quo. Far from being disturbed by the presence of the church, the power structure of the average community is consoled by the church's silent and often vocal sanction of things as they are.

"Maybe again, I have been too optimistic. Is organized religion too inextricably bound to status quo to save our nation and the world? Maybe I must turn my faith to the inner spiritual church, the church within the church, as the true ecclesia and the hope of the world."

Norval D. Glenn, in his work "The Religion of Blacks in the United States: Some Recent Trends and Current Characteristics," says that findings indicate a continued high level of church attendance, confidence in the clergy, and decline in the number of black clergymen.

Happily, the church will probably continue to provide the coping mechanism that blacks need to survive the stresses of today's society. Unhappily, the psychological pressures are, today, so great that even the church seems unable to provide both a stress outlet as well as the propulsion needed to propagate a major new social movement.

The use of radio and television for church services is probably the most effective psychological means available of perpetuating and modifying religious behavior because:

(1) Thousands of people can participate in a church service in their homes where the church auditorium could accommodate only a few hundred people.

(2) The person who is seated in a comfortable chair at home or who lounges on a bed is psychologically more receptive to the religious ideology than one who must sit in church on a hard bench in a sometimes uncomfortable position.

(3) Films, slides, and diagrams can dramatize the sermon in such a way that the impact will be permanent and subconsciously profound. Television operates subliminally rather than by provoking the viewer into thinking about what is being viewed. The television sermon bypasses the conscious mind and causes subconscious habituated reactions. The viewer not only accepts what is said but acts out the role of those described in the sermon.

(4) Close-up studies of the speaker are shown on the television screen and, interspersed with the lecture, place the speaker in an almost mystical relationship to the biblical materials.

The viewer becomes unknowingly entranced and subconsciously reacts as if he or she had written the sermon and had believed the philosophy from birth. This is essentially the same subconscious control of the viewer's behavior that advertisers of commercial products use to motivate viewers to automatically or peremptorily buy the advertised product. The opening up of this media to television is having an undreamed-of effect in spreading the gospel and psychologically "hooking" viewers and listeners.

The church tells the black person that he or she is a born sinner and is morally unclean. This devastating disclosure is added to the already enormous burden of social inequality and drives blacks to seek church redemption and forgiveness. This invitation is wholeheartedly welcomed by the black person who is promised forgiveness by the heavenly Father who asks only that one believe in "life in the hereafter."

Lawrence N. Jones, in his work "In God We Trust: The Black Experience Beyond The Red Sea," notes that blacks are becoming more and more millenarian in that they tend to believe that only God can bring a reign of justice and peace to America. He also suggests that a decline in religious participation of black youth contributes to the visible deterioration in the quality of life in their communities.

Carl H. Marbury, author of "Biblical Faith, Ethics and Quality of Life Quest Among Black Americans: Implications for Research," presented at the American Educational Research Association's Annual Meeting, not only recognizes the leadership function of the black church but encourages it. He reviews the role of the black church in black American history and suggests ways in which its role must change to help blacks cope with our modern and technological society. He suggests that the black church increase its role of leadership in directing black parishioners toward a high spiritual quality of life which, he says, "may not necessarily be the same as the modern American materialistic approach to life."

This turn-the-other-cheek philosophy has produced a modern passivity that places social movements in the hands of a force outside of man. The acceptance of this doctrine reaffirms the father-son relationship between the black person and God. The white person justifies his or her perception of blacks as being childlike with an interpretation of semi-relevant biblical passages. The black person "confirms" it with the turn-the-other-cheek philosophy which, although possibly viable in the hereafter, has little impact upon the negative plight of the black person today.

Sutter's book *Religion and Psychiatry* points this out clearly. "The sinner comes as the child to its father, seeking forgiveness and expecting punishment. He has already learned through experience the coins of penance he must pay for various degrees of sin, and there is little inner growth experience in this well-worn routing of confession and ecclesiastical reproof."

The church not only keeps its members "in line" by reprimanding them for violating the moral code but also makes disobedience a matter of conscience. Thus, when one disobeys a commandment, he or she feels a strong sense of guilt. Day-to-day existence requires one to fight back. But the church serves as society's policeman. This form of policing requires that the black churchgoer abide by many of the very laws that have caused the social inequities or suffer psychological stress.

Religious philosophies that mount serious social programs have tended to lack permanency and are even victimized by more conventional religious philosophies. The "Black Muslims" were targeted for destruction until they "cleaned up their act" and became just plain Muslims.

An employer keeps the worker peaceable and pacified with promises of promotions and raises. The church keeps its members peaceable and pacified with promises of better things in the hereafter.

This passivity is often unintentional and indirect. It would not appear that black church leaders plot to make their members passive. Nevertheless, the philosophy of refusing to strike back at one's tormentor results in social inaction that, in pragmatic terms, is identical in its effects.

The Bible offers moral guidelines. The black preacher castigates those who fail to adhere to the guidelines. Biblical idealism directs the believer to "love thine enemy" but the so-called "enemy" practices a more realistic philosophy of stomping the weak into submission. Thus, the black church propagates love and self-abuse while those who control society practice a form of amorality, domination, and manipulation.

Could it be that the black church is an unknowing partner to injustice? Could it be that blacks are spiritually ill-equipped to exist in a society that responds only to violence and threats of violence? Although the emotional inclination is to answer each question with a resounding no, the logic of the conditions that exist seem to produce a contrary response.

Many of the characteristics of the black church are found also in the white church but the effects are different. The church offers a primary source of emotional fulfillment and hope for the black person. The white person uses the church, at best, as a secondary means of emotional reconstitution. Few white people dream of equality of opportunity or of a society in which blacks and whites will walk hand-in-hand into the sunset.

The church has greatly increased its physical facilities in most large cities, but there seems to be no similar increase in the social programs to match. Many churchgoers boast of the apartment complexes and auditoriums that have been recently constructed by their churches. Their boasting presumes a contribution to a national social movement.

The facts do not support these presumptions and, indeed, seem to contradict them. If the contribution of churches to an actual improvement in the social plight of blacks was actually taking place, as one would like to believe, an easily discernible social movement would be in evidence. The opposite is true.

The implicitly contradictory nature of the plight of the black person who is taught as a child to be kind and forgiving in a world that is brutally unkind and unforgiving is psychologically devastating. The historical religious background of most black people drives them to search for an escape. It engenders a hope for an answer to the difficult questions of life that cannot be addressed by the limits of science or the limits of reality.

In studying religion in the black community we are made aware of the desperate plight of the black masses. Their powerlessness in society at large has brought about the following occurrences in the black church: (1) increased attendance among blacks, other than college students and ghetto youth; (2) heightened concern in larger middle class churches about the problems in their immediate communities; (3) greater "trust in the Lord" feelings among the black masses attending smaller churches and churches that exemplify fundamentalist philosophies; and (4) closer ties to, and greater need for, the psychological comfort of religion, generally.

The society in which the black church exists is perhaps more ruthless and inconsiderate than we had reason to expect. If the faith of the black masses is a drug or a psychological medicine, we know that television, education, reading, and money making can also drug us into a social coma—if they are not viewed in the proper perspective. The way to treat this age-old addiction is not to tear the victim away from the beloved church but to entice, if at all possible, the heartless society that controls, restricts, and manipulates the influence of the black church and its influence on the masses.

Dr. William Jones, an outstanding black scholar at Yale University, writes in his book *Is God A White Racist?*:

It is not my intention to eliminate the category of hope from black theology. Hope is necessary to motivate an oppressed people to undertake its liberation. What I insist upon is some clarity about the different types of hope. Must a black theology appeal primarily to an extrahuman or suprahuman ground? Is hope in God, as they interpret him, the only basis for black religion? If this is what black theologians affirm, then they are obliged to justify hope in this suprahuman factor in light of the intolerable surplus of black suffering, which is their own point of departure for theologizing. If they invoke God as their ultimate hope, they had better be certain that God is on their side.

15

The Quest for Humanist Values

Ishmael Jaffree

In 1982 I filed a complaint to keep prayer and other religious activities out of the public schools of Mobile, Alabama. As a lawyer and an agnostic who strongly believes in the separation of church and state, I was seeking to maintain the integrity of the Constitution and to keep public officials from making decisions about my children's spiritual upbringing. A simple enough request, I thought.

In a decision handed down in 1983, however, U.S. District Court Judge W. Brevard Hand ruled against me. On appeal in 1985 the Supreme Court characterized Judge Hand's ruling "a remarkable deviation from principles firmly embedded in our constitutional juris-prudence." The case set off a national controversy about the nature of secular humanism and the separation of church and state.

Initially, I encountered hostility in the African-American commu-nity; the press had reported that I was attempting to take prayer—and, by extension, God—out of the public schools, often without focusing on the larger issue of the constitutional principle of sepa-ration. That I would file this kind of lawsuit was an embarrassment to the African-American community, which expected me to be a "good Christian."

From *Free Inquiry*, 10, no. 2 (Spring 1990): 17. Reprinted by permission of the publisher.

I received a great deal of flak from African-American ministers, none of whom offered to debate me on the topic. I did have the opportunity to debate some Southern Baptists and born-again Christians. These debates mainly centered on the First Amendment—that is, on freedom of religion versus freedom *from* religion—and were for the most part legal rather than theological.

Unfortunately, not everyone on the other side was so rational. I was threatened, slandered, and vilified by mail and phone and on radio talk-shows throughout the city. My children were ostracized from the schools to the point where they asked me to dismiss the case. Some of the judges disliked what I was doing, and so I found it difficult to litigate cases before them. This went on for about two years—again, until after the Supreme Court ruled in my favor. At that point things began to subside and my family and I more or less peacefully coexisted with the rest of the community of Mobile until 1989, when we moved to Youngstown, Ohio.

African Americans as a group are among the most religious people in the world. Religion offers us hope—hope that we will receive some benefits in the hereafter, though the cruel realities of the present may seem like living hell. Many of our people have little hope that our lives on earth will improve, and for some of us religion acts as an opiate. We African Americans are among the most repressed people, and religion helps us to cope with the everyday struggles of living.

But perhaps the susceptibility to religion goes beyond that. The early heritage of African Americans focused very much on the supernatural; this may contribute to the feeling that religion is the one thing that can give some hope that our miserable lives will improve in the future.

It is my hope that the African-American community will become less fragile. If we were stronger, we would not look to other sources for the answers to our problems. We would realize that "the answers lie in ourselves and not in the stars." We would not seek to use religion as a crutch; we would not need to rely on a hoped-for deity to make our lives better. We would realize that we can make things better for ourselves, and we would cease being the followers that we are, believing in some charismatic leader who has his or her own agenda. We would no longer be led like lambs to the slaughter, simply obeying commands without question or investigation.

It is my wish that people would analyze things in a logical, rational way and make logical, rational decisions based on intelligent observations. I wish that people would be more open to the scientific method of inquiry and not so given to mysticism.

But these wishes may just be flying in the wind, because unfortunately we live in a community where people have a need for religion. People need their opiate. Indeed, it is true that if religion did not exist, we would invent it.

I believe in the expression, "Know yourself and you shall be free." People should learn to accept the consequences of their own acts or omissions. They should be aware that we live in the here and now, and that we are responsible for what happens to us. If more people realized that, then we would all treat one another better and it would be a better society in which we live. To the extent that I can, I encourage people to think for themselves and not allow others to do their thinking for them. And to my dying breath I shall always attempt to do just that.

Part Three

Essays by African Humanists

16

Thoughts from Africa's Leading Secular Humanist Activist

Emmanuel Kofi Mensah

WHAT RELIGION HAS DONE IN AFRICA

Since Africa came into the limelight of the world, much has been said about the continent in the media. Some refer to it as the dark continent; some call it the underdeveloped continent. To the uninformed, Africa brings to mind a safari, people residing in trees, and jungles in which travelers use knives and axes to move from one area to another.

Africa, the second largest continent in the world, has a land mass of 30.5 million square kilometers and constitutes one-fifth of the total land surface of the earth. Added to the continent itself are seven island nations: Cape Verde, Comoros, Equatorial Guinea, Madagascar, Mauritania, Sao Tome, Principe, and the Seychelles. The land is rich in many resources. It has an estimated population of 601 million, of whom 236 million are Christians, 216 million are Muslims, and 64 million practice traditional religion. These are official figures; but there is ongoing speculation that the real figures are higher. Religion, according to the official figures, is practiced by 86 percent of the continent's population. The official statistics are a clear indication of the strong religious affiliation throughout the continent.

Historically, Africa has been a force to be reckoned with. As a result of archeological findings spanning the last three decades, there can be little reasonable doubt that it was on the African continent that man-like creatures first evolved. In *The Descent of Man* Darwin wrote, "It is therefore probable that Africa was formerly inhabited by extinct apes closely allied to the gorilla and the chimpanzee, and as the two species are now man's nearest allies, it is somehow more probable that our early progenitors lived in Africa than elsewhere." Africa is mentioned when the birth of civilization is brought into discussion. Even before 4000 B.C.E., Egypt was a thriving kingdom. Azum and Cush were also great ancient African civilizations. And one of the first universities—if not the first—in the world was established on the continent.*

African wild animals are world famous: the continent has the largest ungulates and fresh water fish. One also finds the world's largest desert, the Sahara, in northern Africa, as well as the world's second largest mountain range. The continent's known mineral resources place it among the world's richest repositories of raw materials. Africa supplies 50 percent of the world's gold, 40 percent of its platinum, 80 percent of its tantalum, more than 50 percent of its phosphate, 33 percent of its manganese, while mining the bulk of the world's diamond supply. These minerals are only a few of the many resources that account for Africa's vast mineral wealth.

Africa also has a vast and priceless stock of cultural artwork. The artists of Ife, Benin, and South Africa, in particular, are world renowned for their brilliant craftsmanship.

This brief description offers some insight into the potential of the vast African continent. In spite of its great promise, Africa remains riddled with poverty, deprivation, want, disease, and hunger. One cannot help wondering why. I am reminded of a school boy who was having a difficult time drawing maps in his geography class. He devised an ingenious plan to overcome the problem: whenever he drew a map of Africa, he would first make a big question mark, and from there he would shape it into a map of Africa. Africa is indeed a question mark. Why is there so much hunger, poverty, and want? When will these problems come to an end? Who is to blame for these ills? Who can help Africa end this quagmire of hopelessness?

---

*The Grand Lodge of Luxor housed a museum of science, a library containing 400,000 volumes, and a faculty of priests/professors—Ed.

What has actually gone wrong with the continent and its people? Which economic system is best: communism, capitalism, radical governing? These questions have brought about a great deal of speculation, research, and argumentation over the years.

Economists, political analysts, and others have delved into these problems but solutions seem to elude them. Every known method has been tried to combat the hydra-headed problems of Africa: the need to industrialize, lack of diversification in agricultural products, cutbacks in government spending, structural adjustment, and a host of economic programs. Some politicians blame imperialist ploys while others cite a lack of enterprise as the culprit. These are all ideas which may accrue some advantages if carefully studied and followed. About fifteen African countries have adopted the International Monetary Fund's Structural Adjustment Programme. Nonetheless, when the much-publicized African problems are viewed critically, one finds that they are, more or less, the effects of a deep-rooted cause.

Religion is inextricably woven into the very fabric of African life. The main religions of Christianity, African traditional religion, and Islam are accepted in varying degrees throughout the continent. Within African traditional religion, there is much diversity, which is also true of Islam, most notably the Orthodox and the Ahmadiya. African traditional religion, which is the original religion of the indigenous African, is held in high regard. South of the Sahara there are an estimated 700 ethnic groups, each having its own tribal religion, although they bear similarities which show a common origin. They all believe in one supreme god and a number of lesser deities, comprised of personal, family, clan, or communal gods. "These ethnic religions," wrote Ronald Bernett, "reflect the various concerns of the people in everyday living. They focus on social relations, on the crisis of human existence, and on practical matters of survival." The emphasis tends to be on personal safety or communal well-being. Within these religions are superstitions: unreasonable beliefs and irrational fears forming an integral part of traditional religion. Almost all occurrences have their attendant superstitions. In his study of this phenomenon, the African sociologist Adefula Ademogun remarked, "Superstition plays a major role in the lives of almost everybody on the continent. This phenomenon has gripped not only the inhabitants on the continent but all the Africans in and out of Africa." Witchcraft, sorcery, charms, and magic are commonly practiced:

charms to offset evil forces, to nullify hazards, and to facilitate the gaining of deserved ends are ubiquitous. Ceremonies and rituals are tied to African traditional religion. These are performed regularly or as the need may arise. There is always a sacrifice during these rituals. In lesser ceremonies or rituals, animals are sacrificed, but during major ceremonies human sacrifice is offered.

The African traditionalist religion and its attendant superstition, sorcery, and other practices date from prehistoric times. These practices are very prominent in the rural areas where it seems the umbilical cord of primitive thinking has yet to be completely severed. Many of these practices also exist in the urban areas and cities where there are clear evidences of modern life.

The witch doctor and the fetish priest are the spiritual superintendents in the traditional religion. They are regarded as infallible. Every happening has its direct connection with the supernatural, and these guardians of the gods are the only ones capable of unraveling the mysteries.

Christianity and Islam share some similarities with the traditional religions. Due to these similarities, traditional forms were easily adopted. These foreign religions foster belief in a higher power, a big brother who oversees earthly events and helps in times of crises. They stress faith, which is unsupported by empirical evidence, and these religions have spread like wildfire. In some instances, Christianity and Islam displaced the traditional religion; in others they coexist. Islam has a stronghold in north Africa. Countries like Libya, Morocco, Egypt, and Nigeria are Muslim countries. Historically, many Muslims used threats and violence to convert the African. Christians operated successfully in the south where they used a soft but subtle method of winning followers.

As has been previously mentioned, religion is an inseparable part of the life of the African. Consequently, whatever the African does has a direct or indirect religious undertone. The traditional religion with its attendant legends, myths, and magic, and the foreign-oriented religion with its beliefs and irrational faith, negatively effected the progress of the individual and the community as a whole. Take a case in Ghana, for example. There was a guinea worm epidemic in one area. A borehole was dug for the village by the United Nations through the auspices of the World Health Organization and UNICEF to help avert the river-borne disease. It was later learned, however, that the villagers were not using the borehole because they claimed the river, which runs through the village and was causing their problem, was better than the borehole for drinking and for domestic usage. They alleged that the gods lived in the river and that anybody who shunned the river would eventually die. Consequently, they clung to their religious beliefs and the epidemic continued.

Children who are said to be possessed by the gods are not sent to school; they are denied formal education. Their only recourse is to learn the ways of a witch doctor and to try to gain respect in the practice of witchcraft. In this way some of Africa's great minds are lost, and the people continue to stagnate and suffer. This contributes to the scandalous illiteracy rate, which is as high as 75 percent and, in some countries, even as high as 90 percent.

Taboos are the children of superstition, and Africa has a wide range of taboos. Despite the continent's food shortages, there are many nutritious food items that could be eaten, but are forbidden because of religious customs. This obviously compounds the existing food problems.

According to Yvonne Brace, "Africa has the highest annual [population] growth increase in the world—2.9 percent. Despite the increasing rate of population growth, family planning has not had any substantive success in Africa." This retrogression is due to the fact that children are believed to be gifts of God, and that it is He alone who has the right to decide how many children will come into the world. Women therefore have as many children as they can bear. This negatively affects the lives of the children and places unnecessarily heavy burdens upon the shoulders of the mothers in particular.

In rural areas the fetish priest and the witch doctor are highly revered where medical issues are concerned. They are even regarded as superior to those who practice modern medicine, because in addition to being able to cure the sick, they are believed to be able to delve into the unknown to foretell or forestall future events. Owing to that claim, no disease is believed to be beyond their power. At a fetish shrine in Ghana, for example, it has been announced that a cure for AIDS has been discovered. In Nigeria a spiritualist agreed to heal a woman who had acute fibrosis merely by consulting the oracle and praying. The witch doctor depends on faith, magic, myth, and the power of suggestion. Patients believe that the alleged infallible knowledge of the healer is as important to their cure as the medication used. Sometimes the "medication" may have no therapeutic value, but the witch doctors take advantage of the ignorance of their clients. The fetish priest tries to show that he has an immediate understanding of the illness, its cause, and its prescribed treatment, as opposed to practitioners of modern medicine who start with uncertainty and inquire into the nature of the illness. Owing to this perceived infallibility, the death rate of those who attend the fetish shrine for treatment is alarmingly high.

Ceremonies and rituals have a negative effect on development. In Yorubaland, when the time for the famous festival of Oro is nearing, a curfew is imposed on the town that happens to be playing host to the big event. The curfew starts just after sunset, and disrupts many important activities. This restriction continues for about a week or two. Human sacrifices are even carried out!

Christianity and Islam—like the traditional religions—are based upon fear. Believers are taught to fear the unknown and to worship a type of elder brother who stands by to help in emergencies or frightening situations. Karl Marx was correct when he observed that religion is the opium of the people. Muslims and Christians drug themselves with the belief that there is an assured place in the hereafter for the believer. They shape their lives around myths and supposed powers beyond their understanding. They tend to be fatalistic, passively accepting whatever happens to them as ordained by God. They often blame the devil for the hardships and abuses they experience, and they make no attempt to correct their deplorable situations. They view their problems as being insoluble. The problems of Africans (e.g., poor health, hunger, poverty, and want) are great and they continue to worsen.

Women in religion are always looked down upon. The Bible as well as the Koran specifically command women to be subservient to men. Religion—be it traditional, Islam, or Christianity—has denied women equality with men. This is a throwback to a primitive cultural element of the male-dominated societies from whence these religions originated. The modern adherents have naively swallowed everything, much to their detriment. Anything remotely resembling the equal rights amendment or women's liberation are deemed heretical by religious fanatics. And the women dare not speak out against this injustice, having been taught to believe blindly in their religious system. Musa Mahmood, a famous Nigerian politician, remarked that women's studies as well as the education and progress of women are suffering serious setbacks because of religious and cultural beliefs. Many women simply dream about an eternal heavenly abode in which they will sing and play their harps throughout their immortal existence.

The champions of religion—pastors, reverends, fetish priests, etc. —in one way or another, use their positions to perpetrate evil. In many instances, they use their knowledge of psychology to defraud their unsuspecting congregations. Because religion is riddled with loopholes, religious leaders use them selfishly to amass wealth, power, and position. Because those who champion religion are profiting from it, they may also indulge in evil acts in order that their religion can go unchallenged. This becomes a prejudice of interest more diabolical than the prejudice of ignorance, the latter being more combatted and not dogmatically held by any rational human being.

Religion is the brainchild of fear, and fear is the parent of cruelty. The greatest evils inflicted on humankind are perpetrated not by pleasure-seekers, self-seeking opportunists, or those who are merely amoral, but by fervent devotees of religion. The war in the Sudan was caused by disputes between different religious groups—a struggle between Christian and Muslim inhabitants. Egypt is at loggerheads with Israel and its Arab neighbors because of religious differences. A religious riot broke out in northern Nigeria between Muslims and their Christian counterparts. Many lives were lost and property worth millions of naira was destroyed. This is, to say the very least, a disincentive to the development of any region.

Religion is ethnocentric: i.e., people tend to see their own religion as the true expression of divine providence. At the same time, they regard the religions of others as being in error. Racism and slavery arise from this line of thought. And with the exception of hunger, racism (apartheid) is the number one problem on the African continent. Religious adherents close their minds and will not reason critically. Consequently, Africans fail either to identify their problems or find solutions.

Religion does have its positive side, however. Thomas Edison once said, "Nothing is always wrong. Even a stopped watch is right twice a day." If we fail to point out the good to be found in religion, religious criticism becomes as evil as religion itself. Religion is a kind of psychological tool that lifts people up from the depths of despondency. It gives its followers a vision, a dream of heavenly bliss. It sustains, urges, and gives the believers the will and the determination to plod on, in spite of their suffering and difficulties. Africans are able to hold on to life because of the belief in a heavenly reward, and the feeling that God is working his divine purpose year after year; and in this august enterprise, believers have an assured place. A story is told of a very rich couple who could buy anything they desired—they were that wealthy. But they also learned that some things are not for sale. Disillusioned, they committed suicide. They left a note behind which read, in part, "We had no dreams."

In many other ways religion has helped to bring positive changes to Africa. Many schools and hospitals in Africa were set up by missionaries of various religious groups, and the hinterlands were opened up by these same missionaries. During periods of colonial crises, these clergymen became intermediaries between the colonial masters and the Africans. Many problems were averted because of the timely and effective intervention of the missionaries and their mother churches. Sociology teaches us that religion provides the believer with a sense of purpose which serves as an identity. It makes the inevitable reality of death more tolerable, supplies a basis for daily living, and, in general, helps people adjust in times of stress, hardships, and crisis.

Religion is like a knife: when grasped properly by the handle, it can be used constructively and safely, but when it is held by the blade, it can do much harm. It seems that Africa is grasping religion by the blade and is bleeding profusely. This manifests itself in an absence of physical and human development amid poverty, overpopulation, famine, wars, high rates of illiteracy, and ignorance. Religion no doubt has its benefits, but the price is too high, specifically the price of abandoning truth while shackling and perverting man's reason. The main problem of religion is its irrational preference for comfort over truth, and this invariably makes religion very harmful by preventing believers from reaching their full potential. Biased selections of religious ideas and concepts are also very common in religious language. Religious terminology is infested with intellectual dishonesty. But there is widespread evidence that religion has failed to bring a better world to Africans. There is no true and intelligible account of what Christians refer to as faith. Christian faith is not merely believing in God. It is believing in God despite evidence to the contrary. This is not only irrational, but it is a form of hypnotism. In the light of modern science, religion, being a remnant of ancient superstition, will and must one day be completely replaced by a scientific worldview.

In the mid-twentieth century there arose an increased awareness by the African of his own potential, and this was translated into an effective emancipatory effort. During this period, many Africans became convinced that blacks were equal to their white masters. Armed with that knowledge, many African countries became independent. Africans who achieved independence rejoiced, but they found that freedom alone could not solve all their problems. Africa needs this kind of awareness: not only political awareness, but an intellectual awakening that will find expression in the concept of a rational, critical, and objective approach to life. Africans must learn to strive to enjoy life here and now, and to foster an interest in developing humanity's creative talents to their fullest. Africans need to explain phenomena through objective reason rather than through myth, magic, and the Big Brother complex.

During a talk in Lagos, Nigeria, former president Jimmy Carter said, "I do not see any reason why Africa should lag behind." If Africans are to forge ahead, the people should not be taken hostage by theistic illusion. Africans should not fear to speak out or to accept the truth. Regardless of the circumstances, Africans should not fear to be eccentric because of objective dissent. In the words of Bertrand Russell, "Nobody should fear to be eccentric in opinion for every opinion now accepted was once eccentric." When one fears to be eccentric, one not only ceases to grow, but may even lose more ground. For Africans to improve and to allow for moral progress, the immorality of religion must be opposed. Science can help Africans escape the debilitating situation under which the people have lived for so many generations. Africans do not have to look for imaginary supports or invent allies in the sky. They must look within to make the African environment an enjoyable one in which to live.

Bertrand Russell once wrote:

> We have to stand upon our own two feet and look fair and square at the world—its good facts, its bad facts, its beauties and its ugliness. See the world as it is and do not be afraid of it. Conquer the world by intelligence and not merely by being slavishly subdued by the terror that comes from it. The whole conception of God is a conception derived from ancient oriental despotisms. It is a conception quite unworthy of free men. We ought to stand up and look the world

frankly in the face. We ought to make the best we can of the world, and if it is not so good as we wish, after all it will still be better than what these others have made it in all the ages. A good world needs knowledge, kindliness, and courage; it does not need a regretful hankering after the past or a fettering of the free intelligence by the words uttered long ago by ignorant men. It needs a fearless outlook and a free intelligence. It needs hope for the future, not looking back all the time towards a past that is dead, which we trust will be far surpassed by the future that our intelligence can create.

Let us not follow religion to help us out of our predicament. Let us embrace science and advance.

A GIANT IS COMING OF AGE

Some two centuries ago, a group of Americans met to discuss the future of their country. Their minds were charged with ideas. They had concluded that their present system had to be changed. The idea was laudable, but they had obstacles to overcome. They acknowledged the obstacles and the consequences of their plans and actions. They had to push their idea to the forefront.

The idea was not ushered in with fanfare or the blare of trumpets, but rather it met substantial resistance at first. The sword of Damocles hung over its head, poised to strike if the idea did not push through successfully. But the idea was backed by determination, a high purpose, a well-laid plan of action, the will to succeed, and a collective do-or-die mentality.

The American idea might have been nurtured alongside a warm and cozy fire, but it did not remain there. Nor was it shelved or treated carelessly. Rather, it was developed and marketed effectively, and the people at large "bought" the idea. It was pushed through successfully and history was made. The American Revolution was eventually won. Today people can easily—and without sacrifice—appreciate its fruits from the comfort of their homes. The sacrifice and hard work of the early Americans paid off handsomely.

In France, people rebelled against absolutism of both the monarchy and the clergy. Though the storming of the Bastille was said to have been a spontaneous act, it cannot be denied that the whole idea of revolution was masterminded. It was planned by people who knew what they were doing. They risked having their heads lopped off on the guillotine did they not succeed. Their plan did succeed because the architects of the revolution knew what they had to do, and they carefully devised their plan of action. What resulted was the "spontaneous" storming of the Bastille and the successful transfer of power. Others argued that it was the political climate of the time that brought about the French Revolution: the breakdown of law and order, hunger, economic hardship, etc. These things certainly did occur. But one cannot deny the fact that the revolution was the work of human beings. The work of Voltaire, Baron de Montesquieu, Jean Marat, and others cannot be ignored. The success of the revolution can in large part be attributed to a well-formulated and properly implemented plan. This plan was effectively "sold" in the appropriate way, to the right people, at the right time. People talk of the revolution as having been spontaneous when in fact the masses accepted the idea as their own rather than one that had been imposed upon them by others.

An inventor goes through a similar process when he or she has an idea for a new device. The idea must be "sold" to an engineer who then develops it. But the product is still unknown to the consumer until it becomes marketed, advertised, promoted, and eventually sold. The *value* of the product is sold to the public.

The discoveries of land masses or bodies of water by foreign explorers have produced objections from the indigenous peoples whose ancestors had occupied the lands long before the coming of the "discoverers." It is argued, for instance, that the widely accepted claim that Mungo Park discovered the Zambesi River is in error, because even before Park had dreamt of leaving his own country, the natives were drinking from the river. Personally, I accept Mungo Park's discovery because, though the natives knew of the river and used its water, it was only known to *them*. They never took the pains to promote or "sell" the knowledge of such a spectacular river to the outside world. It was Mungo Park who, through his ingenuity, sacrifice, hard work, and effective planning, "sold" the existence of the river to the world.

Novel ideas are not immediately accepted by everyone. Bertrand Russell has asserted that ideas now fully accepted were once eccentric. Before the acceptance of a new idea there has to be a system in need of replacement or a question that remains unanswered. The idea of American independence was not accepted outright and unanimously; some delegates to the Continental Congress accepted that emancipation from the British Empire was the only solution to the grievous wrongs perpetrated on the early Americans, while others strongly disagreed. The idea to seek independence was effectively promoted in many ways and by various means, including Thomas Paine's brilliant pamphlet *Common Sense*.

Secular humanism is a new idea to Africans. The current social system includes reliance on religion, belief in magic and myth, faith in a higher power, fanaticism, and subjectivity. Objectivity, rationality, and the ideals of humanism are the new system. In spite of the predominance of religion in Africa, I am optimistic that humanism will one day secure a stronghold. Africa—the new frontier— offers many opportunities. This vision can only be realized, however, through effective and well-implemented plans of action.

Secular humanism is well grounded in the developed world. It has become a force to be reckoned with, and it has a place among the great "isms" of the world. It has taken deep root. In contrast, efforts are being made here and there to promote humanism in Africa, but they are too feeble to have any real impact.

Some Obstacles to Progress

One might naively assume that all Africans resist humanism outright or deeply abhor anything related to secular humanism. I have conducted a survey and have learned that people hold different perceptions of humanism and for varying reasons.

Outright Resistance

Some people resist or shy away from humanism. They may be a bit receptive but have no real interest in its message. This group includes people who are fanatics, those who are blinded by prejudice of interest, and those who have an undying belief in or reliance on a deity or religion.

In an interview with N. C., an office worker in Ljebu Ode in Ogun state, Nigeria, the following conversation ensued:

EMMANUEL KOFI MENSAH: Why did you choose to be identified with your particular church?

N. C.: Because a new earth is promised to us. God will reward us if we are faithful to Him and obey the Ten Commandments. He has promised us that He will come again.

E. K. M.: I am not pessimistic, but please reason with me. What happens if our wish does not materialize? It has been known to happen. Have you considered the Seventh Day Adventists who were waiting for Jesus' Second Advent in October, 1844? Their expectations obviously did not materialize. And have you thought about the time the Jehovah's Witnesses were set for doomsday? And do you know that the Jews during pre-Christian times were sure that the Messiah would come down from the skies and land in front of the temple to be crowned as the king who would lead them in a war against the Romans? What happened? N. C., we have to be objective. We must live our lives as best we can and suspend judgment when we cannot be certain.

N. C.: You are an Antichrist! Go away!

E. K. M.: I am not an Antichrist. I am a humanist who is committed to the utilization of the fundamental faculties of reason and objectivity.

N. C.: Go, go, go away! You devil!

T. O., a housewife in Lagos, reacted in a similarly repulsive manner:

T. O.: You people must burn by the bunch! You are contributing to the decline of the faith of our fathers. Go away! I am going to call my pastor.

Some minds are like concrete—once mixed and dried, they are permanently set. These women were open to what pleased them, but not to that which was necessarily obvious.

Ignorance

I was in a parked motor vehicle when I seized the opportunity to interview a policeman sitting nearby. A. I.—the policeman—eventually asked me what I thought humanism was. After I explained to him my concept of humanism and its ideals, he asked for literature to study. As my friend and I drove away, he informed me that he had heard the interview. He showed great interest:

DRIVER: Oga ("Big man" in the Yoruba language), I found that conversation to be very interesting. Humanism sounds very good, but I have never heard of it until now. How may I become involved?

I gave him humanist literature to read.

I contacted a Beninois (a citizen of Benin). She had doubted that such a life-stance as humanism existed in her country, because, she said, in Benin one is either a Catholic or a believer in traditional religion, or perhaps even both. But everyone had a religion. She said that she had never known that anything like humanism existed in the world.

Ignorance is mainly responsible for the inability of humanism to take root in Africa. Many people are in the dark as to what humanism is all about. Someone once asked me how I expected him to wade through a river in which he could not see. Many people commented on their lack of knowledge of humanism. I am convinced that many who shy away from it do so simply because they do not have ample knowledge of its ideals.

Fear of Being Eccentric

Another obstacle to the progress of humanism in Africa is a fear of being viewed as eccentric. Africa, as we have seen, is predominantly religious. In light of that fact, some people do not feel comfortable embracing a new idea which has yet to become very popular. In Africa to dissent or to apostasize risks great consequences. The one who dissents from a religion—especially traditional religion—is believed to be cursed. Therefore, dissent from traditional religion demands determination and much sacrifice.

I had the chance to talk with Mrs. Y. O., a senior teacher in Abeokuta. After she had carefully, and with much interest, responded favorably to my questions, I asked her if it was likely that she would identify herself with humanist groups. Here is her response:

"Sir, I see the sense in everything you are saying . . . the ideals of which you speak are laudable. I wish that society would evolve from a world of narrow perceptions to a broader, more objective one. (After a long reflective pause she continued.) How? How do I face my family, my husband, or my extended family if I tell them that I am now a secular humanist. Oh no! Please come again and I will let you talk with my husband. But please call again! Do not forget."

The reaction of Mrs. Y. O. reflects many peoples' attitudes toward a new idea—that is to say, an idea that is not popular. It is only natural that people would treat a new idea with suspicion and mistrust.

Preference

There are people who will prefer to hold on to their line of thought despite sound arguments to the contrary. One point of interest is that some are well informed about humanism and consider themselves to be objective. I do not see this as a problem because, as a humanist, I must allow people to express alternative points of view: that is what is meant by dissent. After I had conducted an interview with S. R., a Nigerian resident, he concluded: "You know that there are many views. You believe in humanism. Won't you accept that what I believe is also right and good for me?"

Passive Acceptance

Some people believe passively—though not reluctantly—in all that is presented to them. This, to me, is a more formidable obstacle than an instance of outright resistance. To quote Bertrand Russell: "Find more pleasure in intelligent dissent than in passive argument, for, if you value intelligence as you should, the former implies a deeper agreement than the latter." With outright resistance, the chances are high that the believer may see the error in his line of thought and change it. If the earth he thinks so solid and firm begins to rock, he trembles as the earthquake intensifies. But the one who accepts religion passively is as a dead log or a wet blanket. Incidentally, those who passively accept religion add to the number of believers, but they do not exert any influence on the society. Their tendency to be passive is usually consistent in everything they do.

Prejudice of Interest

People who are prejudiced in favor of their own interests know the truth, but due to personal advantages to be gained by rejecting it, they do so. In this category fall the pastors, fetish priests, witch doctors, deacons, etc.

I popped into the den of some of the men who fulfill the medicinal and herbal requirements of the trado-medicine men in their unending struggle against demons, gonorrhea, gynecological disorders, and maledictions. I interviewed the leader, who showed considerable interest and responded favorably. When asked if he would join the humanist organization, he said: "Oga, I am not fit to join. And how do you expect me to eat if I do? Will you feed me? Moreover, I am respected and adored as the chief Babalawo (medicine man). Just think about that. . . ." This obstacle is troublesome because it is hard to combat it with information and argument.

Financial Constraint

The issue of financial constraint need not be discussed much because everyone is aware of the economic standing of Africans. Money is hard to come by. Consequently, the acquisition of funds for promotional efforts becomes difficult, if not impossible. This does much to kill the ambition of those who have humanism at heart. Lack of funds obviously creates barriers to the effective implementing of plans for the spread of humanism.

Other Problems

There are other hindrances that are working in one way or another against the progress of humanism in Africa. Religion, the arch-opponent of secular humanism, if fully discussed, would take an entire book. Misinformation, lack of self-confidence (especially among women), indifference, and many other problems thwart the promotion of humanism in Africa. But this bleak picture must be contrasted with the instances of people who *accept* the ideals of secular humanism. The picture is not as gloomy as one might think. Some of the people responded favorably to the questions and showed a willingness to be identified with secular humanism. Their acceptance varied in extent. Some saw the errors in their religious belief systems and promised to start shaping their lives around the humanist values of objectivity and reason, and to solve their problems as well as those of society without myths, magic, juju, and other paranormal beliefs. Others showed a willingness to help in the promotion of secular humanism. But this is just a small step out of the darkness—much more needs to be done.

Possible Solutions

To understand a problem is to have half the solution. We have addressed some of the obstacles to the dissemination of humanism in Africa. Now the central question is "how can humanism be effectively and successfully marketed on the continent?" One possible solution, it seems, is extensive education. Efforts should be made to make humanism more attractive to Africans. Research and development centers should be established and expanded. These centers could be indispensable tools in the promotion of humanism. For instance, humanism is Eurocentric. Consequently, its literature and thinking reflect that of whites. Norm Allen, in his article titled "Humanism in the Black Community," contends that "nonwhites in general and blacks in particular do not pursue secular humanism largely because it is rooted in purely Eurocentric thinking, which has consistently ignored and degraded nonwhites."[1] It is alien to the African culture. Literature and other materials can be made to suit the African context. By so doing, the Africans see and accept it as an African life-stance rather than a foreign way of life being imposed on them. Islam is flourishing among blacks because it has not been identified solely with the white man. The research and development centers should be staffed by skilled workers and professionals who will work effectively to bring about appropriate and workable solutions. In the religious community, Methodist libraries are set up to benefit the literate population. Literary competition on secular humanist topics should be encouraged among the youth. Incentives such as awards should be given to encourage massive participation. This will induce mass involvement by the youth and open them to the world of humanism, thereby making them more rational.

In the contemporary African context, humanism remains a position for the elite. Africa—where only 20 percent of the population can read and write—is at a clear disadvantage. Effective ways to reach every class and both sexes must be found; that is to say, promotional strategies must be devised that will appeal to a broad spectrum of the population. In the case of those who are illiterate, personal involvement, one-on-one promotional methods, public lectures, relief programs (both token and massive), and audiovisual materials should be utilized. Traditional songs and poetry should be composed around secular humanist themes. Dramas and plays showcasing the benefits of humanism in the African context should be written. The media can be of great help in promotional efforts, if humanism is favorably presented. In schools and colleges humanist clubs need to be encouraged—this will provide a forum for an exchange of ideas.

Because securing of funds for promotional efforts is a problem, the well-established groups are requested to contribute as much as they reasonably can. At the same time, local humanist groups should endeavor to be self-sufficient; they should not be dependent upon handouts for very long. Financial independence or self-sufficiency should be attained in the shortest possible time. An appropriate way of funding humanist groups needs to be looked into. This will help check the possibility of unscrupulous people channelling monies meant for the development of humanism away from the various groups. The pooling of resources will help the groups to average out deficiencies and increase their assets. The committee system will help in the proper and smooth planning and execution of organizational policies. It is also important to have volunteers from Africa and abroad. There should be linkage and coordination of efforts by local, regional, and international groups.

These are just a few suggestions. We must realize that the task is enormous, but *we* are able to tackle it. Everyone must be involved in the program. It is not enough merely to talk or dream about humanism in Africa. There is much to be done. More extensive studies need to be conducted if we are to realize our dream. I am not pushing for a kind of militant evangelism or another cult. But I am for a system in which as many people as possible will be adequately informed and have the freedom to choose. Let us all work together to present effectively the ideals of secular humanism to Africa. Some might have already achieved small victories in the various African countries, but greater success awaits us. One day the entire world will come to embrace humanism, including Africa.

I hope to see the day when everybody will be free to live their lives as they see fit, to dissent and to learn all about humanism. I hope to see the day when humanism is no longer viewed as the life-stance of the whites. I hope to see the day when humanist organizations are not viewed as havens for the elite and the privileged. Let us stand by our principles. Let us make this dream a reality. I hope to see the day when Africa will boast of an open society based on liberty, equality, and fraternity—a truly pluralistic democracy with room for different life-stances. I hope to see the day when Africa will grow toward the principle of free inquiry. I hope to see the day when Africa will place great emphasis on the development of reason and a skeptical attitude toward absolutism and untested claims to knowledge. I hope to see the bright morning when Africa's problems will be solved through education and self-reliance rather than spirituality, astrology, numerology, magic, and other paranormal beliefs.

NOTE

1. Norm R. Allen, Jr., "Humanism in the Black Community," *Free Inquiry* 9, no. 3 (Summer 1989).

17

Morality and Religion in Akan Thought

Kwasi Wiredu

One of the ways in which African culture has been misunderstood
has been through exaggerations of the role of religion in African
life. My task [here] is to analyze one particular form of this misconception which is evidenced in the widespread view that in African
societies morality depends upon religion and that this is how morality
is conceived of in African traditional thought. This view is entertained
not only by foreign observers of African life but also by some African
scholars. It is thus urgent to lay it to rest. This is especially so, seeing
that it is an idea which seems to have some part in the subversion
of some of the better parts of our culture. The scenario which seems
to have been enacted is as follows. An African becomes a member
of the Christian flock for one reason or another, or for no reason
at all. He is, accordingly, committed to the Christian way of life.
But an important and essential part of this way of life is the practice
of "Christian ethics." If he or she believes in the dependence of morality
on religion, as many do, he is led to separate this ethic from that
of his own people, which he learns to call "pagan ethics." Christian

Originally published in *Philosophy and Culture: Proceedings of the 2nd Afro-Asian
Philosophy Conference, October/November 1981, Nairobi.* Edited by H. Odera Oruka
and D. A. Masolo. Nairobi, Kenya: Bookwise Ltd., 1983. Reprinted by permission
of the author.

morality on this view depends upon Christian belief, and the pagan (i.e., traditional) morality similarly depends on paganism. Having abandoned this last, he sees the abandonment of the associated morality as a matter of course. Thenceforward his morality is Christian morality, at any rate, according to his "confession." Who has not heard some such protestation on the part of an African convert as "Oh, no! I am a Christian; I would not do that" in a context in which there looms the possibility of his being suspected of some particularly unethical conduct. The hint here is that if he were a pagan, suspicion might be in place. This is not a strict logical implication, but there is no doubt that the hint is one that is intentionally fostered by the protestation.

Now, a culture is a way of life, and morality is the core of any way of life. To suppose that indigenous morality has to be abandoned in favor of a Christian morality, then, is to envisage a very serious negation of indigenous culture. In point of fact, however, this attitude to indigenous morality is, as far as I know, hardly ever consistently thought, or lived, through; since, in any case, conversion to Christianity in Africa has frequently been rather superficial as far as matters of existential moment are concerned. Nevertheless, the earnest strivings of many an African convert towards Christian virtue, viewed as superior to indigenous canons of the good life, have led to serious enough confusions in practical life. Think, for example, of the resultant dilemmas in sexual morality. But there have also been intellectual confusions, and these are what concern us here most directly. In the analysis to be given below I shall consider the issues with particular reference to Akan culture, for it is only of this culture among the cultures of Africa that I have first-hand or inside knowledge through both natural upbringing and deliberate reflective observation. I wish moreover to protect myself against temptations to hasty generalization sweeping over our whole continent.

The intellectual confusions alluded to in the last paragraph are legion. The familiar notion of the dependency of morality upon religion in African society involves misconceptions about the nature of morality and religion in general. It involves, furthermore, confusions about the relation between metaphysical suppositions and practical norms, in addition to some straight-out mistakes in the description of indigenous moral life. With the possible exception of this last, all these are quite complex matters, and we can here only touch on those aspects most immediately connected with our purpose. Take, then, the concept of morality. It refers either to a set of rules for the regulation of conduct or to patterns of conduct viewed in relation to such rules. The simple precaution of noting clearly which of these two senses of the work "morality" is in play in any remark about the relation of morality to religion will be found very useful in avoiding error. It is obvious that with regard to patterns of behavior issues of explanation and justification arise that are importantly different from those that arise with respect to rules of conduct. We can ask for the causes of a pattern of behavior; we cannot ask for the causes of rules of conduct. Moreover, though questions of justification are in place in both connections, they appertain to different levels. Justification of behavior can only take the form of relating it to rules. Obviously, the rules cannot be justified by reference to themselves but only by reference to higher order rules, where possible, and in other cases, to considerations more general than any specific rule of conduct.

What, then, are the determinants of traditional Akan morality, taking morality to start with, in the second sense, namely, as a certain pattern of behavior? This question treats traditional society too much as if it were a block. In fact, traditional society—and this must indeed apply to any society—consisted of the wise and the unwise and, in between them, a large mass of ordinary humanity moderate in both the abilities and disabilities of the mind. My impression is that the question under consideration has usually been answered only with reference to the attitudes and reactions of the third and largest class. It is, of course, legitimate to leave out of account the class of those who are weak in mind. But since in matters of reflection and insight, especially those of an abstract nature, it is the minority rather than the majority that hold the key in any society, it is a bad mistake to be unmindful of the attitudes and reactions of the wise few in considering the determinants of conduct.

Let us, however, consider first the determinants of the morality of the large mass of traditional Akans. The most striking consideration here is the influence of tradition. One might even include this in the defining characteristics of a traditional society. To ordinary traditional folk to point out that some mode of behavior is what is enjoined by our ancestors or is what has been done from time immemorial is to supply its ultimate justification. It is, nevertheless, important to note that this type of "justification" is not extended to all modes of behavior; it is applied principally to what are known as customs but not generally to moral conduct. If you ask an ordinary Akan why it is that it is the duty of the children of a deceased person, as distinct from any other relations, to dig his or her grave, the answer is most likely to be: "That is how it has always been done." But if you ask him why one should abstain from a neighbor's wife, he would almost certainly reply "Would you like the same if it were done to you?" Or suppose you were to ask him: "Why should one help a person in distress?" The characteristic Akan answer would be aphoristic: "Mortals need help" (*Onipa bia mmoa*) or "The plight of your fellow man is your own plight" (*Wo yonko da ne wo da*) or "It is somebody's turn today; it will be another's tomorrow," literally "Somebody's turn has come; another's is on the way" (*Obi de aba; obide nam kwan so*).

It is worth stressing that no moderately sensible Akan would answer the second and third questions mentioned in the last paragraph by citing the practice of our ancestors. It is equally important to note that there is no reference to sanctions of any sort in these replies. Sanctions are external to morality. It can be said, I think, that morality is on the verge of degenerating into law when sanctions attain a commanding status in its domain. This is not to say that the fact of sanctions does not play a role in the explanation of human conduct. But the point is that in giving an account of moral conduct sanctions can only figure in (psychological) explanation; they have no place in justifications. A mature man may be constrained by the certainty of sanctions to perform or avoid an action, but he cannot, if his action is truly a piece of moral conduct, himself cite the threat of sanctions as a reason for his conduct. If he did, it would be evidence of a relapse into infantilism, and this is certainly how it would be viewed in Akan society. Only a child is expected to say such a thing as "I won't tell lies because my mother will spank me." True, a man of ripe age, sorely tempted to tell lies in some matter, may hold off because lying in that kind of case would call forth severe retribution. But this does not mean that his recognition of the general wrongness of lying has anything to do with the prospect of retribution. The thought of retribution may bolster up a faltering will, but it is not this that creates the *sense* of goodness.

Traditional Akans believed, and still believe, in the reality of both human and nonhuman sources of moral sanctions. Our departed ancestors are supposed to "live" in some form and to watch closely over the conduct of their living descendants, rewarding virtue and punishing its opposite. A variety of "gods" are supposed to play the same role. All this is additional to the more empirical sanctions of social life. Public opinion, especially the opinion of the kin group, exerts a strong influence on the behavior of individuals as does also the opinion of parents, family, and lineage heads. But whether the source of sanctions is human or nonhuman, the point made in the last paragraph stands unaffected: The fact or possibility of these sanctions does not and cannot create the sense of virtue; it can only aid the translation of this sense into practice.

The nearest we can get to the creation, for the ordinary Akan, of a sense of what ought or ought not to be done by mere sanctions is when we come to the field of taboos. A taboo is something forbidden simply because it is hateful to some nonhuman power and will invite adversity if done. Regarding an action that is a taboo, the belief of the ordinary Akan is not that it is hated by the powers concerned because it is bad but rather that it is bad because it is hated by them. No reason is forthcoming for the necessity of avoiding such acts except that their performance will bring disaster. An interesting case of a taboo is sex in the bush. One is not supposed to have sex in the bush under any circumstance whatever, not even with one's own wife. Such an act is supposed to be extremely obnoxious to the "goddess" of the earth *(Asaase Yaa),* and she will visit her wrath not only on the principals involved but also on their immediate community: The earth will refuse to yield fruit in the vicinity. There are cases of taboo that might even appear whimsical. Bishop Sarpong, an Ashanti-born Catholic dignitary and a trained anthropologist very well known for his pride in his indigenous culture, includes the following among the taboos of Akan society. (The Ashanti's are a branch of the Akan ethnic group in Ghana): ". . . singing when you are bathing: one who does that will lose his wife, or if he is unmarried, his mother; singing while eating: to do this is to wish and effect the death of your mother; cutting your finger nails after you have tasted food for the day; shaking hands with a new widow, etc."[1]

There is a category of forbidden things which shares with taboos the character of being specially hateful to the "gods" but which are also recognized as moral evils. Both taboos and such evils are called *musuo* in Akan. This term has a certain connotation of uncleanness; any act that brings disaster to the community through the anger of the "spiritual"[2] forces is supposed to be unclean. The word also connotes the premonition of disaster emanating from estranged "deities." Such threatening disasters can only be averted by purificatory rituals, according to Akan belief. Examples of *musuo* that are, strictly speaking, not taboos are: murder, adultery with the wife of a chief, insulting a chief, and stealing the property of a "god." Because this class of actions shares the affinity just mentioned with taboos, and also because in the Akan language both classes of actions are known as *musuo,* the temptation has arisen to call both classes by the name of taboo. Bishop Sarpong unfortunately succumbs to this temptation when he includes the examples I have just given in his list of taboos.[3] In fact, however, while all taboos are *musuo,* not all *musuo* are taboos. Any ordinary Akan will tell you that adultery with the wife of a chief, for example, is intrinsically wrong. Adultery with the wife of any man is wrong in any case. It is a moral evil, it is unfitting. (*Eye bone; enfata*). But to the Akan there is a special gravity attached to a misdeed of this sort, because a chief is supposed to have a "spiritual" status, and the act defiles him. It is for this reason that disastrous consequences are feared from such acts.

The discussion so far has disclosed three types of rules of conduct, namely, rules of custom, of taboo, and of morality proper. The concept of *musuo* overlaps with all three categories, for a *musuo* is any infringement of a rule of behavior which will arouse the wrath of the "gods" and bring their retribution upon the community or at least an extended family unless *customary* rites of purification and expiation are performed.[4] The way in which sensitivity to all three categories of rules is manifested in a person's conduct affects his social respectability, and that is no small supplementary incentive to compliance. Nevertheless, it has to be emphasized that only one of the three categories of rules belongs to the realm of morals. Once pointed out, this seems obvious, perhaps, but it has been usual to mix all three together in descriptions of moral life in our traditional society; and this has encouraged exaggerated theories of the influence of religion on traditional morality. In fact, the more striking cases of the effect of the fear of "spiritual" sanctions upon behavior are found in the area of conduct ruled by custom and taboo rather than pure morality. Moreover, the following distinction implicit in our account so far needs explicit emphasis: The threat of "spiritual" sanctions presents itself to the ordinary Akan mind as a sufficient reason for action or the avoidance of action in matters relating to taboo. Similarly, the desire to avoid social approbrium is perceived in the same light in matters of custom. On the other hand, thought of sanctions, spiritual or not, does not, even for the ordinary Akan, have the status of a reason for action in moral matters; it only has a part in psychological causation. It is clear thus that the role of spiritual powers as determinants of moral conduct is rather restricted. And not only this; the mode of determination involved here is qualitatively different from that involved in custom and taboo.

If we now turn to the question of the determinants of conduct from the point of view of the wise men of the tribe, the role of the so-called spiritual powers seems to disappear almost completely. The wise man in Akan society is the man who not only knows the rules of conduct, moral or otherwise, but also knows their underlying reasons. It is an important fact about Akan society that any apparently trivial observance, not to talk of the weightier ones, has an underlying reason that can be learnt if one has recourse to the right teachers. These teachers are, of course, relatively few. However, the generality of Akans do not particularly bother to find out; they seem satisfied to do the done things. Concerning the common man in Akan society, then, Bishop Sarpong is right when, talking of the taboos, he observes: "If one were to ask the Ashanti why he keeps these taboos, he will probably not be able to give one the reasons I have propounded. All he is likely to assert is that they have existed from time immemorial, that the ancestors want him to observe them."[5] However, if his reference to "the Ashanti" is intended unrestrictedly, then the remark is somewhat unguarded, for if you go to the wise men (*anyansafo*) of the Ashantis, you will most assuredly be instructed in the rationale of these and other types of rules.

Bishop Sarpong himself offers naturalistic accounts of the social meaning and function of the taboos, even of the most apparently inconsequential ones, such as those concerning singing in the bath or at table or cutting one's fingernails after meals.[6] Here again, I think our divine is right in principle. Consider the following interesting explanation from him of the taboo on sex in the bush: "Those who indulge in it expose themselves to the risk of being bitten by venomous creatures like the snake, the scorpion, and the spider. (It should be borne in mind that Ashanti is a forested region with dangerous creatures whose bite may easily be fatal.) Let a mishap of this nature take place and there is every likelihood that misapprehensions are conceived about the conjugal act itself. That this would be detrimental to the human species is too obvious to emphasize."[7] There surely are other reasons, too. For example, since the fields are unprotected environs, any oversexed or sexually starved citizen can have a field day at the expense of unpoliced damsels by lying in wait in easily contrived concealment if there are no stern disincentives. That this would be detrimental to Akan agriculture is, similarly, too obvious to emphasize. Nor are such considerations lost on our sages.

Let us now suppose that some such naturalistic explanations of the taboos as the Bishop's are true. Then there is a very significant implication that he does not draw. It is this: that the reference to the retributions of the "gods" is superfluous in the sense that the reason why people should not have sex in the bush is not because the earth "goddess" cannot stand it—or, more accurately, cannot support it— but because there are naturalistically undesirable consequences. If, as I maintain, this is the way in which the sages of the Akans conceive these matters, then we have to say that for them there are in fact no real taboos at all. An even more radical hypothesis suggests itself: May it not be that the stories of the dire reactions of the "gods" to certain forms of behavior may originally have been intended by our ingenious sages of old as a way of concentrating the minds of those of moderate understanding on the straight path of acceptable conduct? This hypothesis postulates a degree of rationalism on the part of the traditional sages which cannot, of course, be taken for granted. Furthermore, propagating to others threats of "spiritual" sanctions while not believing in their reality in one's own mind might perhaps strike some as having a touch of deception. On the other hand, this sort of procedure as a pedagogic method is not unknown in Akan society in other contexts. For instance, children are often encouraged to abide by certain prohibitions by being told of very mysterious and unfortunate consequences of noncompliance. A specific example is this: Wishing to have their peace of ear at night, Akan grown-ups have put it about that children who whistle at night will lose their mothers. In truth this is not very different from tabooing singing in the bath for adults on pain of an identical tragedy. Perhaps sages may believe that they have reason to treat nonsages as in some

ways analogous to children. I don't know. My own face-to-face inquiries on this matter remain as yet incomplete. In any case the question need not be settled here, if it can be settled at all.

At all events, one thing is clear. Whether they believe in the
reality of "spiritual" sanctions or not, the wise men of our tribe, unlike
the *hoi polloi,* do not construe such sanctions or any other sort as
reasons for action. And if this is so with respect to the things that
are taboos for the ordinary consciousness, then the same point needs
hardly to be stressed with respect to matters of pure morality. In
this basic fact they do not differ from the Akan masses, as we have
seen. But they differ from the latter by their greater inclination to
rational reflection on the general purposes of moral rules, a form
of thinking which, among the more speculatively oriented, soon
becomes philosophical. At this level the question is no longer "What
are the determinants of morality?" but "What is the basis of that
morality?" And "morality" no longer refers to patterns of conduct
viewed in relation to rules of a certain sort but rather to the set
of rules themselves. This is the important question. Questions of origin
may, of course, have some interest but, from a philosophical point
of view, such interest can only be of a subsidiary nature. We note,
however, that among those who think that morality in general depends
on religion, the idea that moral law originates from God seems to
carry a lot of significance. This is particularly so in the context of
religions such as the Judeo-Christian religion in which revelation is
an article of faith.

We can dispose of the question of origin quite quickly as far
as Akan thought is concerned. Revelation simply has no place in
Akan thought. Morality in this intellectual milieu is founded on rational
reflection about human welfare, and the discovery of the validity of
the rules of morality is ultimately a matter of individual reflection.
This remark is not contrary to the communalistic orientation of the
Akans. Morality is social. This, in fact, is a tautology; for if there
were only one single individual in the whole of existence, questions
of morality could never conceivably arise. Questions of the welfare
of that single individual would, of course, arise for the lone individual;
from which it is clear that the central concern of morality is not
just individual welfare but individual welfare as it fits within the welfare
of the community i.e., social well-being. But the perception of the
conditions of such an arrangement is a mental occurrence, and must,

as such, be in individual minds. In Akan society such a perception is credited to the wise elders, at least. To this class of men the conditions of the harmonious adaptation of the individual's welfare to that of his community are empirical conditions and only require a clear and resourceful mind to grasp. To appeal to revelation would be, from their point of view, to confess an intellectual bankruptcy.

The late Dr. J. B. Danquah, one of the most respected of Ghanaian public men, philosopher, lawyer, politician, man of letters, and specialist in Akan culture, author of the celebrated *Akan Doctrine of God,* has testified thus vigorously to the absence of any reliance on revelation in Akan culture: ". . . [T]he original Akan society did not act according to any Christian conception. We have never had a Christ or a Buddha or a Mohammed. Never in the history of the Akan people, so far as we know, have we had what is known as a revealed religion, a revelation to, or by, a prophet, of duty to a Supreme Master or Lord, residing in your heart or residing in Heaven, who sits there waiting for you at the end of your life, to judge you as either a goat or a sheep, and to send you to Paradise or to Hell, according as you are a sheep or a goat."[8]

To try to disseminate any messages of revealed morality in genuinely wise traditional Akan circles would be unavailing, for any such information would be bound to be appraised in terms of the conditions of human well-being. What is incompatible with these conditions in the way of conduct is evil (*bone*), and evil cannot be prescribed by God, for He hates evil, according to Akan conceptions (*Onyanko pon mpe bo ne*). Thus any suggestion that goodness might be defined in terms of the will of God is ruled out of court—out of the Akan court, and for that matter, out of any judicious court.[9] Any such definition would make it logically possible for goodness to be in conflict with human well-being; for suppose that God were to command something contrary to human well-being, then by this definition, it would have to be accepted as good. An earth-oriented theological parochialism might find it hard to conceive of indifference to human well-being on the part of God, but, metaphysically, there is no reason why the earth with all its inhabitants might not be an insignificant spot in a passing phase of a grand divine project.

The conclusion is clear: If, for the Akan, goodness is to be defined in terms of human well-being—we make no pretense here of articulating the definition itself—then it is logically independent of God;

so that even if there were no belief in God, there still would be rules of good conduct. If follows also and *a fortiori* that morality, as a set of rules of good conduct, is for the Akan, logically independent of the minor "deities." We have already adduced considerations to discourage exaggerating the influence of the "gods" on conduct in Akan society. We now see that the "gods" and even the Supreme God are irrelevant to the conceptual foundations of morality in Akan thought. Indeed, from a moral point of view, the "gods" are in quite a weak position. They are, in our society, subject to human censure, and when considered worthless can sometimes be "killed." Abraham in his *The Mind of Africa* has gone as far as to say that "The proliferation of gods that one finds among the Akans is in fact among the Akans themselves superstitious. Minor gods are artificial means to the bounty of *Onyame* [God]."[10] Busia also says, "The gods are treated with respect if they deliver the goods, and with contempt if they fail. . . . Attitudes to the [the gods] depend upon their success, and vary from healthy respect to sneering contempt."[11] Dr. Danquah, too, remarks that in Akan society, "the general tendency is to sneer at and ridicule the fetish and its priest."[12] All these quotations contain, I believe, large grains of truth, and moreover support the contention that the Akan attitude to the "gods" presupposes an independently grounded morality.

There is an even more radical implication, namely, that the Akan attitude to the minor "deities" implies that those beings are not in fact genuine objects of religious devotion. An object of the typically religious attitude must be believed to be profoundly good; it must also be supposed to have the ontological significance of accounting for the way the world is, and must, furthermore, be conceived as indestructible.[13] No Akan minor "god" possesses all these attributes, and many do not possess any. Therefore, when we find treatises on African religion filled with descriptions of "gods" and fetishes and even charms, we must be sure that some very deep misunderstanding of African life is going on.

When we remove the institutions and practices relating to the minor "gods" from the domain of Akan religion we are left simply with the Akan belief in, and attitude to, God. The attitude is, of course, one of supreme reverence and awe and trust. But there are no institutions or practices of worship as there are in Christianity. The Akans do pray to God, who is conceived as good in the highest, addressing various requests to him, but this cannot be called worship. Within the terms of Akan thought, there is no reason for any institutions or practices of divine worship. Nor is there felt to be any reason for attaching an institution for moral instruction to the Akan attitude to God, though the thought that God hates evil can influence conduct just as in the case of some of the lesser "gods." Moral instruction belongs to the home. An adult Akan is supposed to gain his moral knowledge through his early training in the home and his own later reflection. There is no question of respectable Akan citizens converging regularly to a public place to receive moral exhortations from persons who are not supposed to be in possession of any recondite moral insights. Of course, an Akan who has fallen into punishable error might be given a moral lecture in a court room or at a family or inter-family assembly. But that is a special occasion and the point of it is clear, as it is not in the case of automatic institutionalized moralism. The modern phenomenon of grown-up Akan men and women dutifully and regularly trooping to Christian chapels to be bombarded with platitudinous homilies is a departure from our indigenous culture which has not benefited us, to say the least. Looking at certain notorious trends in my own country, Ghana, I cannot avoid the impression that the hortatory culture which this particular Christian institution has inculcated into our leadership has provided corrupt politicians and others with a ready mechanism for salving their conscience. The unspoken principle seems to be this: Help yourself to national assets et cetera without any undue inhibitions. Afterwards loudly exhort your fellow countrymen to all the highest virtues; and you have done your duty.

Conceivably, this psychological hypothesis might be felt by some to be far-fetched. But one thing seems to be quite clear: In the Akan scheme of things morality is not attached to religion either in its conception or in its practice. There is no reason why it should be, contrary to frequent suggestions that every religion has to have an ethic. Religious beliefs per se are metaphysical claims; they amount to a theory of reality—of what there is. Beliefs as to the nature of certain realities may inspire a particular way of life, but they need not. Whatever the truth about the general relationshp between "is" and "ought," this much appears straightforward. Thus it is that though the Akans believe that God is supremely good, wise, powerful, and kind, still their avowed reason for striving after the good is not because it is pleasing to God but rather because it is conducive to human well-being.

It is pleasing to me that the Akan moral outlook is thus logically independent of religion, for it means that the ethics of our culture can survive the withering away of the belief in God, a belief for which I know no good arguments.

NOTES

1. Peter Sarpong, *Ghana in Retrospect: Some Aspects of Ghanaian Culture* (Accra: Ghana Publishing Corporation, 1974), p. 54.

2. I throw quotation marks around terms such as "spiritual" and "gods" because I do not believe that they give quite accurate translations of the Akan concepts concerned, but it would take us too far afield to try to pursue my qualms and I cannot find any very convenient substitutes.

3. Peter Sarpong, *Ghana in Retrospect*, p. 53.

4. Indeed custom also overlaps with taboo inasmuch as the non-performance or incorrect performance of certain customs is taboo.

5. Peter Sarpong, *Ghana in Retrospect*, p. 58.

6. Ibid., pp. 54–58.

7. Ibid., p. 57.

8. J. B. Danquah, "Obligation in Akan Society," *West African Affairs*, No 8 (1952), published by the Bureau of Current Affairs, London, for the Department of Extra-Mural Studies, University College of the Gold Coast, p. 3.

9. The thesis that "good" is definable in terms of the will of God is thoroughly worsted in, for example, Kai Nielsen's *Ethics without God* (Buffalo, N.Y.: Prometheus Books, 1973).

10. Willie E. Abraham, *The Mind of Africa* (Chicago: University of Chicago Press, 1962), p. 56.

11. Busia, "The Ashanti," in Daryll Forde, ed., *African Worlds* (New York: Oxford University Press, 1954), p. 205

12. Danquah, "Obligation in Akan Society," p. 6.

13. This amounts to a definition of religion, and I must apologize for its apparent off-handedness as it is inopportune to pursue the matter here.

18

The Identity of the African Woman

Freda Amakye Ansah

From the cradle to the grave, African women live in an environment shrouded in superstition. Some of these superstitions provide justification for societal norms, but many benefit no one. Everything is swallowed hook, line, and sinker for fear of being struck down by an unknown superior force. Strict rules govern every aspect of life, and are not questioned for fear of ostracism.

For example, some tribes in Africa practice female circumcision to reduce promiscuity and promote fidelity. Of course, the lack of technical expertise among the "surgeons" can lead to infections that can permanently affect the reproductive system and even cause death. The lucky girls who are able to survive remain sexually insensitive and have little or no libido. Contrary to the beliefs of some African men, female circumcision can actually have an adverse effect on a marriage by making intimate relations unpleasant for at least one of the partners. This practice is not only unnecessary but wicked as well. Yet the young girls of such tribes are looked down upon if they do not undergo circumcision rites.

Another bad practice based on superstition is early marriage. Marriage provides financial and emotional security and is considered

From *Free Inquiry* 10, no. 4 (Fall, 1990): 28. Reprinted by permission of the publisher.

a necessity in almost every African community. But it is not fair to shove a girl of twelve into marriage with a partner the age of her grandfather. Why is this done? Because he is rich enough to pay her bride price. In my opinion, a girl should not marry until she is at least eighteen years old; a man should wait until he is about twenty-five.

Early marriage deprives girls of education. Most African fathers believe that a woman's office is in the kitchen, and that it is counter-productive to waste resources on one whose destiny ends at the front door. A high percentage of dropouts is female. Due to financial and parental pressure, only 20 percent of female Africans find their way to higher education. Those who do are subjected to male hooliganism and even sexual harassment.

Instead, money is pumped into educating the boys. Even the African educational structure is biased against females. Admissions priority is given to men. As a result, information flow is poor.

When one marries, one is expected to reproduce. Yet lack of knowledge about pre- and post-natal care leads to high infant mortality. About 70 percent of African babies die before they reach the age of five. They are afflicted with diseases such as diptheria, tetanus, measles, whooping cough, and polio; a high percentage die from de-hydration. Most African governments are doing their best to eradicate these problems through immunization and education.

Agriculture is the economic backbone of most of the continent, and about 70 percent of the labor force is supplied by African women, directly or indirectly. In order to recruit more farm hands, some men marry as many women as possible. Women have to work hard to feed their families; and they dare not complain to their husbands. They are obligated to accept their position without question.

In the political sphere, Ugandan women can boast of twenty army officers, nine ministers, and thirty-eight parliamentarians. This is encouraging, yet the home lives of these women remain difficult, since there they are considered third-class citizens, after their husbands and children. The woman's position is maintained by tribal super-stitions and taboos.

I once overheard a traditional female say, "She is old enough to make you a grandparent. Why not give her to someone and get some money to look after the boys?"

Is that fair? That is what we face. Yet without education, how can one see reality and wipe out dogma? We must embark upon vast programs of education to enlighten Africans about the way taboos and superstitions hamper progress and development in society in general and in the lives of African women in particular.

19

Shhh! Who Is Talking about Sex?

Franz Vanderpuye

Curiosity, it is often said, makes a child. The increasing number of teenage mothers in Ghana show this adage to be true, for these young mothers play a game they barely understand.

Esi Kom, fifteen, is suddenly taken ill and the doctor realizes she is pregnant. She is transformed into a bundle of fears as she analyzes the consequences of her pregnancy. Can she survive it? What of the prospective father, Kofi Mensah, a Junior Secondary School Form Two student; will he accept the responsibility? Her greatest fear is her parents who have warned her against becoming pregnant. She thinks of abortion, but at what risk? This is common with the youth of today. Teenagers between thirteen and fifteen years swell the number of these young parents.

In rural Ghana, a happy family was one with many children and perhaps lots of cows, too. But while an abundance of children may give a family high status, it has also overstretched the community's and, indeed, the nation's resources to a point where most of the children are malnourished.

Perhaps, population issues rank second only to the debt crises in Africa. In Ghana, it has assumed a high priority in the nation's development programs. When Ghana came out with a population policy in 1969—the second on the continent after Kenya—she had a high ambition of using population control as a variable in arresting the rapid rate at which the economy was deteriorating. Twenty years after that ambitious dream, the policy is yet to show any sign of bearing fruit. If anything, the results have been negative. The population growth rate has increased from 1 percent to 3.6 percent within the intervening decades.

One basic factor contributing to this problem is inadequate information on sex education. Admittedly, population issues have been discussed and appreciated in many quarters. However, what was done only reached the adults who already have had children or are about to stop having more children. But what about those who are yet to have children?

Many young people, regardless of educational level or social class, find themselves caught between silence of parents and teachers, and the often distorted information they get from their peers and the mass media. In most cases, any discussions about sex among children would draw a harsh response: "Shhh! Who's talking about sex?"

Until recently, when foreign cultures penetrated the Ghanaian indigenous cultural heritage, young unmarried girls, to a large extent, led a chaste life. Puberty rites were one mechanism for controlling adolescent fertility. It was a taboo to become pregnant prior to this rite, and the punishment for infringement was harsh and uncompromising.

With modernization, all these came to a halt, for better or for worse. Puberty rites are no longer widely performed. The whole practice was surrounded by considerable superstition. The clash of cultures might have exposed this limitation. Furthermore, it has become ineffective as a result of modern societies' permissiveness. But what is the alternative?

Every child must understand as well as he or she can, the functions by which the race produces itself and by which the family comes into existence and is held together as a unit. How this information is correctly and decently transmitted to the younger generation is a problem of the utmost consequence to the success of the family and the nation.

In the Ghanaian society, the above ideals and purposes of sex education have sparked various results, since this is rather alien to the African mentality which openly shuns and avoids the use of the word "sex" in public.

People are upset when they see a textbook with diagrams that are related to sex. I remember from my elementary school days, when one particular teacher used to say that we should not cut certain plants because the "juice" from these plants could make us blind when in contact with the eyes, we would hide behind each other and laugh, because we thought the word "juice" was filthy: "juice" was discharged from either the male or female sex organ. What a shame!

Then in the secondary school, we would always shout "shiee" whenever the topic in biology class was on reproductive system. It was not our fault.

Many mothers will not provide sex education to their children, because they would say it would be for their children's own good. They would argue that in their time these were taboos, and it would upset their children. There are many mothers who are horrified to hear of sex education and would curse whoever would try to teach it to their sons and daughters.

Within the past few years, the government has been contemplating the introduction of sex education or family education into the school curricula. However, it has been very cautious of this move, fearing reaction from a society dominated by conservative religionists.

There are two schools of thought about the issue. Some believe that the incorporation of family life education in the school curriculum is crucial to solving the teenage pregnancy problem, and others believe that family planning services and counseling should be made available to teenagers.

Sex education is particularly concerned with the development of good mental health and an adjustment to life and adulthood. It is aimed at helping the individual play a valuable role as a contributing citizen in a family situation. Such education must be concerned with the physical development as well as emotional, social, moral, and intellectual aspects.

For the various reasons enumerated—illegitimate births, divorce rates, venereal diseases, maladjustment, immature pregnancies, child curiosity, and increased difference of opinion on matters of sex conduct—there is a need for sex education. However, due to the African concept of sex, the integration of sex topics in other courses that lend themselves to it helps to deemphasize sex education. Students are, therefore, able to study such topics with less embarrassment. Nonsegregation of classes, with both boys and girls, conducted without hesitation, mystery, or subterfuge lend themselves to the best teaching-learning situation.

Courses should include problems that might be of concern to young adults such as petting, masturbation, premarital relations, and abortion. It should be the responsibility both of the schools and home. Since religion has a strong hold on society, churches and mosques should also play a practical role in this educative process.

Most parents are at a loss when it comes to discussing the process of reproduction with their teenage sons and daughters. Parents should cultivate the friendship of their children and forge a close relationship that inspires confidence. The whole subject of sex education should be demystified, otherwise the whole concept of population control will be a joke.

20

Toward a Diagnosis of the Politics of the Western God

Nkeonye Otakpor

I

I do not intend to present arguments for or against the existence of a God. Nor am I interested in the meaning of a God. The meaning of a God and the arguments for or against God's existence, to be seriously intended, must be culturally based. Hence for Joseph Omoregbe, "whether we believe or not that God exists depends on what we mean by God."[1] What we mean by God is intrinsically a question that is culturally determined. This explains why different cultures have different conceptions of a God. It is thus possible, indeed factual, to speak in terms of a plurality of gods just as there is a plurality of cultures and traditions. Thus there is Allah of Islam; Brahman of Hinduism; Tao of Taoism; Yahweh of the Jews; Chiukwu of the Igbo; Olorun of the Yoruba; Leve of the Mende; Juok of the Shilluk; Nzambe of the Bakongo; and God of the Western man. By Western God I mean the God of the Judeo-Christian tradition, hereafter referred to simply as the Western God. This paper is all about the politics of this Western God. The all-important, all-encompassing thesis is that the politics of this God has not only grossly undermined but indeed jeopardized our human otherness. The result is that "the potentialities inherent in the station of man, the full measure of his destiny on earth, the innate excellence of his reality"[2] have all been equally subjected to the politics of this God, to the detriment of the entire human family.

II

Because of different cultural orientations it is clearly evident that CHI-UKWU (God) in Igbo for example is not the same as that in Western tradition. It is equally not the same with the Arabic traditional conception. With regard to the Western conception, the differences with Igbo (and other cultures) are legion. I mention just a few, but first it is important to note that the dogma (or should I say the ideology) of original sin, of heaven and hell, of Adam and Eve, of the mysterious impregnation of Mary, of Limbo and purgatory, of the mystery of the Holy Trinity, etc., are totally absent from conceptions of God in Igbo. CHI-UKWU, for instance, was never born and never died, is not known to have human parents, brothers or sisters. The humanized God of Western Christian theology is thus totally alien to Igbo and African thought. It is totally inconceivable. Rather, the Western God is a selfish, colonial God.

The humanized God of Western tradition led inevitably to Nietzsche's proclamation of that God's death, a death that for the West provided the essential conditions for human liberation and freedom. Most significantly, the death of this God has had severe consequences for the West: the divinization of Western man, which has primarily a political end-state, that is, the domination of non-Western people around the world. "The project of modernity," according to James Bernauer, "was a divinization of man, the passion to be. Although Descartes' roots in scholastic thought and vocabulary enabled him to avoid drawing the implications of his meditations, the discovery of the *cogito* was actually the transference to man of God's function in medieval metaphysics as source of the world's reality and intelligibility."[3] On this basis Hiram Caton suggests that "I think was to become the divine I am."[4] After Kant and Hegel had done with the transference and Nietzsche had completed the demolition exercise by declaring the death of God to be a Western cultural fact, Bernauer believes that "it was Foucault who saw that the death of

God necessarily entailed the death of the figure who had taken on his role as the absolute."[5] Bernauer may be correct with his assessment but with this difference: that while the Western God *is supposed* to have died for all men, the Western man is metaphorically dying mainly because of his sins of exploitation, domination, and destruction of non-Western peoples. In being humanized, the Western God died. In being divinized, in playing God to other peoples and cultures, dissolving them, ceaselessly unmaking them, making it impossible for such people to create and recreate their positivity, the death of Western man is chronicled. So, parallel to the death of Western God is the divinization and death of Western man; one died for the supposed sins of all men, the other dying mainly because of indulgence in self-abnegation that results from the wanton but conscious destruction of his otherness.

The divinization of Western man provided as well as nurtured the necessary, sufficient, and essential conditions for the development of ideas and attitudes that enabled him to view himself as the master of the world. With the death of his God, the new God of the universe became Western man. Simply put, the divinization of Western man gave birth to his predatory ideology. The period of colonial adventures, of gunboat diplomacy, of the subjugation of non-Western peoples and their cultures, of slave trade and Nazism are lucid examples. In a nutshell, the death of the Western God presaged the culture of domination, exploitation, subjugation, and destruction of non-Western peoples and cultures on the grounds that Western man is not only superior but divine. In other words, the divinization of Western man is the medium for the full-scale unjustified exploitation and domination of non-Western peoples and cultures.

With domination, as Murray Bookchin argues, "there is a general condition of command and obedience, of unfreedom and humiliation, and most decisively, an abortion of each individual's (people's) potentiality for consciousness, reason, selfhood, creativity, and the right to assert full control over his or her (their) daily life."[6] The religion of Western man, derived from and founded on a dead God, is not an accidental correlate of Western colonialism, exploitation, domination, and the rape of other traditions and cultures regarded as primitive by them. Jomo Kenyatta, late president of Kenya, poignantly made this point when he argued that when the British colonial administrators came they brought the Bible. They taught Kenyans to pray with their eyes closed. Kenyans did so but when they opened their eyes, the British administrators left the Bible for them but had taken their land and everything. This statement is true not only of the Kenyan situation; it was a pattern replicated in all known colonial territories whether British, French, Belgian, or Italian.

It is surely necessary to get straight with the grammar and politics of God talk in Western culture and thereby avoid some sort of myopia and radical misconception. Thus God—dead or reincarnated—is selfish. The faithful, it is said, should worship this God only. It is the one and only God and allows worship to no other God or gods. According to St. Matthew (4:1–11), "you must worship the Lord your God and serve Him alone." And in Isaiah (45:21, 22) it is said that "there is no God else beside me, there is none beside me, for I am God, and there is none else." In effect, the Western God is a one-dimensional God. And this has led to the one-dimensional conception of the world, religion, culture, history, art, music, philosophy, technology, and the fabrication of man on the part of Western society. The selfish, predatory, and paternalistic bearing of Western man is, thus, a replica of his selfish God. The elaborate arsenal of exploitative and dominating techniques which has characterized the Western mind since its contact with the rest of the world, particularly Africans, Asians, and Latin Americans, is a clear manifestation of this selfishness. It is not surprising that these techniques are still in vogue and intact judging from the activities of the International Monetary Fund (IMF) and the World Bank. The so-called conditionalities of the IMF in particular are overtly intended to ensure the continuance of Western exploitation, domination, and prosperity, while for the recipient countries (e.g., Brazil and Nigeria) it ensures a socioeconomic death trap. These conditionalities are enunciated not as mechanisms intended to ensure the survival and flourishing of other economies. They are not even intended to promote the good life of non-Western peoples but rather to guarantee that these non-Western economies remain totally dependent just as their peoples have become dependent with dependent cultures, legal and political systems, art, music, educational systems, and so on.

III

In light of this persistent trend, Peter Singer's argument that "if it is in our (Western) power to prevent something bad from happening, without thereby sacrificing anything of comparable moral significance, we ought to do it,"[7] appears hollow if not totally in bad faith. The West cannot prevent something bad from happening without sacrificing anything of comparable importance. But such a sacrifice would be suicidal for the West, something close to self-immolation which is understandably inconceivable on their part. Their objection to the new world information and communication order is, in principle, an objection against sacrificing anything of comparable moral significance. Their acceptance of this new information order would mean giving up their long stranglehold on world information, which in the long-run would prevent Reuters, BBC, VOA, AFP, etc., from "doctoring" news about non-Western peoples and cultures to suit Western whims and caprices. In effect the acceptance of this new information order would mean the self-destruction of some important pillars of the Western ideological foundation, particularly its power base. "Communication can be an instrument of power, a revolutionary weapon, a commercial product, or a means of education; it can serve the ends of either liberation or of oppression, of either the growth of the individual or of drilling human beings into uniformity. Each society must choose the best way to approach the task facing all of us and to find the means to overcome the material, social, and political constraints that impede progress."[8] For very obvious reasons, the West would prefer oppression to liberation, illiteracy to education.

To prevent information from becoming a revolutionary weapon in the hands of others, a tool for "overcoming the material, social, and political constraints that impede progress," the West has to choose for the rest of the world. The acceptance of a new world information and communication order is, to this extent, inimical to Western interests, and the West's objection is obviously in keeping with the gravamen of its position. The acceptance of this order, in large measure, amounts to self-destruction. The West cannot self-destruct; therefore, there can be no new world information and communication order. Just as the equal consideration of all interests has no meaning to their God, so it has neither relevance nor meaning to them in terms of the survival of humankind and world order, except of course by some perverse, deviant logic: by humankind and world order is meant Western European kind and its order.

In the same way that their God appropriated death, which ontologically, biologically, and logically belongs to human beings, so has Western man self-appropriated the world, its knowledge, and its truth. Hence today, the world reduces to Western World; God reduces only to Western God; knowledge reduces to Western knowledge; information to Western information; facts to Western facts; truths to Western truths, while other forms of knowledge, truth, and cognition are regarded as primitive.

It is no accident that the West has gone further to categorize the world into three parts: the first, which of course is theirs; the second belongs to their siblings no matter where their location in the world, while the third has been reserved mainly for marginalized Africans, Asians, and Latin Americans. Parallel to the categorization of the world is the segmentation of the human race with the "white race" at the apex of the ladder. Instead of *one* world with *one* human race, there are now *three* worlds inhabited by different human races; and this segmenting has obviously been intended as a convenient vehicle for racial segregation.

Jesus Christ, son of their God, and a God in his own right,[9] was said to have been born in Bethlehem, not in Rome, London, Paris, Hamburg, or in any part of Africa. He was Jewish, not French, German, British, Italian, or African. Jesus taught a new religion to his people, not to the Romans, the Africans, the British, the French, or to the world per se. "Call his name Jesus for he shall save his people from their sins" (Matthew 1:21–23). So in the beginning was a religion indigenous to the Jews but appropriated by the Romans on the grounds that Rome was then an empire, the center of world culture and civilization. But the Egyptian culture and civilization, which flourished before that of the Romans and the Greek city-states, was not regarded as a world civilization; nor was Egypt regarded as the center of world culture.

The Egyptian pyramids are excellent reminders of this civilization. The Ife, Benin, Nok, and Igbo-Ukwu cultures in Nigeria are as old as that of the Romans, yet none of these were ever regarded as world civilizations. There has also been no such reference to Indian and Chinese cultures and civilizations in spite of their long histories.

With the appropriation of the Jewish religion fully accomplished, followed by the bloody but successful evangelization of Europe, Rome felt encouraged to embark on an unsolicited mission to evangelize and colonize the world. In the name of a dead God, Rome gave both blessing and sanctuary to the early Portuguese and Spanish missionary slave traders to appropriate, evangelize, and colonize the world. The papal bull of demarcation of 1496, for example, divided the world into two: one for the Spanish and the other for the Portuguese. The bloody wars of evangelism presaged the bloody wars of exploitation and domination epitomized in the slave raids on African coastal areas and in the hinterland; the wars against innocent and defenseless Aztecs; the Zulu wars; the extirpation of American Indians; the extirpation of Aboriginals of Australia; the Korean and Vietnamese wars; and the bitter experience of the Tainos and Ciboneys (the aboriginal Cubans) in the hands of Diego Columbus and his men, all Spaniards. These original Cubans were extirpated by Spaniards in search of gold.

The apartheid system in South Africa is a poignant reminder that the long bloody evangelism and wars for colonial conquest, domination, and exploitation are far from over. It is instructive that South Africans of European extraction quote elaborately and profusely from their holy book in support of their apartheid system: a system that divinizes and thus de-Homos* the white man while systematically and methodically degrading and dehumanizing others.

There is hardly any doubt that these myopic and selfishly motivated conceptions and practices function exclusively to help maintain and lubricate the existing Western socioeconomic interests and order. Unfortunately, Foucault's admonition that the West should embrace the "refusal of this kind of individualism (and selfishness) which has been imposed on us (them) for several centuries, and to acknowledge the need to sacrifice the identity of the man it had come to know and trust"[10] has largely been ignored. By ignoring Foucault, the West has also largely ignored "the need for dialogue with the human otherness and the possibility of worthwhile encounter with the other in whose image we may yet see ourselves."[11] Just as individualism and selfishness are primordial human traits, so association and otherness are the complements. The human condition ought to reflect both aspects constituting the ineluctable components of our

---

*I.e., takes away the humanity of—Ed.

one world and *one* identity. Science shows identical human elements as the foundation of human life. "The recognition of the oneness of mankind calls for no less than the reconstruction of the whole world, a world organically unified in all the essential aspects of its life, its spiritual and material aspiration, its original script and language, and yet infinite in the diversity of the national characteristics of its federal units."[12]

IV

Parallel to the acceptance of one Western God is also the acceptance of one religious system, one marriage system, one philosophical system, one system of governance and political economy, and one model of reality as constructed from Western European prisms. The distrust of the West in many parts of the world, especially among the so-called ex-colonial subjects, is therefore not without justification. Many of these non-Europeans are afraid that Western fact, knowledge, and models of reality besmirch and depress, that they tear things apart rather than integrate them, thereby killing instead of creating. The West killed in non-Western parts of the world in order to create in Europe. Their slave traders killed and depopulated the African continent in order to create the wealth of modern Europe.[13]

These models of men and reality are reflected in the various philosophical systems built in Europe and said to have begun with the Greeks, for whom non-Greeks were regarded as barbarians and thus subjected to slavery. Aristotle, for example, stoutly defended the institution of slavery on these grounds. Russell was merely following this centuries-old tradition when he argued that "ever since men became capable of free speculation, their actions, in innumerable important respects, have depended upon their theories as to the world and human life, as to what is good and what is evil. This is as true in the present day as at any former time. To understand an age or a nation, we must understand its philosophy."[14] What was Russell's concern? It was not with the history of African or Asian philosophy. Indeed, it is about Western philosophy, but Western philosophy is not, cannot be, the philosophy of the entire human family. Likewise there is the argument, without empirical or rational evidence, that Western philosophy provides answers or attempts to provide answers to all human inquiries about the meaning of things or what the world is all about. So just as the Western (dead) God is the only God, Western philosophy, inspired by the religion derived from this God, is the only philosophy. Every other philosophical system, to the extent that it does not embrace Western concepts and methods, is primitive and perhaps developing. There is even talk to-day of a developing philosophy, a developing language, politics, economics, law, culture, music, art, and so on, just as there are developing nations and peoples. Since God and man, both by definition and inference, can only mean what is conceived by the West, every other conception follows as a logical consequence.

It is no doubt a conscious design that modern culture refers only to Western personality, fad, and fashion. The spirit of the Western God and its religion is the spirit of Western capitalism.[15] The spirit of Western capitalism is in itself the hallmark of Western personality. It is the spirit of an irreligious exploitation of nature, as well as other cultures and peoples: it regards and treats both as a treasurehouse for Western man, who will create the materialistic ideal on earth and the supermaterialistic ideal in heaven for other peoples. Western man lives in conflict and contradiction, which are the byproducts of their philosophical experience. It is these contradictions and conflicts that Africans, for example, inherited from the economic, political, and religious institutions of the West, and found them compounded by their own inherent African systems: the aggressiveness of the West overwhelmed the less aggressive African experience. Western philosophy is radical in terms of being inherently aggressive because it seeks an ideal here on earth while persuading and coercing other people that their ideal is in a heaven which was constructed and fashioned mainly for this purpose. This aggression is fully expressed in, for example, Machiavelli's *Prince*, where power is for those who have the skill and art to seize and use it. It is also found in Mill's *Utilitarianism*, expressed as the principle of the greatest happiness here on earth.

This aggression to achieve the ideal at the expense of significant others pervades the educational, legal, religious, economic, and political systems of the West. All this has been made possible because by ensuring his own death, the Western God also ensured that the vacuum thus created by His departure is occupied by His chosen one— Western man. The gain, quite apart from material things, is the idolization of an ephemeral self. This has reduced the self to an ontological level at which self-consciousness has become utterly meaningless because the self is no longer able to transcend the material, the mundane, and the less sublime in human affairs. What is demanded and required is neither sympathy nor restitution (expressed in material support-aids), but rather the promotion, preservation, and conservation of variety and pluralism because world progress must be measured and assessed by the degree of differentiation within the world order. But this modest goal is perhaps unachievable at the moment because the West needs the rest of the world to promote as well as sustain its selfishness and supremacy. It needs the rest of the world to ensure its hegemonic position as an insurance against poverty. It needs the rest of the world to serve as a huge toxic waste dump, as a source of raw materials for its industries, and as a market for its finished products. The West needs the rest of the world as a test-ground for its weapons. It needs the rest of the world as an unsuspecting market to dump its expired drugs.

On the other hand, the rest of the world needs the West as an essential complement of its otherness. The difference is profound and exceedingly clear. Humanity today neither wishes nor intends to be the forum in which nations and peoples settle their angry disputes, but a rather commonwealth of different groups joined to achieve respect, decent living conditions, and prosperity for all. This is neither idealistic nor utopian to the extent that humanity in the Northern Hemisphere has already achieved these, though at the expense of the rest of the human family.

The conservation effort is doomed to failure before the initial steps are taken unless there is empathy and dialogue, not merely discussion. According to O. F. Bollnow, "there are two preconditions for the success of this dialogue. The first is that one recognizes the other person as having fundamentally an equal right; and that signifies that the individual who begins a dialogue has to be ready to learn something, that he has to include the possibility that perhaps the other individual might be right."[16] The present inability to listen to the other, to learn from the other, can be remedied if and only if there is the readiness to get away from the self-evident assurance of conceptions that have been nurtured by prejudice. This readiness on the part of Western man is extraordinarily difficult. But the acceptance of dialogue is essential because its success can lead to a new management system of human affairs. On this Bookchin has emphasized that "the World and its future have to be managed, but this management would not be like a game of chess but more like steering a boat."[17] However, in steering this boat, if we use the methods, principles, precepts, etc., of the West to answer all-important questions concerning the human predicament, we can expect answers only within the realm of Western ideology, Western experience, and Western processes. If we sincerely wish to comprehend the whole of reality, of humanity per se, of the phenomena of life as a whole, the only course left to us is to integrate the numerous separate answers obtained by the various cultures and traditions. Each human group makes its own contribution toward the overall image of humanity; none is indispensable and all should continually be sharing, caring, and progressing together.

V

What then is the basic, fundamental difference between the CHI-UKWU of Igbo, the Brahman of Hinduism, the Tao of Taoism, and the Western God; between the politics of CHI-UKWU, Brahma, Olodumare, Tao, and the politics of the Western God? It is that these non-Western gods were never born and therefore never died. For example, CHI-UKWU in the Igbo tradition cannot die because it has no beginning. It is blasphemy to talk of CHI-UKWU's birth or death, because only something having animate form can be subjected to the biological process of death. Only animate things are primarily and ontologically subject to the biological process of coming to be and passing away. So while the proclamation of a humanized dead God is a cultural fact for the West that calls for annual celebration, it is a cultural aberration for the Igbo and indeed for many African and non-Western peoples. And unlike the divinization of Western man, which is primarily political, the deification of man in Igbo and in other African cultures through ancestor worship is both religious and social—not political.

An African God, whether of the Mende, Shilluk, Bakongo, Igbo, Yoruba, or Kasai, is neither one-dimensional nor selfish. No African God is worshiped alone nor is there any injunction that Africans should worship only that which is recognized as God. Indeed, while recognizing African Gods in their individual cultures as the ultimate *ONE*, Africans worship a plurality of spirits that are not on the same pedestal with whatever is taken as a God in the different traditions.

The inherent pluralism in African lifestyles, the emphasis on the community rather than the atomized self, etc., are indices of the African abiding faith in the worthwhile coexistence of the *ONE* and the *MANY*. And just as the belief in the worship of the spirits does not amount to a radical displacement of any African God or the diminution of its status, power, authority, importance, and responsibility, so the emphasis on a community lifestyle is not destructive to the individual African irrespective of tribal peculiarities and nuances.

To the extent that no African God is a predatory being, none of them permitted or sanctioned (overtly or covertly) colonialism, imperialism, and apartheid. CHI-UKWU (God) of the Igbo, for example, never encouraged the destruction, pillaging, and despoilation of other peoples and their cultures. It does not require that non-Igbos self-abnegate in order to worship. It does not require that in order to worship, non-Igbos become Igbo in their thinking, dressing, and names. Simply put, CHI-UKWU does not require any radical psychological transformation of an individual in order to worship. It is against this background that the openness and inherent liberalism in Igbo society in particular can best be appreciated and understood. In other words, the radical amputation, fragmentation, and destruction of our otherness is not part of CHI-UKWU's design in the Igbo worldview. It is equally not in Brahman's design, or Olodumare's design, or Tao's design, or Leve's design, or Nzambe's design for their respective peoples. To dismiss these important differences is to ignore the evidence out of misplaced devotion to a foreign and dead God. The invidiousness and ambiguity in the paradigm of the Western God can only provide facile images of liberation and freedom for the faithful.

The survival of humankind cannot rest on these facile images because a complacent and prosperous Western minority has something important and serious to learn from an "unworldly" vein in the ethos of the peasantry in Nigeria, Brazil, Angola, Burma, India, etc. In the final analysis the inspiring words of historian Arnold Toynbee deserve some moments of reflection: "Western man had brought himself into danger of losing his soul (by being Homo-Di-

vine, playing the Absolute) through his concentration on a sensa-
tionally successful endeavor to increase his material well-being. If he
has to find salvation (liberation, freedom, and authentic-true peace)
he would find it only in sharing the results of his material achievement with the less materially successful majority of the human race.
What part the world's (other) historic higher religions (cultures, philosophies, etc.) might be destined to play in enlightening both parties (but particularly the West) is a question that cannot be answered
yet."[18]

NOTES

1. Joseph I. Omoregbe, "What is God? A Critical Inquiry," *The Nigerian Journal of Philosophy* 3, no. 1 (1983): 1.

2. Bahai Movement, *The Promise of World Peace* (Haifa, Israel: Bahai
World Centre, 1985), p. 20.

3. James Bernauer, "The Prisons of Man: An Introduction to Foucault's Negative Theology," *International Philosophical Quarterly* 27, no.
4 (December 1987): 376.

4. Hiram Caton, "Towards a Diagnosis of Progress," *Independent
Journal of Philosophy* 4 (1983): 11.

5. Bernauer, "The Prisons of Man," p. 376.

6. Murray Bookchin, *Toward an Ecological Society* (Montreal: Black
Rose, 1980), p. 15.

7. Peter Singer, *Practical Ethics* (Cambridge, England: University Press,
1979), p. 168.

8. See International Commission for the Study of Communication
Problems, a UNESCO Project.

9. Catholic Christian theology says that there are three persons in
one God: the father, the son, and the holy ghost.

10. Hubert Dreyfus and Paul Rabinow, eds., *Michel Foucault: Beyond
Structuralism and Hermeneutics* (Chicago: University Press, 1982), p. 222.

11. Bernauer, "The Prisons of Man," p. 380.

12. Bahai Movement, *The Promise of World Peace*, p. 14.

13. Walter Rodney, *How Europe Underdeveloped Africa* (Washington, D.C.: Howard University Press, 1982).

14. B. Russell, *History of Western Philosophy* (London: Allen and Unwin Ltd., 1961).

15. For more details see Max Weber, *The Protestant Ethic and the
Spirit of Capitalism* (New York: Charles Scribners and Sons, 1958).

16. O., F. Bollnow, "The Importance of Dialogue Today: Philosophical Aspects," *Universitas* 30, no. 1 (1988): 15.

17. Murray Bookchin, *Post-Scarcity Anarchism* (Montreal: Black Rose, 1986), p. 71.

18. Arnold Toynbee, *A Study of History*, vol. 2. (London: Oxford University Press, 1978), pp. 378–69.

Part Four

Interviews

Conducted by Norm R. Allen, Jr.

21

Norman Hill: Human Rights Activist

ALLEN: How can humanism benefit the African-American community?

HILL: I think because of the historic and current experiences of African-Americans, having been the victims of and still confronting irrationality in the form of discrimination, prejudice, and racism, an approach to dealing with human beings and the human personality that focuses on rationality, science, and thought can be of direct relevance and benefit to African-Americans.

ALLEN: Because of the emphasis humanists put on critical thinking, do you believe that humanism can be instrumental in attracting more African-Americans to professional fields requiring science and mathematics?

HILL: I would hope so, and I believe that is possible. With increasing emphasis on skill and education to hold and maintain a job and to participate effectively in the world of work, mathematics and science will become increasingly important in the kinds of education that African-Americans seek. These subjects will be relevant to their future, they will be relevant and meaningful to the world of work, and they will be relevant to what is needed to make a better society. Therefore, I think that to the degree this is understood—that is, through humanistic approaches focused toward African-American youth—more African-American youth will be attracted to fields requiring science and mathematics.

ALLEN: What role has humanism assumed in the labor movement and the civil rights movement?

HILL: In the trade union movement, the major aim and focus is not just better wages, hours, and working conditions, but to provide a vehicle whereby workers themselves, through and with their chosen leaders, can gain dignity and respect from a job, and can be recognized as human beings who contribute to the productive process and therefore need to have a fair return for their labor. This requires a rational approach, a scientific approach, and a humanistic approach.

Humanism and its approach have been relevant to the gains that the trade movement has made and the gains that the workers have made through unionization.

In the area of civil rights, which has been about trying to create a more humane society and trying to make sure that all human beings, regardless of race, ethnicity, religion, and sex, are treated fairly and equally, the humanistic approach has been very important. Rationality, critical thinking, and scientific thought have been directly relevant to the struggle for civil rights and racial equality.

ALLEN: Please discuss briefly A. Philip Randolph and his work with the black Pullman porters.

HILL: We are celebrating this year (1989) what would have been the 100th birthday of A. Philip Randolph, who was this nation's outstanding black labor leader, and a fighter for civil rights for over sixty years. In 1937, after a twelve-year struggle, he and a small group of courageous African-American working men made trade union, American, and African-American history when they became the first union with black leadership to gain recognition from a major company—the Pullman (railroad car) company—as a union. Randolph, in so doing, was practicing very much a humanistic approach in his struggle to become a labor leader—a labor leader not just of black working men, but of all working men. By approaching the civil rights struggle in terms of involving people who had directly experienced discrimination, mistreatment, and oppression, and in fighting to change those conditions, Randolph was involving masses of human beings in rationalistic behavior. This culminated in 1963—the height of the civil rights campaign—when he initiated the march on Washington for jobs and freedom. There were from a quarter of a million to 400,000 people, depending upon whose estimates you believe. They

came to Washington, D.C.—both whites and African-Americans—
to march for civil rights, racial equality, and economic justice. This
led to the passage of the most comprehensive civil rights law that
the country has ever known—the Civil Rights Act of 1964. So Randolph *practiced* humanism, both as a trade union leader and as a
civil rights activist.

ALLEN: Is it true that Randolph raised most of his money from
clam bakes in Harlem, and that he never accepted money from white
organizations, and if so, what were his reasons for doing so?

HILL: It is true that Randolph, believing that the people who were
struggling or who were experiencing problems should be involved
in maintaining and carrying on their own struggle, encouraged African-
American porters, the wives, and the women and men who supported
the Brotherhood of Sleeping Car Porters, to put on clam bakes, rent
parties, and fundraisers of various kinds to keep the union headquarters
open, and to enable Randolph to travel, to help organize the Sleeping
Car Porters, and to do other things to help maintain the union.

But it is not true that these were the only sources of money
or support for Randolph and his campaigns, including his struggle
to maintain the union. He did receive grants from foundations and
other sympathetic individuals to help maintain the Brotherhood of
Sleeping Car Porters.

ALLEN: Do you believe that religion and humanism are necessarily
antagonistic, or can they be compatible?

HILL: To the degree that the principles and values of the religion(s)
of a socially conscious people and leadership are encouraged in terms
of making life better right here and now, there is some compatibility.
To the degree that the human personality is encouraged and to the
degree that human relationships are developed, there is some compatibility between the two. I think that that is what must be emphasized
between humanists and those who are carrying forward what they
believe to be religious values.

ALLEN: Are there any closing comments that you would like to
make?

HILL: I think that recent developments, particularly regarding the
overthrowing of totalitarian or dictatorial regimes in Eastern Europe—

East Germany, Hungary, Czechoslovakia, and now Romania—are an indication of the independence upon which humanism is based. We are witnessing a belief in the worth of human beings, the importance of the human personality, and in rationality.

The virtues of democracy are in fact being undergirded by the forces of humanism among the Eastern Europeans, who have fought themselves—in their own way—for the kind of society in which they could practice freedom of thought, freedom of speech, and the basic civil libertarian values that are consistent with humanism. The humanistic approach is becoming increasingly relevant to struggles for freedom throughout the world.

ALLEN: On that note, I would like to add a final question. According to the U.S. Justice Department and various watchdog organizations, incidences of "racial violence" have increased dramatically throughout the United States. What role can humanism play in increasing tolerance and eliminating this kind of violence?

HILL: One of the reasons that I think there has been an increase in the kind of racially based violent incidents to which you refer, has been that we have had—unfortunately—in recent times, a political leadership that has not approached social change among various human beings from the basic tenets of humanism. We must encourage people to engage in political action, based not on their prejudices, passing emotions, or fears, but on that which is in their general interest as human beings. As a result, people will be more inclined to elect politicians who carry forth policies that are consistent with the basic tenets of humanism.

We must also educate people to put forth programs that will speak to their genuine needs. This will encourage respect for all human beings—no matter who they are. It will also lead to a reduction in the kinds of racially based incidents of violence that we have recently seen.

22

Black Athena:
An Interview with Martin G. Bernal

THE AFROASIATIC ROOTS OF CLASSICAL CIVILIZATION

ALLEN: Who were the Greeks, culturally and physiologically?

BERNAL: Physiologically they were and are Mediterranean, which is a thoroughly mixed population—southern European, western Asian, and African. But certainly they were closer to North Africans than they were to northern Europeans in their appearance, so the Aryan image of the Greeks that we've had since the nineteenth century is particularly misleading.

Culturally the Greeks were influenced a great deal by Egypt and the Near East. I'm not trying to challenge the centrality of Greece to the European tradition, but I do challenge the nature of Greece itself. Greek culture is so exciting because it represents a mix of the native Balkan–Indo-European-speaking population with Egyptian and western Semitic populations. The linguistic and cultural mix was extraordinarily productive in cultural terms.

ALLEN: Was the Aryan model ever supported by the ancient Greeks?

BERNAL: No. There is no evidence for the Aryan model in antiquity. The one thing that could possibly be of use to this hypothesis is

From *Free Inquiry* 10, no. 2 (Spring 1990): 18–22. Reprinted by permission of the publisher.

the so-called invasion of the Dorians, but these people came from within Greece—also they came *after* the Trojan War. Therefore we cannot say that the Dorians were *the* Indo-European invaders, because they couldn't have been the first invaders. If they were the first invaders then Achilles and the other Homeric heroes were non-Indo-Europeans, because they came before the Dorian invasion. So there is no ancient authority for the Aryan model.

ALLEN: Is the type of mixed civilization you mention more beneficial than one that is more homogeneous?

BERNAL: Certainly. Comparison and contrast are intellectually and artistically stimulating, so it's more likely that mixed civilizations will be more creative. Even when homogeneous, isolated populations produce great literature or art or philosophy, it is most often when the people have had extensive contact with the outside world through travel or trade. For instance, Iceland is a remote island in northwest Europe that is very isolated and homogeneous, yet it has produced great literature. Actually it has simply preserved in isolation the literature of a much earlier, more cosmopolitan period.

ALLEN: Where did the ancient Greek language originate?

BERNAL: There's no doubt that Greek belongs to the same language family that all European, North Indian, and Persian languages belong to, that is, Indo-European. However, it is remarkable how few Indo-European roots there are in Greek. Only about 50 percent of the Greek vocabulary can be explained in terms of other European languages. Until now, scholars have maintained that the remaining 50 percent derived from the population that was there before the Indo-Europeans arrived, which for convenience is called simply "pre-Hellenic." I believe that this construct is unnecessary, and that the Greek language can be traced to Indo-European, Egyptian, and Semitic roots. The language itself is thoroughly mixed, which is one of the reasons it's so rich and so suitable for poetry.

ALLEN: The anthropologist J. A. Rogers says it is easier to prove that the Egyptians were Africans than to prove that the ancient Greeks were Europeans. What do you think of that assessment?

BERNAL: I don't think it's easier, but it's equally easy. Egyptians lived in a part of northern Africa that was connected by the Nile to central Africa; in a way, we could say they were more "African" than were Algerians or Moroccans, who were living beyond the mountains and deserts. And we know that ancient Egyptians belonged to a language family known as Afroasiatic; so linguistically and culturally there is no doubt of Egypt's African origin. Later, of course, Egypt was influenced by West Asia, in particular by Semitic speakers to the north and east.

As I said, Greek is basically an Indo-European language. But also there was a massive Afroasiatic influence on Greek language and on culture as a whole. So to that extent it is less European than Egyptian culture is African.

ALLEN: Various Afrocentric scholars have said that, properly speaking, there is no such thing as Greek philosophy; that is, Greek philosophy is nothing more than Egyptian philosophy. What are your views?

BERNAL: The Greeks admitted that they were philosophically, mathematically, and scientifically indebted to Egypt. Platonic and Socratic thought looks very Egyptian to me, and certainly they acknowledged their respect for Egyptian philosophy and institutions. On the other hand, I don't think we should say that the Greeks didn't add anything to Egyptian philosophy. They lost some things, and they added some. Aristotle and the Sophists, and to some extent the Epicureans, show specifically Greek developments of a philosophical tradition that goes back to Egypt.

ALLEN: Didn't Pythagoras study in Egypt?

BERNAL: He did indeed. Plato also spent time in Egypt. But it's difficult to know whether the later Greeks went to Egypt to gain status or to actually learn. Some certainly did learn. Eudoxus, probably the greatest Greek astronomer and mathematician, studied for more than a year in Egypt, and is reported to have learned the language and translated texts from Egyptian into Greek. Others, I suspect, just went there to get a gloss, to show that they had culture. But there's no doubt that the Pythagorean school shows many traits that are specifically Egyptian.

ALLEN: You maintain that most of the etymologies you studied have no other explanation, and that there are gaps in the structure of the rest of the analysis of Greek. How was this dealt with before your book?

BERNAL: We call everything that is not European or Greek pre-Hellenic, though we don't know exactly what the pre-Hellenic language was. And that's how it was explained, except that about 10 percent of the words were somewhat exotic, and were admitted to be loans, mostly from Semitic. But I argue that 80 percent of the non-European words are in fact Egyptian or Semitic.

ALLEN: So you're saying that it is only recently that this has been denied?

BERNAL: The Egyptian component was denied before ancient Egyptian was known. Some eighteenth-century scholars were able to point out very interesting parallels between Greek and Coptic, the language of Egyptian Christians that was descended from ancient Egyptian. The decipherment of the heiroglyphics wasn't accepted by classicists until the 1850s, by which time it was inconceivable that Egyptians could have had a major influence on the formation of Greek as a language. So no one ever really looked for the Egyptian roots. The Semitic stituation was rather different in that from the seventeenth century onward scholars have seen many parallels between Hebrew and Greek. So in the late nineteenth century there were denials of previously established etymologies. No substitutes, just denials. It was absurd.

ALLEN: If you deny that, what do you put in its place?

BERNAL: Etymological dictionaries of Greece all say "obscure," "unexplained," "unknown," "difficult to find," and so on. You get beautiful descriptions of the words and their forms, and so forth, but when it comes to the subject of the root of the word, then you run into difficulties. And they just can't find any answers.

THE ANCIENT GREEKS AND RELIGION

ALLEN: As secular humanists, we generally look toward Greek roots for our ideals. Your theory has a great impact on how we view the ancient Greeks.

BERNAL: I think that in fact humanism is rooted in the late-Egyptian religious concept that human beings can become "god." The belief that humanity has divinity within itself is essentially Egyptian or

African, and was transmitted to modern Europe through the hermetic texts. These texts drew on Egyptian tradition, are mystical, and place great stress on the divinity of humanity. Some of these texts were known in the West and were referred to by the earliest humanists, but the big wave of neoplatonic thought came about during the 1470s, after a mass of these texts was discovered. They were extraordinarily influential. They influenced magic, for instance, which in a way is related to humanism in that the magician supposedly has the power to control outside forces, rather than praying to those forces. But they also had a more general influence. So though you could say that the atheist tradition can only be traced back to Greek and Latin thinkers, humanism, in the centrality of the "person," is a very Egyptian idea.

ALLEN: How important was religion or spirituality to the Greeks?

BERNAL: I think it was very important. The idea we have of the rational, humanistic, or agnostic Greeks is culled from thousands of texts that mention belief in spells, witches, and so on, throughout Greek society. It's only in the late nineteenth century that we came upon the idea that the Greeks were entirely rational; though the image was there early in the eighteenth century, it was not fully developed. The Greeks were sometimes cynical, sometimes humorous about the gods, but that didn't mean they didn't have belief in or concern for them.

ALLEN: What is the connection between Egyptian and Greek mythology?

BERNAL: The myths are very close indeed. Herodotus, for example, specifies that the names of most of the gods came to Greece from Egypt. Also, I think a lot of myths contain Egyptian puns, particularly when certain words appear that seem incongruous, as is quite often the case. Punning is seen as a deep, mystic connection between entities.

ALLEN: Many religious people have maintained that Greece fell because it abandoned religion. How accurate is this perception?

BERNAL: I don't think there's much truth in it. It's much less true than the argument that Rome fell because it became Christian, which is what St. Augustine inconclusively attempts to answer in *City of God*. The Romans weren't notably more religious than the Greeks.

I think Greece fell because of its lack of unity and its lack of economic resources in comparison to those of the Western Mediterranean and surrounding areas. I don't believe that the relative lack of religion played a part in that.

ALLEN: Nineteenth-century historians claimed that Phoenicia fell for basically the same reason—because it became decadent and ir-religious.

BERNAL: I think it actually fell because it was too close to the land empire of Mesopotamia. The Assyrians, the Babylonians, and others put much pressure on it, which cramped Phoenicia's political and economic opportunities. Greece survived because it was relatively isolated from the near East, where Phoenicia was crushed.

But nineteenth-century historians thought it failed, I think, because they believed the Semitic spirit to be essentially a "feminine," passive one incapable of "hard" achievement or "masculine" activity. The two contributions that the Semitic "race"—they saw the name not in terms of language but of race—had given to the world were religion and poetry. But whereas the Israelites had had a monotheistic religion, the Phoenicians had had the most decadent type of sacrifice. So the Semites were not given the respect accorded the Jews where religion was concerned. Nineteenth-century historians believed the Phoenicians failed because they *deserved* to be crushed completely. A lot of the Nazi images for Jews of the 1930s and 1940s were already being applied to Phoenicians in the 1850s and 1860s. For instance, the idea of the Jew as a disease-carrying rat, as part of a people who moved from place to place without proper roots of their own, infecting, mixing. This whole idea of cleanliness, that everything must be put in its proper place with no intermingling, is essential to racist thought. It's a primary source of racism. This type of thinking made the mer-cantile people seem offensive, and I think that's why the Phoenicians suffered, and the Jews later. And that's why a lot of right-wingers have become pro-Zionist: because this gives the Jews a homeland and a proper romantic role. They have become a proper people at last. That is apart from the notion of Israel as a bastion of Western civilization. So you have this double appeal to the right in regard to Israel.

EGYPTIAN INFLUENCES ON HEBRAIC CULTURE

ALLEN: How indebted were the Hebrews to the Egyptians?

BERNAL: We have to be very careful about the historicity of the Bible. I believe, with a number of other scholars, that the so-called sojourn in Egypt is a folk memory of the Hyksos invasion, in which tribes from the northeast invaded Egypt and held most of it for 100 to 150 years. It's difficult to sort out because the inhabitants of Palestine were in contact with the Egyptians from before 3000 B.C.E. Hebraic culture borrowed heavily from Egypt, but also in reaction to Egypt. The Egyptians, for instance, worshiped graven images, whereas the Semitic speakers tended to worship at rocks and grottos that were unhewn. The Egyptians payed a great deal of attention to the preservation of the body and to mummification; the Semites on the whole were very casual about bodies, burying them as quickly as possible. Egyptians were very concerned about the immortality and the soul, and no doubt the Greeks were influenced by that, whereas the Old Testament pays virtually no attention to immortality. There are contrasts as well as similarities between the two cultures. But the Israelites seem to have seen Egypt as wealthier and more sophisticated, and although they often felt hostile toward the Egyptians, they always respected them.

Interestingly enough, I think the ways in which Hebrew and Phoenician differ from other Semitic languages, such as Arabic, Mesopotamian, or Ethiopian, is in the Egyptian influence they contain. Phonetic simplifications were made that would seem to be the result of high-status Egyptians trying to speak Semitic languages and not managing all of the subtleties of it. I think there was a major and continuing Egyptian influence on Israelite culture.

ALLEN: Many people believe that the Hebraic culture gave birth to monotheism. How accurate is this perception?

BERNAL: It is widely known that the earliest example of monotheism is that of Akhenaton, the Egyptian pharaoh of the fourteenth century B.C.E. And the earliest trace of monotheism in Judaism is really from the eighth century B.C.E. You can see its development in the Bible out of the concept of a tribal or people's god whom the Israelites worshiped, which in no way denied the existence of the gods of other peoples. The idea that their god was a transcendent world god comes much later. I very much doubt that we can go as far as Freud did in his book *Moses and Monotheism,* and say that Moses took monotheism from Akhenaton's reforms in Egypt, but there seems to be no doubt that Egyptian religion had both polytheistic and monotheistic trends, and that Judaism borrowed from it.

Interestingly, many of the ways in which Christianity diverges from Judaism can be specifically attributed to Egyptian influence. The god who dies and is revived three days later is very clear in the Osiris tradition, as is the symbolism of the Eucharist. Iconographically, the representation of the Virgin Mary and the baby Jesus appear to come straight from representations of Isis and her son Horus, and a number of the saints in early Christianity have very clear Egyptian prototypes. Although some of these were Hellenized by the time of the formation of Christianity, I think that the Egyptian component in Christianity is massive and has been systematically underestimated.

ALLEN: Why do you think that has happened? In the early church history did the Neoplatonic philosophers bring it about?

BERNAL: I think that even before the collapse of the Egyptian temple system, a large number of philosophies were growing up. The Neoplatonic, Gnostic, and hermetic philosophies merged with Christianity—particularly the satiric Gnostic texts. One thing that is characteristic of Egyptian religion and not Judaism is the emphasis on knowledge. In Judeo-Christian thought the emphasis is on faith. And the idea of knowledge—which again is humanistic in that human beings attempt to understand and manipulate spiritual and other systems—is very different from the position of subjugation of the worshiper who accepts with blind faith whatever happens. Also, organizationally, monasticism started in Egypt with a church hierarchy, rituals like the shaving of priests' heads and things like that. Egypt provided the model of Western religion and religious institutions and structures.

SCHOLARSHIP AND AFRICAN-AMERICAN HISTORY

ALLEN: Do you believe that the historical role of people of African descent is suppressed by the U.S. educational system?

BERNAL: There's no doubt, but it is not merely the U.S. educational system. The entire European–North American system has systematically suppressed history. This was absolutely necessary in order to maintain slavery and the post-slavery oppression of people of African descent. It dehumanized them; anything that might attribute a high level of civilization to blacks had to be suppressed and continues to be suppressed. I'm not saying this was conscious, but it was inconceivable to white scholars that blacks, whom they "knew" to have been the epitome of savagery and barbarism and to have been rescued from this by slavery, could have been civilized. Therefore, evidence that Egyptians and Africans had been very civilized and had been central to the formation of Greek civilization simply was not recognized.

ALLEN: Do you believe that Afrocentric scholars can be as biased and dogmatic as Eurocentric scholars? What major mistakes have you found in Afrocentric scholarship?

BERNAL: Yes, I do believe that Afrocentric scholars can be as biased and dogmatic as Eurocentric scholars. I'm less worried by it because whites have nearly all the power at the moment, and though I don't care for black racism I don't think that it is a menace to society in the way that white racism is. Some black scholars will say that Socrates was black or that the entire Greek population was black or that Beethoven was black simply because he may have had some "black blood" in him, but I cannot support such contentions. Things have been pushed too far for my taste. However, I think these things are no more extreme and much less pernicious than much of what passes for perfectly normal in everyday "white" scholarship.

ALLEN: Has it been your experience that humanist scholars have been as biased in their research as those who are more religiously inclined?

BERNAL: It depends on the issue. If you're dealing with the biblical period I think humanist scholars have been much more detached and more likely to build accurate models. On the other hand, if you're dealing with the Renaissance or the eighteenth century, humanist scholars often have their own axes to grind and the "cult" of the Renaissance of humanist scholars in the nineteenth century has a very Eurocentric slant to it. I don't think that humanist scholars are immune to all forms of prejudice when dealing with history. I also would not trust the Catholic historian with Catholic history. The glorification of the Renaissance occurs, but no one can be *completely* detached from their own cultural influence.

ALLEN: Will the day ever come when scholars from all countries and backgrounds will consistently work together for an objective analysis of world history, or is this just a blindly idealistic notion?

BERNAL: I don't know if things will ever be perfect, but I think they are probably getting better. There are very interesting things happening in American education as America ceases to be a white society.

ALLEN: Many scholars maintain that they will not publish their findings on black history in white scholarly publications, fearing a loss of tenure, reputation, or credibility, or even the destruction of their careers. Have you experienced this problem?

BERNAL: Definitely. I had immense difficulty getting my book published. In England, it was published by extremely brave editors who decided to go it alone and not submit the manuscript for peer review. When it did quite well in England, a number of presses in the United States were interested in publishing it—but most of them sent it off to "experts" who turned it down. At Rutgers, the editor Ken Arnold has the power to publish two books a year on his own say-so; he decided to use this for *Black Athena* and took it immediately. But certainly there are publication difficulties.

I have every advantage going for me. Not only am I white, male, and middle-aged, but I'm British in America, which afforded me the role of eccentric. I know that if a black scholar were to say what I am saying, people would think that he or she had an ax to grind, and that's partially true—blacks are interested in African history, women are interested in women's history, Jews are interested in Jewish history, and so on. But it's untrue that white males are somehow detached and objective, and have no axes to grind themselves, whereas everyone else is biased and partial.

So I have every advantage going for me and I think that has helped. For instance, I was invited to the American Philological Association, a body of professional classicists, and they had a full session on *Black Athena,* which is something they never would have given a black scholar, even now. And twenty years ago they wouldn't have given it to anybody. I think that things are moving—not as fast as I had at first hoped. But the failure of classical scholars to blast me out of the water straight away is critical. They have not come up with effective arguments to silence me, which means that what I am saying is being incorporated into other people's work, and has become a legitimate view within ancient history and historiography. So I think that even black scholars will soon be admitted, which is rather strange given the general intensification of racism in American society. But in a way academia is continuing the movement of the 1960s away from racism, which is one of the few bright spots in what in many ways is an extraordinarily bleak situation. I hope it has a wider significance, but one can't tell.

ALLEN: How much support did you receive from the white intellectual community while pursuing this quest, and did you encounter any hostility or resistance?

BERNAL: None and yes. The Government Department at Cornell was very tolerant about how I spent my time. I had tenure; they couldn't do much about it. Though I wasn't doing research in the field in which I was hired, they were very nice about it, and I didn't get any flak from them. On the other hand, at the very beginning the Society for the Humanities gave me a year to work on Phoenicians and Greeks. When I started studying the Egyptians and applied for grants from the Society for the Humanities—four times I applied to Guggenheim, Rockefeller, and others and received nothing at all. No awards. Often the themes at the center at Cornell were very appropriate to my work, yet four years in a row I was turned down there. I had no support at that stage. I also had some difficulties when I proposed to teach courses in the new subjects. One time an ancient historian objected, saying I wasn't qualified to teach these courses. I was forced to justify them to the Educational Policy Committee, which seldom questions any courses; the last one had been some six years before. So my being questioned was quite exceptional. I did receive personal support from a number of people who told me I wasn't mad, which was quite important for me psychologically. To challenge so much academic authority, rows upon rows of books, does sometimes make one ask, Can they all be so wrong? Who am I to challenge them? But when I started explaining my ideas, white friends would say, Well, it sounds interesting. What's wrong with that? I also got consistent support from the Africana Center at Cornell, which offered to publish some of my materials before anyone else did. But support has become much more general now. Before, I received virtually no invitations from other colleges or universities, but that situation was transformed once the book was out. Now I have to *refuse* invitations to talk almost every week. There is a great deal of interest at colleges, and the administration of Cornell has become extremely supportive. I still haven't received any major awards, but people are curious to hear what I have to say—even quite conservative people.

ALLEN: You make a good point in your introduction about the differences between "radical," "innovator," and "crank." It's a crucial point if you're going to say so much scholarship is either wrong or misinterpreted.

BERNAL: The way I distinguish myself from cranks is that my work generates immediately testable hypotheses. If I say that Egyptian, Semitic, and Greek cultures are in direct juxtaposition to one another, you can test that in hundreds or thousands of ways. A good crank will provide coherent explanations for a mass of scattered data that academia is unable to solve—but having stated that general argument, you can't go further with it. I think you can go further with what I'm saying.

ALLEN: John Allegro's book *The Sacred Mushroom and the Cross* really hurt his reputation. He relied heavily on linguistic analysis. The layperson has to rely on other scholars.

BERNAL: Allegro was attacking biblical scholarship, which is very much confused with religious beliefs and passions. But laypeople need not be afraid of the mysteries of language. One of my mottos is that the obvious isn't always false. Academics *depend* on the obvious not being true; otherwise they would be out of a job. If words in different languages look and sound similar, have similar meanings, and there is no other explanation for their origin, it seems to me inherently plausible to suppose that they are connected in some way. The general response to my work has been that the historiography is fine and reasonable, the archaeology may well be right, but the linguistics is wrong or crazy. And that's a very satisfactory liberal response to what I am saying.

Our view of European Greece was conceived in what we now

consider to be the ideological error of the early nineteenth century, but that in itself does not make it untrue. Darwinism was created in very much the same intellectual atmosphere of racism and laissez-faire capitalism, and has been quite useful in understanding natural history. So the fact that classics was created in that atmosphere does not in itself make it wrong. But I argue that, in fact, classics does not provide a helpful scheme. We can't understand much about Greece if we work in the model that was set up during the nineteenth century. New scientific disciplines have been impinging on archaeological conventions—radiocarbon dating, neutral activation, and so on have shown that conventions in ancient history have been wrong in many ways. And there's a good deal more uncertainty and therefore flexibility among archaeologists in response to what I'm doing.

ALLEN: Do you believe that if the contributions of all civilizations to world progress were accurately taught in the educational systems of all nations, there would be a decrease in prejudice and a corresponding increase in tolerance and understanding?

BERNAL: Yes, I do. I have that amount of faith in human nature and in human society.

ALLEN: What advice would you give to students and teachers of history who want an objective analysis of past and present events and how they affect the future?

BERNAL: To trust their judgments, but to try to make them systematic and capable of argument. I know it is difficult. A lot of blacks have "learned" this about Egyptians, Africans, and others, but have not been able to sustain an argument about it, because whites have all these books and arguments against them. You can say that blacks were at the center of early civilization. That statement alone when asked to refute white scholarship is a positive step, but I think African-Americans should go beyond that. They should be willing to see contradictions within different black views and be prepared to make some concessions, while maintaining the central core of their own beliefs.

23

Charles W. Faulkner:
Psychiatrist and Syndicated Columnist

ALLEN: How can humanism be effective in uplifting the African-American community?

FAULKNER: I believe that humanism can be effective in uplifting the black community by providing blacks with an insight into themselves as human beings, detached from any phenomena that might be nonhuman. That is to say, I believe that once people look into themselves as human beings and see the strength that they have as individuals, they can move ahead. And very much a part of the problem with black Americans is that we give so much of ourselves to religion, astrology, and other paranormal beliefs without looking into ourselves and seeing that we have what is necessary to be what we want to be, if we give our best efforts.

ALLEN: What negative influences has religion had on the African-American community and on the overall psyche of African Americans?

FAULKNER: Religion has had the negative impact of providing a psychological crutch for people. Of course many people will argue that religion gives them strength—and I'm sure that it does give many people strength. But it tends to provide, in my estimation, boundaries and limitations to the behaviors of people and to their capabilities of achieving individual performances outside of boundaries that might be externally imposed. But I also believe that when we look at religion and the importance that we give to prayer, for instance, it's almost as if we are praying to an unseen being for whose existence we have no strong evidence. And we give ourselves to this being as a child gives himself to his parent. We become the son and the supposed being becomes the master. And this has clearly had a negative impact. We have become accustomed to being servants, and it has become much more difficult for us to view ourselves as masters.

ALLEN: Many people claim that, historically, religion has been absolutely necessary to the success of the African-American community. They cite such examples as the establishment of black colleges and the beginning of the civil rights movement. They also insist that most of our great African-American leaders have been religious. What do you think of this assessment?

FAULKNER: I think that it is a half-truth. And what I mean by that is, it is partially true. I don't devalue the importance of religion in the history of our race. Our race and the races of others in which the church has played a major role have produced many great people. But we have never had the opposing arm of black assertiveness whereby people *outside* of religion have had the mutual opportunity to be leaders. Blacks have taken the role of being great churchgoers imbued with the "spirit," so to speak. Blacks generally follow politicians who are religious leaders. But there are many people who are outside of religion, or in any case, who take a nonreligious perspective, who could be great leaders. But they are unable to pull together large enough forces of the body politic to be strong. And I think that in promoting its leaders as political leaders, the church has had a stranglehold on the progress that others such as scientists and humanists could have.

ALLEN: What do you think accounts for so many African Americans being attracted to religion?

FAULKNER: First, tradition obviously plays a very large role. I think beyond that is a need for us to flatter ourselves by believing that we can be saved. And because of the very negative crisis afflicting blacks in this society, many blacks will do *anything* in the hope that they'll find a better life, if not in this current world, perhaps in the "afterlife." But I believe that as many people use drugs, or any kind of substance of that nature, black people use religion as a psychological crutch.

ALLEN: What do you think of the current African-American religious leaders such as Louis Farrakhan and Al Sharpton? How do their teachings affect the overall psyche of African Americans?

FAULKNER: I think that if you look at Louis Farrakhan, you propably have a man who expresses a strong sense of masculinity or manhood that other blacks are not able to express. So in that sense, he's very good. Farrakhan is able to say—without repercussions—much of what practically all blacks feel, but fear to say because they believe they will be reprimanded either by their bosses or by the society in general. Farrakhan has espoused an amazingly wonderful philosophy. He doesn't seem to intertwine religion as strongly in his effort to mobilize blacks into economic freedom.

Al Sharpton is similar to Farrakhan in the sense that he's militant. The likelihood of blacks ever getting themselves out of the turmoil that they're currently in becomes stronger with the use of militancy. But I wouldn't want to generalize black religious leaders. I think that Farrakhan and Sharpton stand out as being unusual personalities who have had more of a positive than a negative impact upon blacks.

ALLEN: The Association of Black Psychologists unanimously passed a resolution stating that white religious images such as those representing Jesus, Mary, and the angels have had a very negative effect on the collective self-esteem of black children. What are your views on this type of imagery?

FAULKNER: Oh, I agree with the resolution totally. If a person is strongly connected to religion and he finds that no black person has had a strong impact in terms of spiritual leadership, he's going to feel that it's okay—he will feel justified in establishing a father-son relationship with the church. Blacks need some kind of role model. We talk of role models, and the role models that we have are white—even the most deeply spiritual role model—Jesus—we are told, is white. And the acceptance of Christ as being white simply parallels the lack of black sophistication or black input in our history books. I think that blacks are outcasts in religion just as much as they are historically. But I think that the most important point is that millions of blacks are very close to the church, but still pray to a white leader.

ALLEN: How can humanism be made more attractive to African Americans?

FAULKNER: I think that humanism has to be in a position to produce a practical program that has practical, easy-to-evaluate results. If you look at astrology, for instance, many black people hold very strongly to astrology because they need a crutch. What kind of inspiration can humanism provide? Humanism has to provide some means whereby blacks can feel that if they accept it, they will become more successful and happier.

ALLEN: You once wrote a column on religion and how it was used to manipulate black jurors at the Oliver North trial in Washington, D.C. Would you comment on that?

FAULKNER: I sure would. And in addition, I'll use the same theme relative to the Marion Barry trial. As far as the Oliver North trial was concerned, both the prosecuting attorney and the defense attorney, in the closing arguments, appealed to the religious needs or religious philosophies of the jurors. They both quoted from Scripture. And it was *clear* that they had made no prior quotations from the Bible. They only did so in their closing arguments. They were both trying to make it appear that if the jurors voted a particular way, they would indeed be voting the way that the Lord would prefer that they vote.

And if you look at the trial of Marion Barry, you'll find that these things occurred when the closing arguments were made. And you can also see that both sides were careful in selecting jurors who had close religious connections or who regularly attended church. You'll find that an appeal to their religious needs and philosophies was made in the closing arguments of the attorneys.

And I'll make one further point. The defense used a strategy whereby they wanted Louis Farrakhan and Father George Stallings to sit in the guest spots behind Marion Barry. Obviously, this would have had a very positive impact for the defense, because when people would look to the defense table, they would see outstanding religious leaders who were in support of the mayor. Therefore, they would more likely believe that if they found the mayor guilty, they would be dishonoring the Lord.

ALLEN: Would you like to make any final comments on humanism or black psychology?

FAULKNER: Yes. Norm, I think that it's important that you and this *magnificent* organization—African Americans for Humanism—

make yourselves better known. Because there are many people who would do anything in their power to join or to rub shoulders and elbows with people who hold views such as yours. But it's very difficult for a person to isolate himself from astrology, particularly when he feels that all his friends will make him a pariah. I feel that we need to make people aware of what humanism is and how valuable it can be on a practical level. I also believe that for humanism to have the great value that it has to you and me, it has to be broken down into a more simplified philosophy, maybe even using a term that would be more appealing to people.

Finally, I believe that as long as we hold to nonhumanistic concepts and spiritualism, we're going to maintain the father-child relationship whereby we (African Americans) are the child in this society.

Leonard Harris on the
Life and Work of Alain Locke

ALLEN: How important was Alain Locke to the Harlem Renaissance?

HARRIS: Alain Locke was a major figure in the Harlem Renaissance. In 1924, he edited a special edition of a magazine called *Survey Graphics,* which included many of the literary figures of the time, such as Langston Hughes and others. From that he developed an anthology called *The New Negro,* which was published in 1925. It was an anthology of works by African Americans, as well as whites. It included artworks by Winold Reiss, poetry by Langston Hughes, articles on black history, and examples of black spirituals. It was one of the first works to do a full pastiche of black culture and to present it as an example of the creative power of the culture, which at that time was previously ignored, or was considered to be a kind of example of Negro existentialism, or Negro spiritualism, or Negro emotionalism, without any content or studied method. So Locke argued that the art of the African-American was a classical work. He maintained that jazz and the blues were works that were due serious consideration.

Another feature of *The New Negro* which is not very often noted is that it included artwork of Africa. Locke considered the artistic product of African sculptures as a classic art form. Consequently, we find photographs of carvings by Africans in the anthology as examples of artistic productions of African people. *The New Negro,* then, becomes a standard bearer of what was then an already existing

269

movement. Booker T. Washington had written about "the New Negro," and E. Franklin Frazier's doctoral dissertation was on "the New Negro." The idea was that there was a different kind of attitude occurring among African Americans. And that attitude was one of self-respect and self-regard. These people had different versions of what that attitude should be in the future. Locke's version was the one that was to be the most influential, because Locke focused on the diversity of cultural manifestations.

So *The New Negro* becomes very well-known and gains recognition throughout the world of black art as well as white art.

ALLEN: Did Locke have much to write and say about Marcus Garvey and the Universal Negro Improvement Association (UNIA)?

HARRIS: Yes. Oddly enough, in his own self-description—in the description of his own life—Locke pointed out that Garvey was an influence. In fact, to some degree, he had supported Garveyism. He described himself as being paradoxical. Having been raised in Philadelphia, he came from a well-off, always independent family. Locke's family was free on both sides for three generations back. That is to say, they were not slaves; they were free persons. But from that background he finds himself involved in a cultural world. He becomes supportive of a variety of nationalist movements. He supports the independence movements of Turkey, Egypt, India, and to some extent, the nationalism supported by the Garvey movement. He also supported the NAACP movement and other movements because they represented for him a moment in historical time where Africans and other peoples were grasping for a sense of their own self-identity. The Garvey movement had already constituted that stage.

Now remember, the Harlem Renaissance doesn't become effective as a viable movement until 1925, whereas the Garvey movement had already been well-established and popular. So the Garvey movement was definitely a precursor to the Renaissance. The Garvey movement was national and international. There were UNIA offices in Jamaica, Liberia, Birmingham, England, Dubuque, Kansas, Alabama, and throughout the United States. Consequently, the sense of internationalism had *also* been promoted before the Renaissance became a viable movement in terms of cultural awareness; and Locke became one of the many inheritors.

ALLEN: Was Locke widely respected among the leading white philosophers of his day?

HARRIS: No! There is a strange paradox here. Locke attended Harvard University and studied under William James, Josiah Royce, Hugo Munsterberg, and all of the main figures of American philosophy. They were his instructors at Harvard. He then became a Rhodes Scholar, that is, he received the scholarship to Oxford University. There were many letters written condemning the awarding of the Rhodes Scholarship to Locke. One had to be competitive in order to get the scholarship. And because Locke was black, many white scholars of the time asked themselves: "Could it be possible for a Negro to be that intelligent?"

Locke goes to England and again confronts that kind of racism within the context of academia. He met quite a number of scholars at Oxford like Satya V. Mukerjea, a supporter of the independence movement of India. He also meets P. K. Isaka Seme, one of the founders of the South African Native National Congress—the precursor to the African National Congress—and a number of other nationalist-oriented scholars, like D. B. Burckhardt from Norway who was beginning to promote Norwegian independence.

Upon his return to the United States, Locke joined Howard University, which was at that time the premier black college in the United States. He completed his doctoral degree under Ralph Barton Perry in 1917 and graduated from Harvard in 1918. But having become one of the most well-educated persons—regardless of race—in the world, in a fairly closed field—philosophy—there was no place for him to go. Nonetheless, he maintained close relationships with certain persons in the field of philosophy thoughout his life, including Ralph Barton Perry, his former advisor. He also maintained relations with Max Otto, Horace Bernard Stern, Leeman Bryson, and many other whites, in what we would call the humanities. It was then known as the pluralist movement, which maintained that: (1) there was something common among all humans, (2) various cultural orientations should be respected and that people ought to be given regard for their preferences, and (3) those preferences should not be prioritized.

So the pluralist movement was where he found his theoretical and practical home. But the field of philosophy was and remains one of the most closed and racist fields in the world. Locke's participation, much like the participation of other American philoso-

272   Part Four: Interviews

phers such as John Dewey, occurred, in many respects, outside the field. That is to say, they didn't spend most of their time being professionals. They spent their time being philosophers and being active in the community of ideas. So in the sense of Locke participating in the profession of philosophy, that didn't occur until the early 1950s, when he was invited to various universities to lecture. He did present lectures on occasion. For example, in 1930 he lectured before the Howard philosophy club. But those were rare occurrences, and the profession was primarily closed to all but white males.

ALLEN: What were Locke's views on the scientific method?

HARRIS: What I do in my book *The Philosophy of Alain Locke* is to look at Locke's underlying philosophical motivation, because Locke is known for the Harlem Renaissance and for having promoted the scholars of the Renaissance. He is also known for his work *The New Negro* and for his publication of the Bronze Booklets, and many other publications concerning black culture. He is *not* known for his work in philosophy. Consequently, I look at what was behind his promotion of and associations with George Padmore, Paul Robeson, Richard Wright, Langston Hughes, Zora Neale Hurston, Claude McKay, Sterling Brown, Jean Toomer, Aaron Douglas, Wallace Thurmond, Roland Hayes, and the other literary giants of the era. I also look at what was behind his promoting the Harmond Foundation in New York and African art. What was behind it was a conception of reality, values, and science. His view—what he termed "critical relativism"—is a view of how we ought to approach reasoning. It is one thing to talk about science, but quite another to talk about its content and what is or ought to be its specific methodologies. What occurred in the 1930s and 1940s was that Africans and African Americans were considered to be inferior because they were not scientific; that is to say, they were deemed inferior because they were not producers of scientific products. They were also seen as being emotional. Locke, in a way, reverses this whole process and rejects the foundation upon which these claims are made. First, he says that to be scientific is not to be without emotion. That is to say, to be objective is not to be outside of the world, but to be a part of the world, and to look at the world in a certain critical fashion. Locke claimed that that critical fashion is itself an emotive characteristic. So we can't neatly make this division. We have to be objective in a way that recognizes the importance of continually being self-critical. On the one hand, he is rejecting the foundation of the distinction between emotions and facts. On the other hand, he is recognizing the importance of maintaining a critical attitude to be associated with science and many other fields. We have this seemingly dual approach.

So Locke's notion of critical relativism is marshalled against the pragmatist view, which held that all decisions should be based on instrumental reason or purely objective considerations of outcomes. At the same time this is marshalled against the view that only persons who are associated with the scientific culture are normal humans. Consequently, his view of critical relativism recognizes the importance of the diversity of reasoning modalities in arriving at warranted claims. He recognized the variety of ways in which people must evaluate their circumstances, political policies, and objective reality to arrive at methods that work. He is a pragmatist. He is within the pragmatic tradition in that he is concerned with what works, and not strictly with concocted mythologies and the like. In terms of science, that was the kind of activity in which Locke was engaged—that was the kind of battle he was fighting. And those were some of his views on science and the scientific method.

ALLEN: Your book *Philosophy Born of Struggle: Anthology of Afro-American Philosophy from 1917* sounds fascinating. Tell us about it and some of the philosophers and ideas it covers.

HARRIS: *Philosophy Born of Struggle* was my first anthology. It includes works by a variety of philosophers including Bernard Boxill, Angela Davis, Lawrence Thomas, Berkeley Eddins, William Jones, Maulana Karenga, and Houston Baker. The various authors in the anthology address issues of the nature of philosophy and the nature of experience. Each author is concerned with a particular idea, and they try to present their views of what the nature of philosophy or experience is or should be. They take into substantive account the history of racism and the way in which it has altered human relationships, and the way in which it has been used to misguide evaluations. *Philosophy Born of Struggle* is predicated on the assumption that a good deal of philosophy from the African-American heritage is a function of the history of the struggle to overcome adversity and to create. My book asks: "What is it that you create and what do you believe to be true about the nature of experience?" It is one thing to say that some white person is wrong. It is another thing to express what you believe is in fact correct. What ought to be the beliefs we should have about reality? What should be our notion of experience? *Philosophy Born of Struggle* departs from the history and heritage of simply responding to others and challenges African Americans to promote their ideas. What do you think is right, and what are your arguments for understanding philosophy and for understanding experience? It is one thing to say that pragmatists are too caught up in promoting science or that Marxists are too caught up in the class struggle to recognize the importance of identity, or that integrationists are really assimilationists, and are too caught up in what would be defined as Euro-American culture. But it is another thing to ask what views are true and important, and why are they important. *Philosophy Born of Struggle* presents for the first time an anthology of philosophers who take up that challenge, and who present what they believe ought to be the relevant canonical views.

ALLEN: Feel free to express any final thoughts you might have on African Americans and humanism.

HARRIS: Humanism has a very long history within the African-American community. In one article by Brodus Butler in *Philosophy Born of Struggle,* he argues that the principle modality for the African-American viewpoint is that of humanism, and that a great deal of the American vision is a function of humanism. And he shows how Frederick Douglass reinterpreted the Constitution by giving the term "man" new meaning. It could not just mean "white" man, but humanity. He redefined America and showed how it could not only mean a nation inhabited by those who came from Europe and were white, thereby excluding the descendants of those who were Africans and who were already here. "America" had to be redefined to incorporate the diversity of identities which comprise and create the country itself. And that form of humanism expands the meanings of terms to *include* human beings rather than exclude them.

So the history of humanism takes on a whole new dynamic in the context of this history and heritage. What is of importance is what Alain Locke saw as the "common cognates" of our humanity, or the common variables that link us to one another, as definitive of what it is to be a person. It is that foundation—not a metaphysical foundation but rather a heuristic one—that we can use to build our commonality, or what Locke called our "communicative competency," to understand our unity and oneness.

One final thought on humanism comes from Frederick Douglass in 1857:

> Let me give you a word of the philosophy of reform. The whole history of the progress of human liberty shows that all concessions yet made to her august claims have been borne of earnest struggle. That struggle may be a moral one, or it may be a physical one, and it may be both moral and physical, but there must be a struggle. Power concedes nothing without demand. It never did and it never will.

Notes on Contributors

FREDA AMAKYE ANSAH is a member of the Rational Centre in Accra, Ghana. She represented the Rational Centre at the 1990 International Humanist and Ethical Union (IHEU) Conference in Brussels, Belgium.

MARTIN G. BERNAL is professor of government and Near Eastern studies at Cornell University. He is the author of *Black Athena: The Afroasiatic Roots of Classical Civilization*.

FREDERICK DOUGLASS (1817–1895) was a runaway slave and leading abolitionist. He was one of the greatest orators of the nineteenth century and a close friend of the great freethinker, Robert G. Ingersoll.

W. E. B. DU BOIS (1868–1963) was one of the most distinguished African-American intellectuals of the twentieth century. He was a co-founder of the NAACP and an active Pan-Africanist. His book *The Souls of Black Folk* is a classic work of African-American literature.

MICHEL FABRE is one of the world's leading scholars on the life and thought of Richard Wright. He has taught African-American literature at many American universities including Harvard and Wellesley. In 1973, he won the Ansfield Wolf Award for his book *The Unfinished Quest of Richard Wright*. Today he lives and teaches in Paris.

CHARLES W. FAULKNER is a psychiatrist and syndicated columnist based in Washington, D.C. He has written many columns on religion and the need for critical thinking.

LEONARD HARRIS is professor of philosophy at Purdue University. He is the world's leading authority on the life and philosophy of Alain Locke. He is the editor of *The Philosophy of Alain Locke* and *Philosophy Borne of Struggle: Anthology of Afro-American Philosophy from 1917*.

NORMAN HILL is a human rights activist in New York City. He has been very influential in furthering the legacy of A. Philip Randolph.

DAVID HOWARD-PITNEY is a lecturer in American history and studies at San Jose State University. He is the author of *The Afro-American Jeremiah: Appeals for Justice in America*.

LANGSTON HUGHES (1902–1967) was one of the leading poets of the Harlem Renaissance of the 1920s. He was regarded as black America's poet laureate; and he was actively involved in the fight against racism throughout his life. His famous books include *The Big Sea* and *I Wonder as I Wander*.

ZORA NEALE HURSTON (1903–1960) was an anthropologist and a leading Harlem Renaissance novelist. Her popular writings profoundly influenced many African-American female writers including Alice Walker. During her life she published more books than any other black American woman. Her works include *Dust Tracks on a Road* and *Their Eyes Were Watching God*.

ISHMAEL JAFFREE is an attorney from Dothan, Alabama. He started a national controversy by filing a complaint to keep prayer and other activities out of the public schools of Mobile, Alabama, in 1982. He won the case on appeal in 1985.

MIKE MCBRYDE is an actor, artist, and writer from Pittsburgh. He has been a serious student of black history since 1978. Today he is the leader of a study group in the Pittsburgh area.

CLAUDE MCKAY (1890–1948) was a leading poet of the Harlem Renaissance. His most famous poems were filled with protest and revolutionary rhetoric, but he also produced lesser-known works in which he examined his thoughts and beliefs.

EMMANUEL KOFI MENSAH is the president of Action for Humanism in Ikeja, Lagos State, Nigeria. He is studying for his doctorate in philosophy at the Adventist Seminary of West Africa in Nigeria.

NKEYONYE OTAKPOR is a senior lecturer in philosophy at the University of Benin, Nigeria, and a member of the Executive Board of the Nigerian Philosophical Association.

JOEL AUGUSTUS ROGERS (1883–1966) was one of the most important and influential anthropologists in African-American history. As a secular humanist, he was highly critical of spirituality, yet his writings had a profound effect upon such leaders as Marcus Garvey, Elijah Muhammad, and Malcolm X.

MELVIN B. TOLSON (1898–1966) was a poet, a writer, and a columnist for the now defunct *Washington Tribune* newspaper. He was appointed poet laureate of Liberia in 1947 by Liberian President V. S. Tubman, and he was awarded the Order of the Star of Africa by Liberian Ambassador Simpson in 1954.

IVAN VAN SERTIMA is the editor of the *Journal of African Civilizations*. He has done much research into the African past, and his extensive knowledge in the fields of science, linguistics, anthropology, and human paleontology makes him a leading African-American scholar.

FRANZ VANDERPUYE is a member of the Rational Centre of Accra, Ghana. He has written extensively on the need to develop humanism on the African continent.

KWASI WIREDU is a professor of philosophy at the University of South Florida. His writings have appeared in many philosophy journals.

BRUCE WRIGHT is an outspoken critic of racism in the U.S. criminal justice and political systems. He is a New York Supreme Court justice who gained notoriety early in his career because of his policy of setting low bail where he thought it was appropriate. He is the author of *Black Robes, White Justice*.

Bibliography

Abraham, Willie E. *The Mind of Africa*. Chicago: University of Chicago Press, 1962.

Allen, Norm R. "Humanism in the Black Community." *Free Inquiry* 9, no. 3 (Summer 1989).

Aptheker, Herbert, ed. *Against Racism: Unpublished Essays, Papers, Addresses by W. E. B. Du Bois, 1887–1991*. Amherst: University of Massachusetts Press, 1985.

———, ed. *Annotated Bibliography of the Published Writings of W. E. B. Du Bois*. Millwood, N.Y.: Kraus-Thomson, 1973.

———, ed. *The Autobiography of W.E.B. Du Bois: A Soliloguy on Viewing my Life from the Last Decade of its First Century*. New York: International Publishers, 1968.

———, ed. *The Complete Published Works of W. E. B. Du Bois*. 37 volumes. White Plains, N.Y.: Kraus-Thomson, 1973–1986.

———, ed. *The Correspondence of W. E. B. Du Bois*. 3 vols. Amherst: University of Massachusetts Press, 1973.

———, ed. *Creative Writings of W. E. B. Du Bois*. White Plains, N.Y.: Kraus-Thomson, 1985.

———. *The Literary Legacy of W. E. B. Du Bois*. White Plains, N.Y.: Kraus-Thomson, 1989.

———, ed. *Prayers for Dark People*. Amherst, Mass.: University of Massachusetts Press, 1980.

———, ed. *Selections from "The Crisis."* Millwood, N.Y.: Kraus-Thomson, 1983.

———, ed. *Soliloquy on Viewing My Life from the Last Decade of Its First Century*. New York: International Publishers, 1968.

Aptheker, Herbert. "W. E. B. Du Bois and Africa." In *Racism, Imperialism, and Peace,* eds. Marvin Berlowitz and Carol Martin. Minneapolis, Minn.: MEP Publications, 1987.

————, ed. "W. E. B. Du Bois and Religion: A Brief Reassessment." *Journal of Religious Thought* (Spring–Summer 1982):5–11.

Bahai Movement. *The Promise of World Peace.* Haifa, Israel: Bahai World Center, 1985.

Bernauer, James. "The Prisons of Man: An Introduction to Foucault's Negative Theology." *International Philosophical Quarterly* 27, no. 4 (December 1987).

Blassingame, John W., ed. *The Frederick Douglass Papers.* New Haven, Conn.: Yale University Press. 3 vols., 1986.

Blight, David W. *Frederick Douglass's Civil War: Keeping Faith in Jubilee.* Baton Rouge: Louisiana State University Press, 1989.

Bollnow, O. F. "The Importance of Dialogue Today: Philosophical Aspects." *Universitas* 30, no. 1 (1988).

Bookchin, Murray. *Post-Scarcity Anarchism.* Montreal: Black Rose, 1986.

————. *Toward an Ecological Society.* Montreal: Black Rose, 1980.

Brotz, Howard, ed. *Negro Social and Political Thought, 1850–1920.* New York: Basic Books, 1966.

Caton, Hiram. "Towards a Diagnosis of Progress." *Independent Journal of Philosophy* 4 (1983).

Clarke, John Henrik, et al., eds. *Black Titan: W. E. B. Du Bois.* Boston: Beacon Press, 1970.

Danquah, J. B. "Obligation in Akan Society." *West African Affairs,* No. 8 (1952), published by the Bureau of Current Affairs, London, for the Department of Extra-Mural Studies, University College of the Gold Cross, p. 3.

De Marco, Joseph P. *The Social Thought of W. E. B. Du Bois.* Lanham, Md.: University Press of America, 1983.

Diop, Cheikh Anta. *The African Origin of Civilization: Myth or Reality?* Trans. Mercer Cook. Westport, Conn.: Lawrence Hill & Co., 1974.

————. *The Cultural Unity of Black Africa.* Chicago: Third World Press, 1978. (The English translation was published originally by Présence Africaine in 1963.)

Diop, Cheikh Anta. *Precolonial Black Africa.* Trans. Harold Salemson. Brooklyn, N.Y.: Lawrence Hill Books, 1987.

Douglass, Frederick. *Life and Times of Frederick Douglass: Written by Himself.* New York: n.p., 1892; reprint ed.: n.p., 1962.

Dreyfus, Hubert, and Paul Rabinow, eds. *Michel Foucault: Beyond Structuralism and Hermeneutics.* Chicago: University Press, 1982.

Du Bois, Shirley Graham. *His Day Is Marching On: A Memoir of W. E. B. Du Bois.* Philadelphia: J. B. Lippincott, 1971.

Du Bois, William Edward Burghardt. *Africa: Its Geography, People and Products.* Girard, Ks.: Haldeman-Julius, 1930.

———, ed. *Atlanta University Publications on the Study of Negro Problems.* Atlanta University, 1898–1913.

———. *Black Reconstruction: An Essay toward a History of the Part Which Black Folk Played in the Attempt to Reconstruct Democracy in America, 1860–1880.* New York: Harcourt, Brace, 1935.

———. *Color and Democracy: Colonies and Peace.* New York: Harcourt, Brace, 1945.

———. *Crisis.* New York City, 1910–1934.

———. *Dark Princess: A Romance.* New York: Harcourt, Brace, 1928.

———. *Darkwater: Voices From Within the Veil.* New York: Harcourt, Brace & Howe, 1920.

———. *Dusk of Dawn: An Essay toward an Autobiography of a Race Concept.* New York: Harcourt, Brace, 1940.

———. *The Horizon.* Washington, D.C., 1907–1909.

———. *In Battle for Peace: The Story of My 83rd Birthday, With Comments by Shirley Graham.* New York: Masses & Mainstream, 1952.

———. *John Brown.* Philadelphia: George W. Jacobs, 1909.

———. *Mansart Builds a School.* New York: Mainstream, 1959.

———. *The Ordeal of Mansart.* New York: Mainstream, 1957.

———. *The Philadelphia Negro: A Social Study.* Boston: Ginn and Co., 1899.

———. *The Quest of the Silver Fleece: A Novel.* Chicago: A. C. McClurg, 1911.

———. *The Souls of Black Folk: Essays and Sketches.* Chicago: A. C. McClurg, 1903.

———. *The Suppression of the African Slave-Trade in the United States of America, 1638–1870.* New York: Longmans, Green, 1896.

Du Bois, William Edward Burghardt. *The World and Africa: An Inquiry into the Part Which Africa Has Played in World History.* New York: Viking, 1947.

Foner, Philip S., ed. *The Life and Writings of Frederick Douglass.* 5 vols. New York: International Publishers, 1971.
————, ed. *W. E. B. Du Bois Speaks: Speeches and Addresses.* 2 vols. New York: Pathfinder Press, 1970.
Forde, Daryll, ed. *African Worlds.* New York: Oxford University Press, 1954.

Harding, Vincent. "W. E. B. Du Bois and the Black Messianic Vision." *Freedomways* 9 (1969): 44–58.
Harrison, Hubert Henry. *The Negro and the Nation.* New York: Cosmo-Advocate Publishing Company, 1917.
————. *The Voice of the Negro.* Vol I, no. 1 (April 1927). New York: International Colored Unity League.
————. *When Africa Awakes.* New York: The Purro Press, 1920.
Hatch, O., and Mark A. Noll, eds. *The Bible in America: Essays in Cultural History.* New York: Oxford University Press, 1982.
Horne, Gerald. *Black and Red: W. E. B. Du Bois and the Afro-American Response to the Cold War, 1944–1963.* Albany: State University of New York Press, 1986.
Huggins, Nathan I. *Slave and Citizen: The Life of Frederick Douglass.* Boston: Little, Brown, 1980.

Ingersoll, William T. "Reminiscences of William Edward Burghardt Du Bois." 1963. Columbia Oral History Collection, Columbia University.

Lester, Julius, ed. *The Seventh Son: The Thought and Writings of W. E. B. Du Bois.* 2 vols. New York: Random House, 1971.
Logan, Rayford W., ed. *W. E. B. Du Bois: A Profile.* New York: Hill & Wang, 1971.
————. *What the Negro Wants.* Chapel Hill: University of North Carolina Press, 1944.

McCabe, Joseph. *Keys to Culture.* Book 3. Girard, Kans.: Haldeman Julius Publishing Co., 1927.

Marable, Manning. *W. E. B. Du Bois: Black Radical Democrat.* Boston: Twayne Publishers, 1986.

Martin, Waldo E. *The Mind of Frederick Douglass.* Chapel Hill: University of North Carolina Press, 1984.

Meier, August. *Negro Thought in America, 1880–1915.* Ann Arbor: University of Michigan Press, 1963.

Moore, Jack B. *W. E. B. Du Bois.* Boston: Twayne Publishers, 1981.

Moses, Wilson J. "The Poetics of Ethiopianism: W. E. B. Du Bois and Literary Black Nationalism." *American Literature* (November 1975): 411–27.

Omoregbe, Joseph I. "What is God? A Critical Inquiry." *The Nigerian Journal of Philosophy* 3, no. 1 (1983): 1.

Preston, Dickson J. *Young Frederick Douglass: The Maryland Years.* Baltimore, Md.: Johns Hopkins University Press, 1980.

Quarles, Benjamin. *Frederick Douglass.* Washington, D.C.: Associated Publishers, 1948.

Rampersad, Arnold. *The Art and Imagination of W. E. B. Du Bois.* Cambridge, Mass.: Harvard University Press, 1976.

———. *The Life of Langston Hughes.* 2 vols. New York: Oxford University Press, 1986–1988.

———. "W. E. B. Du Bois as a Man of Literature." *American Literature* (March 1979).

Rodney, Walter. *How Europe Underdeveloped Africa.* Washington, D.C.: Howard University Press, 1982.

Rogers, Joel Augustus. *Africa's Gift to America.* New York: Helga M. Rogers, 1961.

———. *As Nature Leads.* Baltimore, Md.: Black Classic Press, 1987.

Rogers, Joel Augustus. *From Superman to Man.* New York: Helga M. Rogers, 1968; reprint 1978.

———. *The Ku Klux Spirit.* New York: J. A. Rogers, 1923; reprint Baltimore, Md.: Black Classic Press, 1980.

———. *Nature Knows no Color Line.* New York: Helga M. Rogers, 1952.

———. *100 Amazing Facts About the Negro.* New York: Helga M. Rogers, 1957.

Rogers, Joel Augustus. *The Real Facts About Ethiopia*. New York: J. A. Rogers, 1936; reprint Baltimore, Md.: Black Classic Press, 1982.

———. *Sex and Race*. 3 vols. New York: Helga M. Rogers, 1952.

———. *World's Great Men of Color*. 2 vols. New York: Helga M. Rogers, 1947; reprint New York: MacMillan Publishing Co., Inc., 1972.

———. *Your History: From the Beginning of Time to the Present*. Pittsburgh, Pa.: The Pittsburgh Courier Publishing Co., 1940; reprint Baltimore, Md.: Black Classic Press, 1983.

Russell, Bertrand. *History of Western Philosophy*. London: Allen and Unwin, Ltd., 1961.

Sarpong, Peter. *Ghana in Retrospect: Some Aspects of Ghanaian Culture*. Accra: Ghana Publishing Corporation, 1974.

Schwartz, Barry N., and Robert Disch. *White Racism: Its History, Pathology, and Practice*. New York: Dell Publishing Co., 1970.

Singer, Peter. *Practical Ethics*. Cambridge, England: University Press, 1979.

Toynbee, Arnold. *A Study of History*. Vol. 2. London: Oxford University Press, 1978.

Van Sertima, Ivan, ed. *Egypt Revisited: Proceedings of the Nile Valley Conference, Atlanta, September 26–30, 1984*. New Brunswick, N.J.: Journal of African Civilizations, Ltd., Inc., 1985.

———, ed. *Great African Thinkers, Vol. I: Cheikh Anta Diop*. New Brunswick, N.J.: Journal of African Civilizations, Ltd., Inc., 1986.

———. *Ils y étaient avant Christophe Colomb*. Paris: Flammarion, 1981.

———. *Nile Valley Civilizations*. New Brunswick, N.J.: Journal of African Civilizations, Ltd., Inc., 1985.

Weber, Max. *The Protestant Ethic and the Spirit of Capitalism*. New York: Charles Scribners and Sons, 1958.

Woodson, Carter G. "Journal of Negro History," 11, no. 2 (April 1926).

———. *The Miseducation of the Negro*. Philadelphia: Hakim's Publications, 1939.